D1433666

CRUISING
JAPAN
TO NEW
ZEALAND

CRUISING JAPAN TO NEW ZEALAND

THE **VOYAGE** *OF THE* **SEA QUEST**

TERE BATHAM

S
SHERIDAN HOUSE

LINCOLNSHIRE
COUNTY COUNCIL

Published 2004 in the United States of America by
Sheridan House Inc.
145 Palisade St
Dobbs Ferry, NY 10522
www.sheridanhouse.com

Copyright © 2004 by Tere Batham

Maps by Peggy Preindel
Photographs by Tere Batham

All rights reserved. No part of this publication
may be reproduced, stored in any retrieval system
or transmitted in any form or by any means, electronic,
mechanical, photocopying, recording, or otherwise,
without the prior permission in writing of Sheridan House.

Library of Congress Cataloging in Publication Data
Batham, Tere
    Cruising Japan to New Zealand : the voyage of the Sea Quest /
by Tere Batham.
       p. cm.
    Includes index.
    ISBN 1-57409-182-4 (alk. paper)
       1. Batham, Tere—Travel—South Pacific Ocean. 2. Batham,
Michael—Travel—South Pacific Ocean. 3. Yachting—South
Pacific Ocean. 4. Sea Quest (Yacht) I. Title.
GV817.S66B38 2004
797.124'6'091648—dc22   2004006977

ISBN 1-57409-182-4

Edited by Janine Simon
Designed by Jesse Sanchez

Printed in the United States

In memory of my parents

Jack and Ruth Carstarphen.

This voyage began with them.

And to

Michael.

CONTENTS

ACKNOWLEDGMENTS

One of mysteries of the Orient is an enigmatic sense of formal obligation. On that day in 1997 when Keiko and Munihiro Hanada inquired politely if we would take Miki-chan with us to New Zealand, and we felt compelled to agree, it was impossible to foresee that the acceptance of *obligation* would lead us into an unforgettable adventure.

Thus we lead our acknowledgements with thanks to Munihiro Hanada and his wife Keiko. Their caring helped us make the grand leap into Japanese life. *Arigato gozaimashita.* To Seiko and Norio Takada who welcomed us into their home and family life we owe deepest gratitude. Acknowledgements go also to Shu Tanaka whose fist-full of personal introductions became magic keys to the sequestered heart of the Seto Naikai. Thanks also to indefatigable Sayu Kusayama, mechanic Tanaka San, Yoshi Torimoto, of Kao Corporation, Hashimoto San for the weekly bouquet, Tomoko Takahashi for repeatedly sharing her Kyoto home with us. Also Jiro Taneguchi, of Tanabe, fish dealer, who put Michael to work during our first week in Japan crating thousands of tuna!

After departure from Wakayama each and every port seemed to offer up some special person who took it upon himself to become our friend. To those people, too many to mention, but despite this fact, each no less important, thank you for your generous kindness that we never had any hope of repaying. I feel inadequate also in expressing my appreciation to the people of the Micronesian atolls where our presence must have felt like an alien intrusion. Special thanks go to Joe and Katherine Yetigmal, Thomas and Mary Hapitmai, Monica on Puluwat, and Etelinda Thomas, as well as Chiefs Lewis and Pakalimar.

Throughout my life people have remarked, "You should write a book!" To all those who believed in the romance of our seagoing life, I salute you. However there is a great leap to be made between first draft scribbles and anything that could be published. To my nautical in-laws, Jean and Allan Batham, go my thanks for peppering the early drafts with astute and helpful comments. Deep appreciation goes also to my friends, Vanessa and Antoon de Vos, he a doctor of environmental science, she an English major, who, with their superb academic backgrounds did some real cut-it-out and stick-to-the-point editing.

At my weekly yoga classes led by 83-year-old Lindsey Nichols I met Peggy Reindel. In New Zealand on a six-month work experience from Germany, she introduced herself as a cartographer at the very moment I was struggling to put into printable form my hand drawn maps. I mean how many *cartographers* do you meet? To you Peggy go my thanks and gratitude for the skill with which you re-created my many maps. The body-mind aligning yoga ritual performed after long hours at the keyboard and my interaction with Lyndsay, fellow teacher Ines Piroth, Caroline Mills, and other denizens of Russell township in the Bay of Islands all served to inspire me.

At the eleventh hour, with our departure from New Zealand imminent, retired publisher Brian Moss sailed in aboard his century old wooden sloop. "Let me see that book of yours," he said. His practical assistance at that particular moment when the book was about to be shelved to make way for our passage to French Polynesia, can only be described as serendipitous. Thanks also to others in the publishing business: Michael Fleck and Daphne Brassel and to Herb McCormick, editor of *Cruising World*, whose acceptance of my cruising articles encouraged the larger project. It is, however, to my publisher Lothar Simon, his love of sailing classics and to his wife Janine's capable editing, that I am most indebted.

From the moment when we bid *sayonara* to Japan, Miki felt like a daughter to us. The opening of Miki to the wonders of the outside world was as through a brilliantly hued kaleidoscope, so bright it sometimes hurt the eyes. Thank you Miki-chan for sharing your terror and your joys as you crossed from your sheltered youth to your emerging adulthood: across that mighty chasm between Orient and Occident.

None of this would have happened without the partnership, adventurous spirit and unending support of my sweet husband Michael. Thank you for keeping the computer running, building my office space in the fore cabin, and for repeatedly double-checking facts. Thank you for your stalwart support in readying this book, like a sturdy ship, for launching.

INTRODUCTION

Wearing baggy British Army shorts, Michael strode confidently down the dock, a day late for my "coming home from school" party. His hands, the first things that I noticed about him, were big; almost clumsy, but the clever sort of hands that I had the impression could manage even the most delicate jobs. Spread across his face was a broad self-deprecating grin. He was seventeen and I was sixteen.

Michael had sailed out to the Caribbean from England on an ancient 36-foot Falmouth quay-punt, FALCON, with his parents, Jean and Allan Batham. The yacht had been recently lost, wrecked by a hurricane in Jamaica. Their only asset destroyed, the family was working hard to attract yachts, both private and charter, to the small resort they were attempting to establish on a remote islet in the British Virgin Islands. Their only contact with the outside world was by marine radio. Messages often had to be relayed—hence the reason Michael had got the wrong date and arrived a day late to my party.

Though born on opposite sides of the globe, Michael and I had many seagoing childhood experiences in common. His family had enjoyed summers sailing across the North Sea from England to Denmark where they would navigate the inshore waters until the holidays were over. In 1958, the Batham family decided to immigrate to Canada and set off by boat across the Atlantic. Had they not lost FALCON in Jamaica, Michael might have ended up in Vancouver, as they originally intended—and this story would never have been written. However, the family stayed in the British Virgin Islands and poured their considerable energy into building up Marina Cay Hotel.

My own parents were outright romantics and cruising was a lifetime occupation. When they first met in California, Dad owned a sailboat and Mom was already an experienced daysailor. Wartime conditions forced upon the couple a whirlwind courtship and a wedding during shore leave. Soon after Dad's discharge from the navy at the end of the war, they sold their accumulated property and set sail aboard TIKI, a 34-foot cutter, to explore the West Coast from Mexico to Panama. The fact that by now Jack and Ruthie had two bundles of baggage, my brother Tim and I, did not deter them. In 1949, after nearly three years in the tropics, we returned to southern California where they promptly purchased a 38-foot ketch, SHELLBACK, to better accommodate my brother and me.

To earn a living, they leased the old Coronado Boat House premises and its fleet of small rental sailing craft. The docks, finger piers and ample workshop facilities in the many-storied Victorian boathouse, along with Dad and Mom's seafaring reputation, attracted would-be cruisers. Over time the existence of this high-spirited nucleus of yachtsmen attracted other long-distance cruisers, which in 1953 spawned the Seven Seas Cruising Association. Today this same SSCA has a membership of around 10,000 sailors!

Growing up aboard boats almost guaranteed that both Michael and I would be adventurous. We learned to swim early. We fearlessly paddled or sailed our skiffs in both harbor and stream. On the waterways we fantasized that we were castaways surviving dire hardships. In time, we graduated to larger sailing boats. We grew up with the warm sun on our skin, the whispering ebb and flow of the tide, the coarse ropes and the heavy canvas, the smell of caulking tar and paint, the feel of our bare feet in the scuppers and the ratlines between our toes.

Though life was sweet at the boathouse, Jack and Ruthie's dream was not to run organizations, but to sail away. In 1954, when the kitty seemed full enough, they disposed once more of all they had acquired and set sail. Half a year later we reached Panama. On an expedition Dad had arranged aboard a banana trading boat, we journeyed up the Sambu River, chugging up the savage reaches of the remote Darien country. There we met Choco headhunters and Indian girls, ten years old like me, already physically developed and married! One of the fleet from the Coronado Boat House, TROPIC BIRD, joined us, and together we cruised pristine San Blas Islands. Tiny Kuna Indian women with flashing eyes, cropped black hair and heavy gold nose rings played with me. They brought me into their long house, dressed me in a bright appliqué clothing and drew upon my nose and across my brow a heavy black line in imitation of their own paint. Then I was set lose to run after my parents!

Each enchanting Caribbean port enticed us to stay longer. Charlotte Amalie, the old Dutch-Danish town on St. Thomas, beguiled us with a fine harbor and an opportunity to replenish the kitty. Chartering SHELLBACK during the brief five or six week tourist season brought in enough income to pay the family bills for a year. When not chartering we roamed where we pleased, Tim and I either enrolled in a correspondence school or attending one of the local church schools until we reached high school age.

I had just returned from my first year away at school in California when I met Michael. He was also just back from school in the States. Having no money for airfare, Michael had hitchhiked 2,000 miles to and from Massachusetts by yacht. Before coming to the Caribbean, he had attended private boarding schools in England. When his parents were ready to leave he was just 15. Michael left school to join them for the Atlantic crossing aboard FALCON.

A year later at Marina Cay an American visitor remarked, "What is a fine young man like you doing out of school?" After Michael explained the present tight circumstances, he added that he quite liked being out of school. The man made a "harumphing" sort of sound. "We shall see what we can do," he had said. Weeks later a scholarship at Phillips Academy at Andover had arrived in the post.

Despite all this, when we next met, school was far from our minds. As soon as SHELLBACK's anchor had splashed down into Marina Cay's lagoon, Michael sailed alongside in LILY, his long-boomed 9-foot native Tortolan sloop.

"Tere! Want to come for a sail with me?" he called out. How could I know then that the sail would last a lifetime!

The following summers the shady banyan grove near the water's edge was my bower, a string hammock my bed. By then Marina Cay had accommodation for paying guests and a functioning kitchen. Michael's mother no longer needed to cook food for her visitors in an old oil drum oven on the beach. We spent the bright days exploring the surrounding islands, diving on the reefs, and wandering among the tumble of house-sized granite boulders called "The Baths."

With the magical place to ourselves we climbed and swam

3

from shadowy cave to sun-drenched pool, crawling through narrow passages beneath the gigantic stones. We discovered in each other a matching optimism and love for life and adventure.

Our wedding in 1965 was a simple service at the stone Anglican Church on St. Thomas. Afterwards so many friends crowded aboard my parents' recently acquired Brixham trawler, MAVERICK, that the ship's massive 76-foot waterline was fully submerged. Waterfront sightseers loitered near by, fascinated by our celebrations. When I joined Michael to cut the three-tier wedding cake my 5'1" felt petite alongside his 6' bulk, but the look in my new husband's proud eyes told me that I had made the right choice.

The old stone dwelling, Tamarind House, was to be our first home. Michael's family had taken over the leases for Beef Island Shipyard and Trellis Bay Hotel. Michael managed the old shipyard with its rickety rails where he hauled the last of the old trading schooners and even occasionally patched bullet holes in the hulls of smugglers' ships. After Michael's parents acquired a 99-year lease on a large portion of Great Camanoe Island, Michael formed the Island Construction Company. He began to build roads, jetties and vacation homes. There was so much work to be done. Over a period of several years, we built our own rambling West Indian-style home. While Michael kept the construction company and the shipyard going, I played the part of secretary and bookkeeper. I also rented the homes we had built to vacationers on behalf of their owners. When I could, I practiced commercial photography.

Had not Michael's parents got itchy feet, we might have carried on like this indefinitely. However, in short succession they installed Michael's English-born uncle to manage the hotel, bought a well known New Zealand boat called WHITE SQUALL, changed the name to AIREYMOUSE, and set sail across the Caribbean into the Pacific. "We will return," they promised. We wondered if they would. We were still only in our twenties and sorely missed them. Without their encouragement and the enthusiasm generated by our shared projects, our own latent escapism was triggered, although by now we had our own children, Marina and Conrad.

"Do you think New Zealand might be a nice place to live?"

I asked Michael one day ever so innocently. "Good schools—no racial tensions," I continued. "Our house here should be worth a bit. Perhaps along the way we could travel . . ."

Eighteen months later we were exploring southern Europe in a Land Rover, our children tucked up with their school books in the back seat.

We arrived in New Zealand aboard a liner on a sea voyage from Italy in 1972. Though faced with some big adjustments, we adapted. Michael had a lifelong love for woodworking, and learned to build furniture well. When the children grew older, we bought a shop in Auckland and I ran the retail side of the business. With our growing children, we enjoyed New Zealand's matchless countryside and explored every corner of the two big islands. The children were the focus of our lives. We camped, we hiked and we skied in the winter. The children rode horses in the pony club and learned to sail small boats. When Marina and Conrad grew bigger, we rented yachts in the summer and took them cruising. Soon they were no longer children.

We were unprepared for the break-up of the family. Naturally our children had been raised to be as independent as we were, but the void they left behind when they set off on their own life adventures happened to coincide with a deep business recession in New Zealand. Since we no longer had schooling costs to consider we asked ourselves, "Why remain in business?" We decided to sell up and buy a boat.

Thirty-five foot TEQUILA was perfect for coastal cruising. To feel the deck of a boat move under our feet was the most natural thing in the world. It brought back into focus that whole other life aboard boats that had remained dormant for 20 years as we raised our family. The sense of unlimited freedom was unexpected after years of being bound to family, house and business routines.

"Should we consider cruising offshore?" Michael asked.

The genie was out of the bottle.

Within days, TEQUILA was back on the market and the hunt was on for a vessel more suitable for passages across the wide oceans of the world.

We were taken with SEA QUEST before we even set foot on her. She was moored in one of Auckland's tidal estuaries. "She would be a good boat for you," said the agent, "but unfortunately the owner has withdrawn her from the market."

We stared with binoculars from the beach. "She's a little ship," I said.

"Twenty-eight-tons and 47 feet of little ship," countered Michael. " Not the sort of toy yacht you would find at a prestige boat show."

Eventually our persistence paid off when the sentimental owner-builder decided we were suitable future owners. We were ecstatic. Her all-steel construction was what we were looking for and we knew that her heavy displacement would help to make her safe. Although our budget would not stretch to insurance, we hoped SEA QUEST's hearty build would provide us with some. Robust enough to round the Horn, she was nicely turned out with heavy-duty stainless fittings. She had just completed her maiden voyage, a two-year jaunt around the Pacific.

"Might her size be a bit much for just us two to handle?" I queried Michael after I had stepped aboard.

"No. I don't think so. She has a sensible rig. None of her sails have excessive area. And this really heavy-duty trim-tab steering system will take the work out of the watches."

Antipodean cruisers, who voyage in the vast reef-strewn and lonely reaches of the Pacific with no one but themselves to rely on, have developed an understandable love affair with steel boats. Though some are built in professional yards, others, like SEA QUEST, have been built by talented individuals on their own lots.

SEA QUEST's builder planned to sail her to England around the Horn. The 42-foot design by Auckland's Colin Childs was stretched an additional five feet. The expanded midships got a couple of feet and three more were added to her counter. The extra length provided a bigger cockpit, a roomy engine room and a handy lazarette, giving more lift aft.

Her deck design offered some added security with the comfort of steel bulwarks around the foredeck with both bow and stern enclosed with heavy stainless steel rails helping to ensure that both sails and seamen did not slip past the lifelines. The cockpit was semi-enclosed by a wooden doghouse and zip down curtains offered protection from both heavy rain and tropical sun.

SEA QUEST proved to be as good as her first impression. For the next five years we traced lazy zigzags across the broad expanses of the Tasman and Coral Seas, from Tonga to Australia and as far north as Papua New Guinea and the Solomon Islands. The easy tradewind sailing and extensive practice navigating around coral reefs refreshed the skills of our early years while providing us with new confidence.

We never expected, however, to cruise for so long. A one-year shakedown cruise grew to two. Fiji was exceptionally interesting, we thought, so we remained over cyclone season. We grew to love the independence of the seagoing life. We found cruising an affordable way to visit remote places where we could remain long enough to become part of the local community for a while.

One day I blurted out, "I would love to sail to Japan!"

"Me too," replied Michael. "But Japan gets lots of typhoons and it *snows* up there! Still, we might manage it. If we do head that way we could stop at some of those really out-of-the-way atolls in Micronesia. Not many yachts go there."

It was decided.

Our newlywed daughter and son-in law joined us for the first eight months of our voyage. The youthful enthusiasm of Marina and Mark added much to our own sense of fun and adventure. We were sorry to bid them good-bye in Guam and sail on alone to Japan.

Via Saipan we hopped up the uninhabited Northern Mariana Islands to Ogasawara, Japan's southeasterly island group, where we entered at Chichi Jima. From there we sailed 600 miles to the mainland and entered again at Tanabe on Honshu's Kii Peninsula.

"Osaka is the official port of entry! Why have you come here?" the Customs officer demanded.

"We came here because it is the first port we have a chart for."

The Japanese officials like to follow the rules to the letter. We found that as *gaijin* (literally "white man," a faintly derogatory term, which threw them into paroxysms of embarrassment when we applied it to ourselves), we had a wonderful ability to confuse and in a sense, run circles around them. During our two-and-a-half years in Japan we discovered that officials would either avoid us if possible (fine by us), or stonewall us with the words *dekinai*, it is not permitted! At other times they would give us what we wanted so that we would become someone else's responsibility.

Japan proved to be exotic beyond our wildest fantasies. We expected to find a heavily industrialized country. Instead, we found, in this part of the country at least, industry well contained, integrated into compact towns surrounded by steep, uninhabited wooded hills, glittering with Shinto shrines and Buddhist temples. Japanese, who seemed bowled over by the fact that we had *sailed* our yacht to their small coastal villages, made us very welcome.

Many of the people we met in Tanabe and later in Japan's huge Inland Sea, the *Seto Naikai*, had never before met any Europeans. They vied with each other to be our hosts. We enjoyed their interest and took the opportunity to immerse ourselves in Japanese culture; said yes to every suggestion they made, and spent our spare time memorizing words and sentences in their language. Our three-month visa was extended to six while our presence continued to cause a stir wherever we went. Newspapers, magazines and even television interviews followed. New friends from Wakayama, some 35 miles south of Osaka, invited us to return to teach a small group of very keen sailors all we could about how to cruise overseas. Their efforts on our behalf provided us with the work permit we needed to stay on. One year became two and we became integrated into the local community, scooting around town on our motorbikes, supplementing our income by tutoring English to groups while using our weekends to make excursions to the ancient treasure cities of Kyoto, Nara and Koyosan. Finally the day came when we knew we should break out of our comfortable routine or remain under Japan's heady spell forever.

A Wakayama beachfront café provided the focus point for the local yachtsmen. We met Miki Hiramatsu there at her twenty-third birthday party. I remember the way one of her many male admirers described her. "If other girls are a poem, Miki-chan is a song." Like other well brought up Japanese girls, she always listened with rapt attention during our conversations but seldom voiced an opinion of her own.

Nevertheless, there was another side to Miki. Always a bit of a rebel, after an early episode of bullying at school she had opted, despite her family background, to attend a vocational school for mechanics where as a girl she was a distinct minority! Somehow she grew up and became a kindergarten teacher and I suspect, a highly creative one, at a university training center. Unfortunately the Japanese system rarely rewards individuals, especially when they are young and female. She was doomed to frustration and knew it.

Miki's socially conscious parents intended that both she and her younger sister marry young. Her family was on a mailing list for prospective husbands of impeccable lineage—not an altogether unusual situation in a country where 80% of marriages are arranged. However, Miki made paper darts of the proposals her mother carefully selected, and irreverently sent them flying across the room! A brief engagement to a doctor ended in a breakup. Miki's attitude towards traditional Japanese marriage with its locked-in roles hardened. "Miki not marry salary man!" She put her foot down and was fighting her parents. Nothing would dissuade her. She moved out into her own apartment and began to plot her escape.

Marriage is really the only situation available for a well brought up young woman in Japan. Nevertheless, like a growing number of youth who had been influenced by the culture of the West, Miki dreamt not of a strong silent *samurai* type who would appear cloaked in mystery late at night and then disappear by day into the realm of his own manly adventures. Instead she longed for a real life-companion. Merely having a partner with whom to beget a child followed by a life of prescribed obligations was out as far as Miki was concerned. With the help of the café owners, who like us were old enough to be her parents but had become her loving friends, Miki determined to sidestep her parents' plans. Her mentors had themselves lived and worked abroad for nearly a decade. They knew that if Miki were to spend enough time abroad, she would gain her independence.

"Why not sail with Michael-san and Tere-san?" they suggested one day as they sat together floating ideas for a solution to her problems. "You be their crew to New Zealand!"

When we eventually heard about the wild proposal, we thought it was a joke. That this glamorous girl, this fashion-crazy, headstrong beauty would have the faintest desire to go cruising seemed to us quite ludicrous. We teased her about the hardships. However, when the idea did not go away Michael asked me, "What do you think we do about it?"

"I think that when it comes down to brass-tacks they will all see how crazy the idea is and drop it. If not, there is only one answer."

In Japan people are usually very polite to each other and go to great lengths to avoid saying "no." Miki's mentors were the very same people who had opened the door to our own incomparable experiences in Japan. Social custom obliged us to return any favor we could.

We had not taken into account the fact that Miki was more desperate than we realized. She really could see no way out of the dead-end life her family and Japan's cultural traditions imposed on her. Under the influence of her many friends now urging her on, Miki began to see the voyage as not only a solution to her present parental impasse, but the vision of herself fleeing to New Zealand aboard SEA QUEST assumed great romantic appeal. The die was cast.

Miki's mentors set to work preparing her. She was taken out on day sails in near windless conditions and made to do a fitness run every morning before breakfast. She was having fun shaping up, but we felt pretty certain that her parents would intervene.

We invited Miki to come day sailing with us. We would put the boat through its paces. If Miki got seasick and broke her nails, she would give up the idea, we thought. However, as though she read our intentions, she sidestepped repeated invitations. Just 24 hours before our scheduled departure Miki finally showed up to stow her gear aboard. It seemed an inauspicious beginning! But there was still time. Before leaving Japan for good, we would be cruising Japanese coastal waters to Okinawa. When reality finally hit home, we were certain Miki would change her mind.

But could she?

1

The Seto Naikai

SEA QUEST maneuvered through Wakaura's inner fishing harbor past inquisitive anglers staring down from the breakwaters. Friends, who had gathered on the docks, some now in tears, waved good-bye. It was an emotional moment. Even the old *guji-san* priest from the local Shinto shrine was there. His presence reminded us that we had immersed ourselves in Japanese culture through the friends we had made. Not only had we visited ancient palaces and shrines but we had also taken part in religious ceremonies, feasts and street dancing. We had studied Buddhism and communed with monks. During the festival of *O-bon* we had accompanied our friends as they ritually washed their family graves.

At cherry blossom time, we sat beneath falling petals and admired the blossoms, while drinking beer and sake. When the hills were ablaze with rich scarlet and gold from maple and lacquer trees, we wandered the countryside in open admiration.

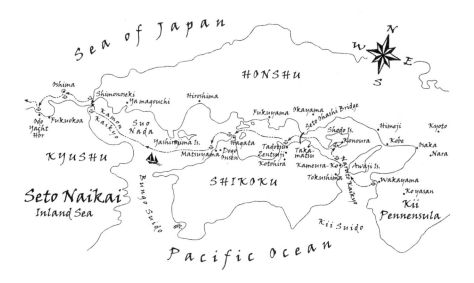

With the first rice harvest we joined in a family group to pound the grain and then helped form the sticky rice balls dipped in ground sesame, as pleased as everyone else with the delicious results. We too had hunted the *take noko*, joining the throngs who climbed high into the forest to dig for plump bamboo shoots in the spring.

Even more surprisingly, we learned how to bow as the Japanese did (well, almost), a skill as necessary as riding a bicycle in Japan. We were willing participants in countless tea ceremonies where our folded legs became as numb as wooden stumps. We rose to every culinary challenge, even *nauto*, a fermented soya bean paste, as well as jelly fish, raw liver dipped into raw egg, and *fugu*, the poisonous puffer fish. Our willingness to try out and savor without reservation won us the admiration of our friends and made it easy to remain in Japan for as long as we liked. Yet for every cruiser, there must come farewells. Leaving these friends was particularly sad. They had contributed so much, and would linger in our memory.

Just outside of the breakwater, the beautiful mountainous landscape of the Kii Peninsula floated in mist above the bay. Michael hoisted our mainsail and genoa. In a waving, shouting buzz, the local yachts belonging to our friends swarmed close by while our sails unfolded to billow in the breeze.

"Michael and Tere, Good Luck" read a banner, and beneath, in *katakana* letters, "*Miki-chan, sayonara.*"

Miki Hiramatsu, our young Japanese novice-crew stood silently waving, arms outstretched, tears streaming down her face. A horn blared a last farewell, shattering the morning stillness and causing Mizzen, the ship's cat, to leap below, quivering. The three of us wrapped our arms around one another as our friends, and the unparalleled experience of our lives in Wakayama, drifted into the past.

We were embarked on a 10,000-mile return voyage to New Zealand where Michael's parents and our old friends awaited us. When even the most stalwart of our well-wishers had turned back, Michael and I, though feeling suddenly bereft, knew the time had come to resume our own journey begun so long before.

We were at that emotional time between endings and beginnings, which we had experienced so often in our years of cruising around the Pacific. To avoid cyclone and typhoon seasons we had stopped for months at a time in the Fijian Islands, in Queensland and in Guam, but never before had we remained in one place for so long, nor been befriended by so many. Leaving required determination. It is hard to turn away from so likable a place, an easy job, a secure routine and the warmth of Japanese friends for a life of day-to-day uncertainty. Nevertheless, we were growing a little too comfortable. We had observed that when we break away from our complacent routines, magic seems to happen. Following our hearts, and not our pocketbook, has thus far rewarded us with riches beyond our dreams.

Yet this time we left with a souvenir of Japan. Miki had been entrusted to our care by her resigned parents who had arrived at SEA QUEST, under duress I am sure, to give their permission, as we had told Miki we would not sail without it.

SEA QUEST had already brought us far and gained our respect. We remained confident that she would take us home again. She was a little tired though. A few weeks earlier her 110-hp Ford had started to pour out black smoke. A proper rebuild was financially out of the question. Nonetheless, a Japanese friend, a mechanic, volunteered to help Michael overhaul the valves and replace the main head-gasket.

Apart from our initial summer of exploratory cruising, most of our days in Japan had been spent in the fishing village of Wakaura on the outskirts of Wakayama. Traveling south from industrial Osaka is like stepping back a century. By Japanese standards, Wakayama is only a medium-sized city, its population of 400,000 neatly concentrated into an area that in New Zealand might house 50,000. It sits at the foot of the rugged Kii Peninsula. Secreted in the nearby mountains is a city of Buddhist monasteries known as Koyasan, once forbidden to women. Scattered amongst the orange, plum, and persimmon plantations and surrounded by rice paddies are wattle and daub farmhouses, little changed since the days of the *samurai.*

Offshore, continuous big-ship traffic flows to and from Osaka through the Kii Suido. With timing as precise as a ballet dancer's, we wove our way across the two lines of vessels,

13

slipping behind one container ship and then skittering in front of a huge oil tanker. We waited for the tide to turn in a deserted cove three miles east of an immense suspension bridge leading to Shikoku Island.

When we judged that slack tide was near, we motored out to join the queue of northbound cargo ships, making their way towards the narrows of Naruto Kaikyo, a gateway into Japan's great Inland Sea, the Seto Naikai. During times of the strongest ebbs and flows, sightseers board large cruise boats to venture close to the swirling whirlpools. Jet skiers, who like to test their courage, are occasionally drawn too close, capsize and are swallowed by the vortex.

Full darkness descended. As we neared the churning narrows my heart hammered. The current caught SEA QUEST. She surged heavily, but the engine gave sufficient maneuverability to press on safely. We continued under the great looming bridge and through the narrows with a bright spotlight at hand to illuminate our sails, the better to be seen by large ships bearing down on us. When we were sufficiently clear, we again crossed the shipping lanes, ducking under the stern of a cargo vessel that was slicing through the currents at 16 knots. We rounded the headland for a night tied alongside a disused barge in the cove of Kameura-Ko.

The morning dawned bright and serene, but by midmorning, 30-knot gusts were heading us out of the northwest, forcing us to tack and tack again. SEA QUEST, built for heavy weather, leapt to life and plunged gaily into the frothy seas with her rigging rattling and stays straining. Michael and I felt a thrill, but below decks sloppily stowed gear slid to the cabin floor where it lay in untidy heaps.

Miki, as expected, was soon prostrate, huddled on the lee bench of the doghouse. I was not in such good shape myself. In the twisting eddies of the Naruto Narrows I had strained my elbow tussling with the helm. A sharp stab left me momentarily crippled. Miki's nausea and my pain were the inevitable price we paid to adjust to our new environment. By the end of the day, though, our trials were forgotten. We had found anchorage in the still waters of sheltered Konoura that reflected a fine shimmer of gold from the deepening sky. From a cluster of fishermen's huts on shore came the sounds of a barking puppy and an answering child.

The following afternoon we passed under Japan's longest bridge, the Seto Ohashi. This seemingly endless bridge leapfrogs half a dozen islets connecting the mainland of Honshu with Shikoku to the south. Historically the Seto Naikai, the navigable heart of Japan, has served as a marine highway. Road transport over Japan's rugged topography has always been slow and dangerous. Warlords, until just over a hundred years ago, demanded tariffs and tributes from travelers. Commoners could not own horses. Only the Imperial Family was permitted to use wheeled transport. Despite the pirates who sometimes preyed on travelers, sea passage was thus easier and quicker than by land especially as the swift tidal currents carried boats easily between the islands. Today Japan's maritime traditions are reflected in the thousands of cargo ships that provide efficient shipping service to the length and breadth of the country.

The Seto Naikai, Japan's Inland Sea, laps the shores of Japan's three central islands, Honshu, Kyushu, and Shikoku. It has just three narrow exits through which the tides race: the Kii Suido, Bungo Nada, and the Kanmon Kaikyo. From Osaka in the east to Shimonoseki in the west, the sea, which is more like a lake, is about 225-mile long. At its narrowest point, it spans only three miles: at its broadest about 30. The entire Inland Sea is strewn with thousands of heavily wooded islands, large and small, most of which are adorned with copper-roofed shrines and vermilion-painted *torii* gates. In years gone by the emperor and his entourage made pilgrimages to the important Shinto shrines located on the islands there, so the seaway has served as a conduit, not only for trade, but also for culture, art and music.

The region has until recently provided Japan's population with a rich harvest of edible seaweed, fish and other creatures. Though red tide algae caused by industrial pollution are now destroying the inland fishery, it is not quite extinct. Wooden fishing boats, little changed for centuries, still ply these waters along with sleek, fast, fiberglass launches.

Thickets of monstrous cranes jut at every angle from shipbuilding yards along the coast. The ruthless spread of industry, the relentless construction of new cargo ships, docks and sheltered fishing harbors have gobbled up the picturesque foreshore islands in pitiless land reclamation. We entered the old harbor of Tadotsu past the original hand-hewn sea wall, now located far from the pull of the tide; the ancient stone lantern is now obscured from the sight of passing ships.

At the heart of the town basin, dilapidated wooden buildings housed tiny soba noodle shops and dusty purveyors of marine and fishing gear. Small craft moored bow-to near the ferry landing while the larger boats lay alongside the wharf. In a gap just big enough to fit, we wedged SEA QUEST alongside.

The next morning, for the huge sum of two hundred yen (about two dollars), a train carried the three of us from the ancient seaport to Zentsu-ji, a town of crumbling farmhouses surrounded by rice fields. History records that Kobo Daishi, the legendary Japanese saint who in the eighth century made Buddhism accessible to the commoners of Japan, was born here. Before his time, Buddhism was primarily the prerogative of the emperor's court. Although pilgrims arrive on foot or by the busload we were the only foreigners in sight. We had learned enough Japanese and dos and don'ts after two-and-a-half years to get around without drawing undue attention to ourselves and of course having Miki with us was an advantage.

From a triton-shell horn a slender young acolyte sounded a long haunting note. Devotees followed a shaven, rotund old monk dressed in a saffron silk robe and purple pompoms down a colonnaded walkway, where they lit candles. Over burning incense in the heart of the centuries-old wooden temple, the group intoned ancient chants amid treasured art and sumptuous brocade hangings. Raised red lacquered seats were reserved for the highest-ranking monks. In a small room cluttered with ancient scrolls, thoughtful monks brushed special prayers in fine calligraphy. As each fresh wave of worshipers arrived, the wooden-grilled collection boxes rang with the clatter of coins.

A life-sized bronze statue of Kobo Daishi, the "Great Teacher," stands atop a stone hill. He appears to be gazing out across the centuries. Surrounding the statue are eighty-eight images of Buddha. Under each is buried a handful of sand from the temples that Kobo Daishi founded around Shikoku. Devout Japanese aspire to a pilgrimage once in their lifetime to all these temples, a two-month journey by foot. Devotees too old or too crippled to make the pilgrimage believe that circling this stone hill and its 88 Buddhas just once, while at the same time fervently praying, will earn them the same heavenly benefit.

Our ultimate destination, one of the most sacred of Shinto shrines in Japan, was Kompira-San dedicated to Okuninushi-no-Mikoto, the protector god of seafarers, voyagers and travelers. He is the Japanese Neptune. In Greek mythology Neptune is the god of the sea and is known as the god who created the horse. In a strange parallel Okuninushi-no-Mikoto is also the god of horses. His shrine contains a separate building that shelters a full-sized equine effigy.

Japanese Buddhism and the Shinto religion are so intertwined that it can be difficult for an outsider to separate one from the other. Eventually we discovered that the Shinto religion gives expression to the instinctive feelings of the Japanese for nature, just as in times past, before Christianity dominated our culture, our religions too reflected similar concerns and respect for the gods and goddesses of wind, water, sun and moon. The teachings of Buddhism, on the other hand, reflect more sophisticated abstractions of religious thought.

Today the pragmatic Japanese use the Shinto religion to bless weddings, babies, new cars, new boats and all new ventures. I went to a shrine with a Wakayama friend, who bought a prayer board on which she wrote a request that her child pass his next exam then hung it on a rack with hundreds of others. By contrast, the rites of Buddhism are concerned primarily with the welfare of ancestors, funerals, and the after life.

In Japan, ancestor spirits are not only thought to remain close by but continue the bond between the living and dead. These spirits, the Japanese believe, return annually to visit during the big August festival of *O-bon*. At the end of the holiday, lighted candles in paper boats are sent down waterways and across lakes and bays to symbolize the return of the departed ones to the netherworld.

The train took us another three miles inland to the bustling town of Kotohira, at the foot of Kompira's mountain. Here supplicants, traders and tourists have since ancient times brought prosperity to the town. Local artisans fashion every souvenir

17

imaginable, from the tacky to the sublime. Fine woodcarvings, sacred ritual objects, bronzes, silks and brocades take their place alongside plastic devil faces with rayon hair, paper fans, and cane walking sticks lettered with *Kompira-San*. In a land of 126 million xenophobic people, who mainly think that any place outside of Japan is unsafe, domestic tourism thrives.

The mountain on which the Sea God's shrine is located is densely covered with cedar, pine and camphor trees. The miles of avenues and the wide, granite steps are lined with great hand-hewn stone lanterns. The sound of mountain water gurgling into stone basins, the melodious birdsong, the tap of a pilgrim's walking stick, gongs, bells and drums, was music to our ears. On an earlier trip we had climbed the 785 steps to the main shrine and then later continued panting upward 500 more to the summit of Mount Zozu. There we found a quiet sanctuary of red and gold, where a great burnt ochre long-nosed *tengu* goblin mask stared out from a nearby cliff-face.

By the time we arrived, it was already too late to climb to the summit. We had come instead to leave a sentimental offering for the Sea God. A photograph of SEA QUEST, a map of our planned course and a prayer from each of us had been prepared as an offering. His shrine was already crowded with countless representations of ancient watercraft alongside handsomely framed photographs of commercial shipping and naval vessels. On a timeworn roof beam, we found space to pin our modest offering.

In times past, barrels were set adrift on the Inland Sea, addressed to Kompira by travelers too far from the temple to visit there themselves. A pottery sake barrel would be outfitted with a mast and flag and a few coins wrapped up with their prayers. A fishing boat would pick up such a drifting barrel and send it via relatives on to the shrine. In so doing, they would insure their own prosperity. Fishermen reasoned that were the messages *not* delivered, luck might turn against them.

The sun set early behind Mount Zozu, cloaking the ancient woods in gloom. Yet in the dim light thick green mosses on cedar bark roofs seem to glow more intensely. The terraces around the main shrine were quiet. Only a few visitors remained. Tonight, the most sacred ritual of the year was to be performed. The god would be called out of his mountain to be paraded in his golden *mikoshi* palanquin down the 785 steps into the town where his sacred presence would purify and bless all. A quiet murmuring came from richly-garbed monks meditating in the dimly lit rooms of the temple. One such group suddenly appeared in the dusk-filled courtyard, calling out to any strong man.

A monk gestured to Michael. "You carry *mikoshi* to the main temple."

Michael was pleased to be asked to help to move the portable shrine from its house of storage. There, in a simple ceremony, the god was invited to enter the waiting *mikoshi*. Though not large, the *mikoshi* with its dazzle of intricate gold work, surmounted by a fabulous phoenix, was extremely heavy, requiring at least 50 men to carry it any distance. In Wakayama, to the surprise of many of the locals, Michael had been one of the men chosen to carry their large *mikoshi* during the annual festival.

Later that night troops of men emerged into the lantern-lit streets to carry out dexterous acts of pole balancing and throwing, baton twirling or gong beating. Preceded by flaming torches, ceremonial horses carried a toddler, a child, a man and a sage: the group representing the four stages of life. The medieval pageantry served both to emphasize the continuity required for these rites as well as to remind the onlookers of how transient man's life is. Then the shrine maidens arrived, dressed in white linen, their faces serene and still.

The crowd's attention seemed to intensify in the already electrically charged atmosphere. The spine-tingling blast from a triton shell horn suddenly filled the night. The god in his glittering *mikoshi* drew near. Sweating, golden-robed men struggled down the last of the steep steps, muscles straining to keep the shrine from tumbling out of control. When they reached the street they stopped, their chests heaving. As they rested, to my acute embarrassment, a monk stepped forward to single me out from the densely packed crowd, insisting that I be photographed in front of the magical *mikoshi*, surrounded by the performers.

The *mikoshi* continued to move on and the crowd just followed, jamming the streets. We were eager now to catch the last train. But try as we might we were unable to break clear of the slow-moving throng as it wound its way through the streets of Kotohira. If we missed the last train, we would have to huddle on the streets until dawn. Stepping past supplicants kneeling in attitudes of prayer, we pressed on wherever we saw an opening. Rounding a corner, we suddenly found ourselves in full view of several hundred prostrate devotees. Unable to retreat we ran past them, feeling very big, very foreign and very conspicuous.

We arrived panting at the train station where Miki translated a large hand-printed sign that read, "Late trains will run."

2

Onsen of the White Heron

Sailing along the hilly Shikoku coastline we were buffeted by headwinds. After a long day beating to windward, we made our way into a small crowded harbor. Circuiting slowly, we searched for a berth amid launches, small freighters and rafted fishing boats.

A man waved to attract our attention, then scrambled to shove aside fishing boats and dinghies to reveal an unoccupied floating dock. He gestured for us to come in alongside but before we had secured the last mooring line, he had disappeared. Why had he not stayed and introduced himself? Experience suggested he wanted to avoid any ensuing obligation. His initial generosity was in itself remarkable. Fishermen in Japan are a close-knit, autonomous group, with a generally very narrow worldview. And few are interested in extending themselves to *gaigin*, like us.

The port where we found ourselves was Hagata-Ko. Located in the narrows of Kurushima Kaikyo, one of the main east-west transits for ship traffic, it might very well have been a Mediterranean seaside village. Only the freighter under construction at a nearby shipbuilding facility spoiled the illusion. I watched a bent old woman push a heavily-laden fish barrow along the waterfront, stopping now and then to chat with passers-by before disappearing into an alleyway. Men tended fishing poles and hooked protesting worms on lines before casting them into the bay.

Once SEA QUEST was secured, we searched for a *sento*, a Japanese bathhouse. Though these bathhouses were once common in all villages, newer private homes now have their own bathing facilities. The nearest *sento*, we were informed, was a long taxi ride away. With our hopes for a hot bath dashed, we followed the winding lanes into the countryside past terraced rice fields and over low hills from where we admired a tapestry of farms and cottages below. We discovered one of Kobo Daishi's 88 temples, but it was little more than a ruin, neglected except for the fresh flowers placed before a small image of Buddha.

The next morning we set off towards the western end of Shikoku. Again, we were beset by headwinds. The ship traffic was tremendous; at any one time there were, within sight, up to 70 vessels and fishing boats. By late afternoon, our eyes watering from the sun's glare and weary from keeping a close lookout, we rounded past a sentinel rock at the entrance to a short navigable river. The ancient port of Matsuyama nestles in the river's mouth with an old castle standing guard over the city.

Squeezed between docks and fish processing facilities were a ferry terminal and freighter wharf with a raft of small ships moored stern-to. One dock appeared free, so we came alongside. We were rudely ordered to leave.

"No yachts here!" the dockmaster shouted.

Too late, Michael realized his mistake. He had brought Miki along to translate, but since she was female and unmarried, she had no status. Had Michael approached alone, the dockmaster would not have dared to be so rude.

Leaving the dock, we anchored offshore from a beachside amusement park where the screams of happily terrified children on roller coasters drifted across to us. A suburban train rumbled to a stop at the nearby station. Landing our dinghy below it, we hopped on the train to ride into town.

In the heart of Matsuyama lies Dogo Onsen. Japanese literature has immortalized these hot springs. Like so many spas, springs, temples and shrines in this country of long memories and sentimental people, the locations themselves have gathered myth like furniture gathers dust. When neolithic farmers and fishermen lived here, a white heron appeared at the spring. He had a damaged leg and repeatedly returned to be soothed and healed. The wise old heron's repeated visits gave rise to tales of miraculous properties of the waters of Dogo. Word spread. Even emperors journeyed here not only to heal their bodies, but their minds and spirits as well. A section of the spa still remains reserved for the private use of today's Imperial Family.

We entered the spa's rabbit warren of inter-connected chambers where a hostess ushered us into a large 24-*tatami* room. In traditional Japanese houses, both old and new, the floors are covered with matting made of layers of rushes, edged with narrow strips of black brocade. These *tatami* are all of a standard size equivalent to one sleeping space. The number of *tatami* mats a room holds describes its size. This room of 24 mats was very large by Japanese standards, about 16 by 22 feet.

A kneeling hostess placed red-lacquered baskets before us. Inside we found soft towels and fresh kimono robes called *yukata*. Miki and I shed our city clothes in a locker room, then stepped naked into a large steamy stone-paved chamber. We had to support each other across the slippery granite floor polished by generations of bare feet. A large oval pool dominated the room. Ivory-skinned women knelt under scorching water that streamed from a large fountain. Others sat on wooden stools or squatted on the floor where they vigorously scrubbed themselves until their pale skin reddened.

Nudity in public bathhouses does not concern the Japanese. There is, however, a polite etiquette. They never seem to look directly at other bathers and naturally do not expect to be stared at, but they miss nothing from the corners of their eyes.

Picking up a wooden bucket and stool from those heaped by the door, I sat near the pool and next to me, a woman proceeded to rhythmically massage her legs. I scooped water, as the others did, from the pool and sloshed it over my body, involuntarily grimacing at the searing heat. When I relaxed, though careful not to stare, I could not help but notice a row of neat Japanese derrières across the room balanced upon their tiny seats. No sign of cellulite ripples there, I thought. Though middle-aged women bore a soft cushion of belly fat, their legs and lower hips stayed slender and firm. However, elderly women were excessively bent with backbones like a twisted railway-line of knobby protruding vertebrae. I am told that after the war, a lot of Japanese starved, and girls especially suffered. Even today, girls like to pretend to eat very little.

With a bar of super-soft Japanese soap I worked up a tremendous lather over my body, followed by buckets of water. When I was thoroughly rinsed, as convention dictated, I held a wash cloth modestly before me and lowered myself into the granite pool, shuddering in the 103° F water. I discovered profound satisfaction in this companionable public bathing. Miki slid in beside me, twisting her wet hair high on her head, bracing too when the heat touched her skin, but then rapidly immersing herself until the water lapped her chin.

After the bath, wrapped in the cotton *yukatas*, we joined Michael in the airy upper rooms to rest and drink tea from small handleless cups. We left the *onsen* feeling like pampered royalty.

Early the next morning an offshore breeze invited us to sail in the first favorable wind conditions we had met since leaving Wakayama. Hastily we got underway. A fine mist curtained the surrounding islands and the Shikoku hills, suspending the landscape in a veil of make-believe that replaced yesterday's cold clarity. We planned to cross the Suido Nada, a gulf at the western reaches of the Inland Sea. If lucky, we might even make it before midnight to the Kanmon Kaikyo, the current-swept strait between the two main Japanese islands of Honshu and Kyushu.

I took the helm when Michael grew tired in the afternoon. As we sailed, I thought of other trips we had made through the Seto Naikai. After first arriving in Japan we had spent three months visiting as many of the islands and mainland ports as we could. Later, we applied for a work visa. While the paperwork was processed we were required to leave the country. We sailed from Wakayama to Pusan in Korea, 100 miles from Japan, again making the Inland Sea an occasion to sightsee.

We had stood atop an island offshore from Hiroshima where our host pointed out a small island nearby. There, he said, is where the teenage boys were taken for their indoctrination as *kamikaze* pilots. In accordance with *Bushido*, the Samurai code of honor, the young recruits were informed, in all seriousness, that they *did* have a choice in the matter. The boys, some as young as 14, could choose to accept the duty they had to honor their God-Emperor (the Emperor is considered a living god in the Shinto religion) by becoming *kamikaze* pilots. Or they could choose to commit *harakiri*, ritual suicide, with dignity and no loss of face in a small building especially set aside for the purpose.

We later met a man who had trained as a *kamikaze* pilot

and survived the war. He remains eternally grateful to the American who shot him down out of the sky. Picked up by fishermen, he spent the rest of the war hiding in the remote Ryukyu Islands.

The sea had been so gentle when we left Matsuyama that Miki had not bothered to take a seasickness pill. Now she lived to regret it. By afternoon, we pounded into heavy swells. In her bunk below, tears of frustration soaked her pillow. This sailing was harder than she thought it would be. Did she curse the day she got herself on a cruising boat?

SEA QUEST pranced along to weather of the scattered islands, riding on a couple of knots of current. In such conditions with 25 knots of wind, SEA QUEST moves gracefully, her heavy displacement a distinct advantage. Two years in port had caused us to misplace the windvane sail, so that rudder was not yet operational. Continuous steering was strenuous work. Nevertheless, alone on deck I felt sheer exhilaration to be again in control of a powerful sailing machine.

Michael woke up when a sail noisily jibed. The wind had died. The sails luffed and the boat drifted. To the south, a soupy fog bank had dropped visibility to only a mile. The rapid weather change pointed to a warm front moving in. We knew what to expect.

The wind hit at around 30 knots and the cat never moved. What after all is a half-gale to a seagoing cat? However, when the wind indicator tipped 40, Mizzen's eyes grew round and worriedly peered up at me from her place under the helmsman's seat, anxious for some reassurance. Books and loose objects shook from insecure positions below. The cat's eyes followed her water bowl as it slid across the cockpit floor. Alarmed now she abandoned her accustomed place, staring around fretfully.

The weeks leading to our departure had been full of commitments. We had rounded off our English teaching jobs while squeezing in a flurry of last minute, highly remunerative weekend charters. Social invitations flooded in, and our pace grew even more hectic. We were unable to complete the usual pre-voyage preparations as thoroughly as we would have liked. We consoled ourselves that the job could be done as we sailed through the sheltered Seto Naikai.

Miki, who was unhappy enough before, was now transported to purgatory. Baam! Baam! Baam! The sound of seas pounding the sides of our steel hull was rather like sitting inside a gong. Miki clung to her forward bunk to stop from sliding out. She had not yet learned tricks that old sailors know, like rigging her lee cloth or stuffing pillows under the edge of a mattress. The new Japanese china rattled in the shelf while shifting bottles in lockers created a cacophony of jingling, jerking, and knocking noises. Stuffing towels and potholders in the most noisome places lessened the din, but I could do little for poor Miki.

By 10:30 PM when I came on watch again, the wind had died and the rain was starting to fall. We plowed on under engine. Our plan to reach the Kanmon Kaikyo straits by midnight was doomed.

All around SEA QUEST red, white and green lights moved confusingly while I struggled to full wakefulness. How could I make sense of them? Some, I knew, were ships overtaking to port showing green lights. Others off the starboard bow showed red and were crossing our course. We must give way to them, I reminded myself. The white lights were probably ships moving away from us—or they might be fishing boats, pair trawlers, anchored ships or navigation lights! I had to constantly assess the course and speed of each set of lights. Three white lights appeared. It was a ship on my starboard bow, now less than a mile away. Watch out, I thought. Those stacked lights indicate a tug and a long tow. It swept towards us faster and much closer than I expected so that I had to round up SEA QUEST to let the seemingly endless towrope and barge pass away into the inky blackness.

A chain of blinking red lights appeared. What is that, I wondered aloud? I used the binoculars to identify it as a fisherman's marker. Farther away, a brilliant flashing white light confused me. Another fishing-marker? No. It was a mid-channel buoy visible from so far away it took an hour to reach it. From behind, behemoth ships crept up silently but swept past in a welter of flying spume and churning wakes.

Some ships ventured too close, forcing me to wonder if I was still in clear view of the helmsman, whereupon I flipped on all the spreader lights to illuminate our white sails. Could they possibly conceive what it might feel to be aboard a yacht moving at only a few knots, unable to get out of the way quickly when an ocean-going cargo ship traveling at eighteen knots runs up close alongside?

We tacked to the edge of the shipping lanes to get out of the ships' wakes, giving way, changing course or holding steady for scores of ferries, coastal freighters, passenger liners, container ships, bulk carriers, and tugs with tows that crossed in both directions. What would the Japanese captains have thought had they known it was a woman at the helm?

Michael came on deck as we approached the coast where we now planned to spend what was left of the night. There we discovered dozens of anchored ships waiting for the morning's favorable tide. Weaving our way through them we dropped the hook close to shore and fell exhausted into our bunks.

Three or four hours later the wakes of departing cargo vessels slapped against the hull, buffeting us awake. At the entrance to the Kanmon Kaikyo an hour or two later the large white statue of the much beloved goddess materialized. The Kanmon stands upon a sea-lapped rock showering blessings upon sailors passing through the straits.

Once within the narrows, the current racing at more than 11 knots took a firm grasp on our little ship. SEA QUEST gathered speed to rush under the massive bridge that joins Japan's great island of Honshu to the southern island of Kyushu. Having already traveled twice through these narrows to and from Korea, we knew just where to get out of the swift current to the protection of the harbor that serviced the port-city of Shimonoseki.

Once inside the harbor we moored alongside a disused police patrol launch that made a handy dock. It was an easy walk from there to the nearby water-police offices from where we telephoned Customs, who in turn alerted Immigration. Authorities like to keep track of foreign vessels traveling between prefectures. However, with few computers and a compartmentalized system, officials find it hard to know where the smaller vessels are that, they worry, might smuggle Korean and Chinese illegal aliens into the country.

Private enterprise is better organized and does not seem to suffer the same inefficiencies. We rang a fuel company. Two hours later a truck was at the quayside pumping 900 liters of diesel into SEA QUEST's thirsty tanks. Chores done, fuel and engine oil aboard, we unlashed our tandem bicycle for a quick trip to the supermarket and a return trip with the bike festooned with bulging plastic bags. After stowing it all we set off again to locate an intriguing red shrine we had noticed as the currents of the Kanmon Kaikyo swept us under the bridge.

On this site 1,000 years ago, the nobility gathered to watch the final decisive battle between the Heiki and Genji clans. These two great families had ruled Japan with a balance of power for centuries. However, in this final confrontation the Genji were defeated and obliterated. Though the material we read did not say, it is likely that the entire family was forced to commit ritual suicide.

The Akama shrine's inner sanctum sits within a shallow jade-colored reflecting pool encircled by a colonnaded walk. Vermilion pillars rise beside shimmering water that casts eerie reflections across the ceiling beams. The serene but unearthly lights made it seem as though we wandered in a temple beneath the sea.

Still on the move next morning, we re-stowed our tandem, cast off from the old patrol boat and headed out again into the swirling current. Caught in its grip we were rapidly swept from the shelter of the Seto Naikai out into the Sea of Japan. Though the congestion of the narrow straits was behind us now, miles of commercial dockage, factories and belching industrial sites continued to sweep past. With binoculars we watched dredges working and several cranes positioning concrete tetrapods for a mammoth harbor under construction. Clearly, the area continues to expand its capacity to handle international cargo from Northern China and Korea.

Once past the port, while we still avoided small fishing boats and flagged net buoys, Japan's frenetic commercial world faded, giving way to sweet mountains and gentle islands. We headed towards the latter.

Oshima, only a few miles offshore, has ancient temples that recently revealed some long-held secrets. Written records tell stories that date back to the Yayoi era, circa 400 BC, the time of the first emperors of Japan. Recently discovered physical evidence suggests that these stories are more than mere myth or legend. The fishing village there is just prosperous enough to be smug and aloof to visitors, but scruffy enough to contain intriguing examples of older farm and village architecture. With Miki's help at day's end we found our way to a hotel bath.

We had only 15 miles to sail to Fukuoka the next day but were unhappy that we had promised Customs we would officially check in there because the guidebook characterized the place as "a city to get out of fast." However, the writer obviously did not come by boat and we were pleasantly surprised. The outer bay was strewn with steep islands where small yachts raced each other in the light breeze. The city itself flaunted its prosperity in a fabulous architectural mix of modern pastel buildings set on reclaimed seaside.

Using Miki's cell phone, we contacted a local man who was expecting us. He said a guest berth had been arranged for us at Odo Marina without charge, a privilege we much appreciated. Because his Wakayama friend had contacted him, he was now obligated to offer us hospitality as if he was our friend.

The marina was old by local standards with coin machines to operate the showers. But just two blocks away was a vast Hyper-Mart, the first we had seen in Japan, with prices so low that for a moment I forgot what country I was in.

A friendly and relaxed Customs officer arrived, obviously more used to foreigners than those in the Seto Naikai. Gone was the sealed Customs packet with the tamper-proof waxed crest to be delivered in the next port. Instead, our papers were returned to us in an open manila envelope.

We walked to Meinohama train station, dodging pedestrians, bicycles and honking traffic. The train was fast and soon deposited us to the first place of interest we planned to visit.

Kamikaze, the name associated by westerners to the suicide bombers of World War II actually means "Divine Wind." The name was originally coined after the citizenry of Fukuoka was threatened in 1281 by the Kublai Khan's invasion force of 100,000 warriors from Korea. The frightened townspeople desperately fought off the first wave of fighting men as they tumbled ashore from scores of ships. Just when it seemed they must be overcome, the *Kami Kaze*, in the form of a sudden violent storm sprang up out of nowhere to drive the Khan's fleet back to sea where they perished.

Hakata, the older section of the city, has been known as the cradle of Zen Buddhism since Eisai founded the movement in 1195. It is commemorated each year in the Dontaku festival that involves hundreds of religious men and weeks of rigorous Zen mental and physical training. The men eat, sleep, and pray together. Even in the damp chill, they wear only a cloth twisted around their loins and a short jacket. Dawn finds groups of them running through the streets, shouting the name, "Ei-sai, Ei-sai, Ei-sai," while aligning body and mind in an effort to transcend normal physical limits.

On festival day these conditioned men do not merely carry heavy carved and gilded floats, but turn the task into an insane workout. They run, swerving out of control at street corners while onlookers scatter. Sweat pours from faces; droplets shake from streaming headbands. Relievers pace the bearers, ready to jump in and heft the load themselves as soon as it becomes necessary. The whole dangerous affair takes a man through the pain barriers to a sense of unlimited self. The festival lends incredible vitality to the city.

Fukuoka's futuristic city-center sparkles with an impressive pride. Canal City boasts shopping arcades, outdoor cafes, computer-driven fountains, and daytime concerts. It is thronged by the upwardly mobile young. We did not remain long enough to discover if this new face of Japan has a soul.

We thought that Kyushu might suffer from provincialism. Instead we continued to be staggered by the grandeur of old temples and astonished by artwork preserved for millennia, much of it carved in wood. Certainly, our original image of Japan as a wall-to-wall megalopolis was utterly shattered. How it manages to fit 126 million people into a country the size of New Zealand, with few natural resources, but an economy second only to America's is astounding. Especially when so much of its industry is so well integrated into towns and cities that it is hardly even noticeable.

One trick the Japanese have mastered is the use of small family-owned manufacturing plants. Even huge companies order components from thousands of Mom and Pop operations.

One couple we knew manufactured metal thimbles. Even Grandma and the smaller kids got involved and of course, they were free to work seven days a week if they wanted to. There are no zoning laws to prevent manufacturing in residential areas, so people are able to maximize the use of their homes and other premises.

Our hostess, the wife of the kind man who had arranged our berth at Odo Yacht Club, drove us into the country for the day. The *guji-san*'s wife at Kokubunji temple insisted on throwing open the doors to its inner shrine so we might admire a highly venerated Buddha image. Though normally it was sealed off from public view, except for a single day each year, because we were *gaijin* who could not return, but probably more importantly, because our hostess was a lady of influence, we were welcomed into the sanctum.

At Kanzeone we discovered eighth-century temples dating to the very origins of Buddhism in Japan. Most of the buildings in this large complex are in ruins. Only a handful survived the ravages of war, invasion and accidental fire. Enveloped now in the kindly light of autumn, the old temples cast a mellow shadow across time.

Gray tunic-clad monks with skin like yellowed parchment are the caretakers of the treasure-trove of giant Buddha images that once graced the temples now in ruin. As we climbed the stairs of the building a sense of serenity spread over us. We rested on a wooden bench, surrounded by 50 gilded wooden images. Heavenly guardians and fierce-looking mythical deities stood 16 feet high.

Later in the day at Dazaifu village, beneath a grove of ancient camphor trees, we found a country fair in progress. Spread out in open stalls were antique robes of silk and cotton, porcelain objects and faded lacquer work. Keen-eyed dealers studied the porcelain with practiced eyes. Housewives, out for a bit of fun, fingered attractive pieces, holding them at arm's length to gauge how enthusiastically their friends responded, before deciding to purchase. Michael studied *netsukes*, ivory carvings small enough to fit into the palm of his hand: baubles every man of substance used to wear in his belt. Then he reached out to touch the shining blade of a magnificent samurai sword.

"*Dekinai.* Don't do that," the stall owner reprimanded him, wagging his finger vigorously.

I was attracted to a delicate Imari porcelain platter but Michael hastily reminded me that it would fit nowhere on SEA QUEST. We found ourselves in agreement over a set of carved elephant bone cabinet figures. Representing the seven gods of Shikoku, they are usually depicted together in a fishing boat as though off on a pleasant expedition. These rustic figures would bring back fond memories of Japan and our sail through the Inland Sea. When I opened the bargaining, in Japanese, I took the stallholder by surprise and then pressed my advantage. He quickly agreed on a good price.

Back on SEA QUEST late that night, after our day of wandering in the countryside and dinner with our host, we welcomed the little gods aboard with ceremony. We had a full ship.

3

Kyushu: Ancient Land of Fire

Hazy days continued. The unwinding panorama of wildly con-
figured hills continued to fascinate us. Ancient basalt plugs,
high peaks, islands pointed like witches' hats, and even square
blocks of living earth pushed from the sea were stark evidence
that Japan sits astride the Ring of Fire, that belt of major earth-
quake and volcanic activity encircling the Pacific Ocean.

We anchored for the night in a boulder-strewn cove, one of
the landing places of Kublai Khan's invading Mongol force almost a thousand years earlier. Though the sun had already set
behind the cove's high bluff, we headed ashore. We waded in
shadowy waters to search the rocky crevices for edible mol-
lusks. By dinghy we skirted the sea-lapped boulders, pausing
now and then to peer below at waving seaweed and darting fish.
Back on the boat we lit the kerosene primus stove and boiled
shellfish, which filled the snug cabin with a salty tang.

The next day, a bright morning awakened us. On this warm
and windless day we motored on to Kujukushima, the Bay of a
Thousand Islands. Romantic castles high on green hills and vermilion shrines with copper roofs stood on the banks of the
winding waterways. With the tide pushing us we threaded a
narrow channel until it opened into a huge bay where lay the
city of Sasebo. A Customs launch zoomed past; we gave it a
friendly wave. Belatedly seeing us, they circled to cross our bow.
The boat drew near to ask for our papers and pass over forms
to fill in. Then they stood off while the officer studied us
through binoculars. When the papers were completed we
handed them over along with our passports. After a lengthy and
detailed inspection they returned the passports and ordered us
to proceed into Sasebo Port.

To the officer's surprise, Michael refused. We had already
been officially cleared to Huis Ten Bosch, a small port given the
name of a Dutch palace in The Hague, and we saw no reason to

North West Kyushu

be required to make our way into a large and inconvenient port. Though all our papers were found to be in order, the officer seemed to be mystified at not being instantly obeyed. However, he relented and agreed to inspect us at Huis Ten Bosch the following day.

The large bay on which Sasebo lies gives way to another narrow channel through which strong tidal currents sweep, leading into the 175-square mile landlocked bay of Omura Wan. Huis Ten Bosch is a Disney-like attraction for Japanese visitors who do not need to risk their safety by venturing overseas to visit a real foreign town. It is the replica of a Dutch village sitting amid canals and tulips. It is replete with windmills, bell towers, tower gates, formal gardens, topiary, the Royal Palace copied from The Hague, and even square-rigged sailing ships in the bay.

We were invited to tie up at the luxury yacht club there. Michael and I thought the primary delight ashore for salty mariners was the unlimited hot water in the shower, but our newest crewmember thought otherwise. She was certain this was fairyland with the impression intensified after dark when the sound and light show began. Laser lights slashed the sky and a tall galleon ship moored in the inner basin suddenly became awash in red flames. From strategically placed speakers came sound effects, while a neon-lit, hydraulically articulated sea-dragon writhed, hissed and belched colored smoke. Miki, sitting astride the mizzen boom, clapped and screamed with the unrestrained delight of a young child.

Our relationship with Miki was gradually deepening, helped in part by her mentors in Wakayama with whom she consulted almost daily on her cell phone. They felt certain that aboard SEA QUEST she would gain experience and skill unobtainable anywhere else. Again and again, they urged her to be patient, to listen, to learn. "Speak out your fears and confusions," they advised. "Ask questions. Don't hold things back until they develop into cankers." Despite our original misgivings, we had become fond of Miki who, when she was happy, had a fun-loving temperament. We sincerely hoped that our voyage together would prove to be her epiphany; that it would pave the way for a rewarding future and a more unusual kind of life. It was naïve however to believe that Miki could adapt painlessly to our way of life and our western culture, not to speak of the day-to-day difficulties of having to live in close quarters. Although we were aware that she felt an intense and rather hopeless dissatisfaction with her own Japanese culture, we knew that the true dimension of ours remained a mystery to her.

By train from Huis Ten Bosch, we headed to the inland hills of Arita and wandered through porcelain shops stuffed with costly ceramic treasures. Though most are decorated with print transfers, there are still gems to be found, painted with masterly freehand strokes and masterly prices to match. Most of *Arita-yaki*, from rice bowls to teacups to all the eclectic variety that the Japanese use for delicate color-matched food arrangements, is produced today for the domestic market. Originally this ware was known in the West as Imari, named for the port from which it was shipped. Collectors from around the world still search out handmade pieces from the eighteenth century. The pottery industry grew at the time of the Opium Wars when China's lucrative trade was interrupted, but the European demand was insatiable. Merchants settled skilled Korean potters in Japan to manufacture copycat chinaware, but gradually the Arita porcelain style evolved and became sought after for its own sake.

A wind ruffled the early morning calm of the yacht harbor at Huis Ten Bosch. The previous evening we had partied on a Japanese yacht, and tried to glean information on ports to the south, but beer and sake flowed too freely. We sat with businessmen who own luxurious yachts that seldom leave the harbor. They all spoke of sailing away one day when their companies finally retire them, though I could not help feeling that the constant overuse of tobacco and alcohol will sail them to eternity before any of them become old enough.

The autumn wind, which swept the sky clear on the late October day we tossed off the lines, was already sharp. Layers of soft blue etched the hills stripped of yesterday's haze. At the narrow straits of the Hario Seto, a fisherman cast his line into whirlpools. In the strong ebb, SEA QUEST was suddenly caught by the pull of racing water and dragged sideways out of control before plunging into an eddy. Locals told us currents can rush through here at 16 knots.

Once outside of Sasebo Bay, a northerly breeze from dead astern filled our sails. Our course lay along the exposed western coast in the East China Sea to the southernmost cape of Kyushu. Although the land of Nagasaki Prefecture was gentler than the countryside bordering the Seto Naikai, we were usually within sight of at least one volcano. The steep tangerine plantations of the Inland Sea were replaced by wild scrub.

Much of the coastline seemed pristine. We caught only glimpses of harbors, bridges and large shipyards tucked well down into deep bays. The offshore islands along this stretch belonged to the military. One abandoned and decaying island resembled a war movie set. Low and gray, it was surrounded by massive sea walls that terminated in a high bluff. A wooden watchtower stood overlooking the abandoned remains of concrete buildings, silent witness to some guarded past. Was the island a camp for forced wartime labor from Korea or China or a prison?

At the southern end of Nagasaki's cape a fishing cove offered refuge from the winds now gusting to 25 knots. The new harbor, unlisted on our charts, was a typical example of the rapid changes being wrought. It is easy to imagine that, in another quarter century, Japan will have little, if any, natural coastline left. We had already observed the relentless destruction of the Seto Naikai's unique environment, but it is not alone. Every prefecture in Japan now seems keen to build harbors, extend them, and then add a bit more. Shallow bays are reclaimed. Islands are ringed at sea level with roads that eliminate every beach and rocky inlet, and then, where possible, they are joined by bridge or causeway to the mainland. Billions of massive concrete tetrapods secure every cove and bay against typhoons. Outside harbor entrances, great 30-foot-high re-curved wave-walls guard against tsunami. Beaches not otherwise eliminated by road works or sea walls are frequently reinforced with concrete paving stones. A truly unimproved stretch of coastline in the Seto Naikai is so rare that our usual response was to reach for a camera to record the place before its unquestioned disappearance.

Strong winds set the rigging to thrumming. A clanging halyard beat its staccato rhythm against the aluminum mast. Miki woke up moody, scared she said, at what the day might bring, unable to face her imagined terrors calmly. She would be seasick today. Of that much she was certain. Barely touching her food, she sat silent at the breakfast table. Would she ever relax and become part of the team?

The tide was well out. High above us on the wharf Nomoura villagers stopped to peer down into the cockpit. A friendly man, owner of the local liquor shop, drove up in a car, hopped out and presented us with a case of canned coffee beverage. He could not know how appreciated his gesture was since, only moments before, another local, a member of the local fishermen's union, had heatedly berated us for using the Nomoura wharf—telling us that the government had built it exclusively for the fishermen's use!

Attitudes are insular in Japan. Little more than a century ago people lived under the yoke of feudalism. They did not even have a last name. Women were just called by a number. Ichiko, number one girl! The movements of peasants and fishermen around the countryside were severely restricted. Habits die hard. Even today most Japanese still stay put. Families are so permanent their name is usually carved in granite outside their front door. We were strangers, and strangers in any country town, whether Japanese or *gaijin*, are seen as outsiders. To an outsider the villager owes no obligation, and no standard form of polite behavior seems to be customary. He can be rude or he can be kind, as his personality dictates. Though unmasked animosity did upset us on occasion, we realized that the behavior stemmed from cultural provincialism. Fortunately, the many good-tempered better-educated Japanese we met more than made up.

Roiling masses of gray cloud filled the sky. The strong wind blew straight from the north, as though urging us to hurry towards the blue skies and warm seas of the tropics. Crossing the Hayasaki Seto, we sailed out of sight of land for the first time in many long months until the coast of Amakusa Shima appeared on the horizon ahead.

A smart-looking launch sped past, its skipper waving on his way from nearby Ushibuka-Ko to retrieve the fishermen he had marooned on rocky islets in the morning. This 60-mile stretch of Kyushu's coast is protected by a string of closely set islands ten to 20 miles offshore. A huge bridge painted electric-blue joining two of the islands dwarfed a seagoing tug and its tow passing under it. At Nagoshima Kaikyo, another narrow inlet gave egress into Yatsushiro Kai. But it was a little further to the south, in the natural surroundings of Tera Shima that we found a pretty bay where we anchored amid roosting herons and black-crested shags.

Fukata, the closest town, lay some distance across the open gulf. But nearby, almost hidden behind the string of islets and a manmade stone sea wall, was the little village of Wakimoto-ko. Although the village looked inviting we were exhausted and planned to stay aboard that night. Michael was already snoozing in a pre-dinner nap when the nearby sound of an engine sent me topside. A boat was standing off, a blue-uniformed policeman in her bows. Michael, rubbing sleep from his eyes, followed me on deck.

Suspicious old men ashore, when they saw the mysterious yacht outside their bay, had jumped to the conclusion that we were both foreign and dangerous. The local constable examined our papers carefully, but probably, never having seen ship's papers before, understood them not at all. We assured him we were in Japan legally and eventually he accepted our word. Chinese and Koreans were frequently smuggled into these parts, he told us. We knew, however, that the excuse served only as a thin mask for local paranoia. But now the formerly suspicious fisherman who accompanied the policeman was all toothy grin. He urged us to come ashore in his boat to join a party already underway in the local hall. We agreed somewhat wearily, but were accosted the moment we stepped ashore by a senior police officer and a plainclothes officer who, alerted, had just arrived from Fukata. They stepped from their car to sternly admonish us.

"You can stay on the yacht, but you cannot come ashore!"

Bowing and displaying conventional niceties while objecting strongly, I retorted in Japanese. "We are free to go anywhere in Japan. We have visas."

Michael was beginning to feel a little irate, but knew better than to let it show. He fumbled in his wallet and pulled out his Japanese driver's license. Seeing it, the officer became instantly contrite.

"You should have shown us this before. There would have been no problem."

We laughed of course over the fact that our legality stemmed from having Japanese driver's licenses! They are something of a prestige item in Japan because getting one often costs two or three thousand U.S. dollars. The testing is stringent and usually must be repeated several times. Fortunately, Wakayama City Hall helped arrange for us to pay a small fee to have our Kiwi licenses replaced by Japanese ones.

I doubt that the people of these little coves will ever become used to yachts. The villagers of Wakimoto-ko told us that SEA QUEST was the first yacht they had ever seen. Even if the locals were not hostile, Japanese yachtsmen prefer luxury locations near shopping malls and hot baths. Few Japanese yachtsmen are as self-contained as we are, and it is rare for foreign yachts to venture into Japan's temperate but typhoon-prone latitudes, although it seemed to us that the experience far outweighed the risks.

Our hosts led us along a road overhung by banyan trees. As we passed people openly stared. At the hall we removed our shoes and stepped into a large room to join a feast in full swing. The hall fell quiet. I felt very foreign, our group rather like an invading alien force as the stony-faced village women stared unsmiling at the three of us. But our friendly escort waved them aside and seated us on tatami mats at the central table where platters of delicacies were set.

"*Kampai,*" they shouted. Toasts were made all around. Soon people relaxed and the pitch of voices grew loud. By this time we were quite famished and set to devouring the food set before us. Several men including the elementary school principal, his retired boss, a diesel mechanic, our fisherman friend and a clerk from the hospital crowded us, asking questions. Their apron-clad wives twittered at another low table, discussing, I am sure, every aspect of our behavior and dress, occasionally bestirring themselves to bring over another dish. How odd we must have seemed to them! One younger woman, bolder than the others, came over, amazed to discover that we used chopsticks and spoke a little of her language. She went back to her friends to report our exchange.

Japanese like to entertain with songs. They prefer taped

karaoke accompaniments but this humble hall had no such set up, so various men, well fortified with sake, took turns to sing. Michael only croaks, but to their amazement and delight, he got to his feet to deliver a speech. In an amusing way in halting Japanese, he told the gathered villagers about ourselves, where we came from and where we were going. Most importantly, he explained why we were taking a Japanese girl with us. Oddly enough, when they discovered that Miki was a true *Nihon-jin*, not a Korean or a Hawaiian as they had first thought, they left her absolutely alone. Since Michael could not sing I was urged on. A really gutsy version of "Waltzing Matilda" had the villagers clapping and humming to the chorus and then screaming for more. The women's faces softened at last, then broke into smiles. We were accepted.

In the darkness of early dawn, we rose to make the best of what would be a long day. SEA QUEST plunged into the swells that rolled into the shoaling waters of the bay. We set our geniker, our lightweight spinnaker-like sail. Instead of filling in the early-morning breezes it backed, collapsed and wrapped itself around the forestay. As the sun climbed higher, the wind grew stronger. By ten o'clock hard gusts were pushing SEA QUEST to eight knots, too much for the light geniker to carry. It was time to get it down. We waited for a lull but it did not come. Eight knots crept towards nine. SEA QUEST screamed along. Miki, happily oblivious to our growing alarm, still slept peacefully in the cockpit.

"Wake up, Miki," Michael called out. "We need help on the sheets!"

I was worried. She lacked experience and her unbound hair was a danger around the winches.

I suggested instead, "Miki, could you steer?"

Not fully comprehending and probably queasy with seasickness, she took the helm from me and gazed fixedly at the compass, as though her staring would steady its dizzy movement. I stripped off my knitted cotton gloves, thinking they might catch in the winch. In our usual routine, Michael goes forward, shouts for me to slack the geniker sheet a little, and then begins to pull the sock down from the top of the sail to collapse it while I play out the sheet.

But under steadily increasing wind, he surprised me. Still in the cockpit he ordered, "Stand by to slack the geniker." He wanted to drop wind out of the sail quickly.

"Slack the geniker now!"

Slack the geniker now? It will go out of control and maybe rip. But I am trained to follow orders so I removed the line from the winch bit. The sheet had only been wound twice, not three times, around the drum in the light morning airs. Now in heavy winds the sail carried extra tons of wind pressure. I began to slacken the sheet. A fresh gust hit the sail, the rope slipped a little through my ungloved hands and then gained speed until a bight of line whipped off the winch drum and ran out unchecked. I dropped the line and stepped back clear as the unsheeted sail flogged riotously like a colorful gay flag against a brooding sky. SEA QUEST slowed and settled.

I lifted my hands to examine them. The skin had flayed from my left hand.

White faced, Michael asked, "Are you OK?" He had seen my look of horror.

"I cannot help you get the sail down."

The boat wallowed heavily in the building seas with the geniker ballooning out beyond the bowsprit. With my good hand I switched on the autopilot because Miki seemed to have completely frozen at the unexpected turn of events. Michael pulled the sock down over the flogging geniker and then lowered it in a heap to the deck. When he returned, I was braced on the cockpit floor considering what to do next.

"Let me see your hand," said Michael gently.

"No, not until you find the things we'll need. Get the Dettol. Add some warm water from the kettle so I can soak it clean."

When the bath was ready I grimaced as I slowly opened my tightly balled hand. Michael blanched. Along the whole length of the fingers the pads were torn, along with part of the palm.

"OK," I commanded, feeling the need for some control, "from under the head sink, pull out the wooden bandage box."

When a clean towel, cotton, gauze bandage and Neobactrim antibiotic ointment were assembled, Michael began the careful cleaning and bandaging, using sterile Vaseline-soaked gauze patches and liberal lashings of antiseptic ointment to prevent the dressings from sticking. Once the fingers were bandaged, I wriggled the tender and still intensely burning hand into a white cotton work glove. From the ship's store of antibiotics, I directed Michael to select a ten-day course of Ampicillin against possible infection.

Miki had watched, as if she was in some terrible nightmare. In her world accidents happened to others and hospitals patched them up. Had it just dawned on her that the three of us were now responsible for each other's safety?

The steady burning of my hand brought back the memory of one summer when Michael and I were still teenagers in the Caribbean. He and I had been spearfishing together when my pinkie finger was nearly severed. In their biggest and fastest boat, a Tortolan sailing sloop, Michael and his worried mother took me to Road Town, a trip of several hours. It was Sunday, the poor old doctor was too inebriated to help. We sailed on in that open boat all the way to the U.S. Virgin Islands, without passports and wearing only swimsuits. The officials refused at first to let us through until I showed them my mangled finger!

As my mind drifted back to the present, I noticed the winds had steadied at around 25 knots to kick up a nice little sea atop a long rolling swell. We sailed past off-lying islands to starboard, and a rugged sparsely populated coast to port behind which rose the towering Sakurajima volcano. This 3,500-feet-high mountain hovers over Kagoshima Harbor, reputedly the loveliest port in Japan. We skimmed past Japan's westernmost headlands: Noma Misaki and Bono Misaki. They are high capes with rocky outliers and lighthouses sitting atop them. Rounding the second cape, another perfectly proportioned volcano hove into view. I had yet to see a more beautiful mountain. Kaimon Dake, also known as Sakaura Fuji, is a near perfect cone rising some 3,000 feet, a serene sentinel guarding the lower reaches of Kagoshima's long seaway approaches.

With a favorable current under our keel, we picked up a gain of almost eight miles on today's run of sixty, bringing us to Makurazaki two merciful hours earlier than expected.

The handmade chart given to Michael at Huis Ten Bosch proved useless. We entered a maze of interconnected fishing harbors. We should have bought a road map. The harbor had recently been enlarged. A road map would have had more details of new waterfront developments than our five-year-old charts. Seeing an empty dock, we tied up. Minutes later a smiling local man informed us we were in the fish unloading area. Nevertheless, he kindly pointed to a disused fishing boat and said we could moor alongside it. Thus finally and properly secured, exhausted by the accident and our stressful day, we gratefully retired to our bunks. There we each reflected quietly on the day's bountiful but painful harvest of experience.

4

Pearls of the East China Sea

The busy bay choked with fishing craft and seabirds hummed. Just outside the interlocking harbors stood graceful Kaimon Dake, her lower slopes spread about her like a skirt. Enjoying the easy movement through the calm water, we motorsailed. Despite the injury to my hand, I had slept well enough, and now only groaned when my hand bumped into something.

Dolphins lazily surfaced, giving Miki her first close look at these enchanting sea mammals. However they seemed more interested in the schools of fish than in SEA QUEST cutting through the water. By the time we passed the flanks of the volcano, gathering clouds had obscured the sun and haze reduced visibility. Across Kagoshima's busy harbor mouth, the light breeze died away.

The rugged southernmost cape of Kyushu, Sata Misaki, was now in sight. The gentle surf barely splashed the dark rocks, which, like a magnet, had drawn fishermen to them. We motored to Odomari Wan, about five miles beyond the cape where the local fishermen pointedly ignored us as we circled the inner harbor looking for a berth. Unwelcome inside the breakwater, we found good holding off a crescent beach where we were later joined by other, friendlier, non-local trawlermen.

The yachtsman who had given us useless maps and erroneous information had mentioned hot springs, close by the beach. The springs, it turned out, were more than an hour's walk away into the hills. Rather than a long hike, we searched for an old-style Japanese *ryokan* inn and found one in the fishing village.

"Could we use your bathhouse?" we asked the *okusan* who opened the door. She was obviously hesitant, but her curious husband stepped up to crane over her shoulder. When he learned we were from the foreign yacht that the whole village was gossiping about, he overrode her objections to invite us in.

The steaming tub set between natural boulders was burning hot. Even Miki, fully accustomed to the heat of Japanese bathhouses, could not get into it. How, I wondered, could anyone enjoy scalding water? Fortunately, there was a shower. While each in turn took a bath, the others were served green tea and coconut candy in a spacious *tatami* room. When we were ready to leave, the proprietor graciously refused our money.

Back aboard SEA QUEST, Miki prepared dinner despite her inexperience with the touchy kerosene stove and our western-style menus. Meanwhile Michael cut away the bandages from my hand so that the more stubborn dressings could be soaked off. The wound was serious, but we thought that if it was kept clean and dry, infection could be averted, though it was our unspoken worry that I might need a skin graft. After the work was over and I had downed a couple of glasses of sake along with some codeine tablets, the pain-level dropped back to tolerable.

We got underway again the next morning under thin clouds. Behind us SEA QUEST's wake reached back, I thought rather wistfully, towards the mist-cloaked mainland of Japan, now quickly disappearing. I felt very emotional. Japan had left an indelible imprint on us. Nowhere on earth had Michael and I been made more welcome and yet, nowhere else had we felt more alien.

Tanegashima lay silhouetted in the path of the sun. It is the most northerly of the chain of Ryukyu Islands, strung like pearls for three hundred miles from mainland Japan to Taiwan. In the west, a young volcano's sulfurous plume wrote its signature in the sky. Io Shima was a fire-mountain in a line of such mountains that stretched all the way from the Aleutians to New Zealand.

Yakushima is a moody and precipitous island with perpetual cloud impaled on soaring peaks. There great stands of *sugi* and *hinoki*, thousand-year old cedar and cypress, of the kind used to build Japan's ageless temples and castles, survive. From our cockpit speakers classical music drifted across the calm seas. The autopilot had taken over and we relaxed, absorbed in the natural beauty surrounding us. Then the roar of jet engines and a blasting horn awoke us from our deep reverie. A strange, almost flying vessel approached close astern, then swerved sharply alongside in a welter of spray. We had been buzzed by a hydrofoil-ferry at what felt like the speed of sound.

Yakushima's main port, Ambo, is no longer a quiet fishing harbor. It caters to the stunning hydrofoils that rush between Yakushima and the mainland at 40 knots. These space-age vessels, designed by Boeing Aircraft Corporation, are manufactured in Japan. Powered by twin 1,400-horsepower jet engines and flying on winged hydrofoils, they barely seem to touch the water.

Nosing into Ambo's outer harbor, we found the fishing boat enclosures too shallow for us while the main wharf itself was too exposed to go safely alongside. We circled slowly. On the waterfront a car horn tooted and a man stepped out waving for our attention, then pointed to a hidden inner bay. Gratefully we nosed our way in.

"Wait. I come back soon," he said after helping us to secure our lines.

Later that afternoon he returned to take us for a drive along Yakushima's twisting coastal roads to his favorite spa where we soaked and steamed in a luxurious marble-tiled *onsen*. When we returned to the boat, the skipper of that same fast-flying hydrofoil hailed us from the dock.

"My crew wants to meet you. Come with me to the ferry house for a beer and sake."

On his routine 50-mile run back and forth to Kagoshima, our appearance had piqued his curiosity. He could not hide his surprise when we told him we had sailed to Japan from New Zealand and were now heading home. But his envious crew was even more incredulous that Miki was aboard.

"She crew? She *sail* with you to New Zealand? Take me instead," one repeated insistently.

"Are you a real Japanese?" the other asked Miki.

That a Japanese girl could or would take up a sailor's life was an affront to their masculinity. The idea seemed so strange, so unnatural. There was something amiss in a young woman wanting to go to sea. Her place, they suggested to her, was *married and at home!*

We rose early to catch the very first morning bus that snaked inland along 3000-foot precipices where thin mountain-fed streams tumbled. How today's island people farm commercial cedar trees on such steep slopes is beyond imagining. The life of a tree farmer on Yakushima is surely a hard one. Nevertheless, farm them they do. The near vertical mountainsides carried a soft velvet mantle of plantation trees.

At the end of the road we left the bus to wander in a sacred stand of ancient cedars. The mountain vastness had been hiding them for eons. Today, the law protects the trees and the people venerate them as gods. Hushed, we walked amongst the thousand-year-old giants. For a few timeless moments in that shadowed glade the largest of them all, the "Buddha of the Forest," seemed to cast a spell over us.

Because we had started out so early, it was only eleven o'clock when we waved our last good-byes to chattering mountain monkeys and returned to SEA QUEST. Another typhoon had developed well to the east, and the weather, the locals informed us, would soon become rough. Though we would have dearly appreciated a couple of days' rest, we dared not linger with the weather closing in and a 90-mile run to the next island. Just after midday, we cast off our lines.

Once we had cleared Yakushima's wind shadow, the boat picked up speed. The lost windvane sail had at last been recovered in its chain-locker hiding place, so for the first time since leaving Wakayama, the wind-assisted steering was put to work.

As night descended Yakushima faded behind us into the general gloom. In the heeling, bucking cockpit, Michael and Miki were grateful for the hot chicken stew hastily prepared just before leaving port and left lashed to the stove. After the taunts of the hydrofoil crewmembers, Miki was wide-eyed and keen with excitement—more determined than ever to master the vicissitudes of seagoing life. Planning to share the night watches for the first time, she even stayed up after dinner, but all to no avail. In the wee hours of the morning the wind increased, and with it her terror.

Tokara Shima's lighthouse, 15 miles to starboard, flashed repeatedly while we kept track of the dozen or so squid boats and cargo ships that hove into our sphere of vision. By 3:00 AM, SEA QUEST roared along at eight knots.

"Michael! Wake up!"

As he came on deck shaking the sleep from his eyes and peering around to see what was happening, I explained. "We've got to get some sail off."

Grabbing the harness he snapped the clip to the safety line that stretched the length of the boat, then stepped outside. Miki, dozing in the cockpit sea-bunk, stared incredulously from him to the roiling seas with their white cresting waves. The wind's rising scream and the hard reality that Michael was going out onto the heaving deck was simply too much. She went into withdrawal.

The wind indicator hung between 20 and 30 knots. I let the sheet go entirely slack. Michael dropped the genoa. The sail fluttered out over the sea and he dragged it aboard sodden. Better wet than to have the sail scoop up a belly full of water and then burst like an overfilled balloon.

With the headsail down, I rounded SEA QUEST up into the building sea until the mainsail started shaking enough for Michael to work it down and tuck in a reef. Then he set the staysail for balance, and on a broad reach, SEA QUEST rushed into the darkness. Under reduced sail SEA QUEST had settled down, the windvane doing most of the work. The windvane is the equivalent of at least one strong and tireless shipmate. A shipmate that never falls asleep, keeps a good course, and is never hungry!

Twenty to 30 knots is just a good stiff breeze. In the open ocean, where there is plenty of fetch, the wind is bound to set up a bit of a sea. The conditions were not something to be overly concerned about. However, when Michael returned to the cockpit and tried to comfort Miki, she was unable to respond.

We approached Amami Oshima's windward side, rounding up to drop sail. Our general chart gave few details of the harbors but the hydrofoil skipper had given us an up-to-date drawing of a little harbor suitable for a yacht. Was the chart accurate, Michael wondered, or was it like the others we had been given that proved so useless? The ocean swells swept around a promontory to roll right into Naze Wan, the gulf outside the harbor mouth. With wind and sea behind us, entering would be tricky. Carefully he compared what he saw with the sketch map before we eased our way across the swell into the suddenly placid waters of Daikuma-Ko. Several Japanese yachts were moored along the breakwater. Seeing us, two men hurriedly cleared some lines and with a wave indicated for us to drop anchor and come in stern first.

We invited them aboard. Over steaming coffee, they introduced themselves. Ani-San was a personable local yachtsman and owner of a fishing shop. Ohta-San was a Hokkaido sailor who, with his wife, had recently sailed their 35-foot sloop MIN MIN to these more gentle climes while dodging the numerous typhoons that this year's El Niño had spawned. The next day Ani-San took us all on an excursion over his island. We climbed mountain trails ringing with birdcalls and gazed out over bays of sapphire and turquoise. Though too far north for extensive coral reefs to form, small chunks now littered the beaches. In tide pools we found tropical cowries, murex and spindle shells that hermit crabs used for homes. After a stop at a sake distillery we gathered at Ani-san's house. Michael and I hid the discomfort we felt kneeling for prolonged periods on the floor, while Ani-San's wife, bowing all the time and on her knees, served us a fisherman's dinner before retiring out of sight. As the dinner ended and Ani-San began to pour out his soul in song, the telephone interrupted.

"My friend, Ishihara-San, wants to come play for you" he said.

Ishihara-San had several CDs of traditional music to her credit. With the grace of someone half her age she sank onto a silk cushion to re-tune her *shamisen*, a three-stringed and narrow-necked traditional instrument fingered like a violin but plucked with a reed. Small drums, taken up by Ani-San's sister accented her plucky rhythms. The lyrics, we were told, spoke of ancestors, myth, and the pride of belonging.

On November 1, we sailed along the length of Amami Os-hima to Satsugawa Wan, a sound formed by a large island off the southwest coast. The waterway, with many seductive bays and white sand beaches, is in places only one or two miles wide. We entered crowded Koniya-Ko at last light and were made welcome alongside MIN MIN, arrived only an hour ahead of us. We were soon squatting around a smoking barbecue eating the fish Ohta-San had caught on the way in. A deaf-mute man engaged Michael in a long, mimed conversation, and each of us sang a song or two until the yawns began to drown out the words.

In the morning, the deaf-mute man arrived with his similarly afflicted wife to take MIN MIN and SEA QUEST's crews on a jaunt. He would treat everyone to a real meat barbecue tonight, he promised. At his relative's farm, a protesting half-grown kid was pushed into the back of the station wagon. As the over-crowded car bumped along the road the goat bleated, leapt about and then jumped out of the window. Our friend, however, was not about to be deprived of his meat. He took off at a run through the scrub and returned triumphantly with the trussed-up kid. Miki and Ohta-San's wife were by this time both dis-traught. On SEA QUEST, where I had stayed behind to catch up on loose ends, Miki arrived almost incoherent, having forgotten what little English she knew.

"I no eat it. I no eat it!"

"But Miki, you eat cow or pig or fish every day. If you are to eat meat you need to come to terms with the fact that animals must be killed."

"I no eat it. I no eat it," she moaned.

"In strange places Michael and I often must eat unusual foods, like turtle or dog," I pointed out. "People may be poor but they will kill a precious animal just to serve their best to guests."

"I no eat it . . ."

"What if when Michael and I came to Japan we had pushed away the sashimi and sushi we were offered? What if we'd turned up our noses at jellyfish, sea cucumber, fish roe, seaweed and sea urchin? Don't you think we would have been seen as rude?"

There was just a whimper. "I hearing *me-eeh me-eeh me-eeeeh!*"

Not really knowing how to handle this outburst and at the same time realizing we must keep heading south, we decided to make it an early night with a 1:30 AM wake up call. Going to bed early was just the excuse Miki needed.

She volunteered, "I tell them we must go bed, can't eat dinner."

With an unusual display of assertiveness she jumped ashore and loudly informed the partygoers that we were leaving.

Ohta-San had planned to sail in company with us to Okinawa, but the evening's weather forecast of 12-foot swells put them off. Ohta-San's wife had announced her limit was eight feet. We could see her point. Their boat was small and light.

The wind was rising, the rigging rattled, setting our nerves on edge. Was leaving now the right decision? Michael and I worried as we fitfully dozed. Typhoon Keith, the twenty-sixth storm of the season, was spiraling westward from Guam but was expected to re-curve to the north, away from us. But it was possible the typhoon might instead charge straight towards us.

Typhoons can occur near Japan at any time of the year but are expected regularly from June through November. We had hoped to avoid getting caught in one in the exposed Ryukyu Islands and knew that at this time of year typhoons usually hit land further north. But should a storm come our way, Koniya-Ko, the halfway point on our island-hopping voyage to Okinawa, was the only harbor that afforded us any real protection.

In the inky blackness before dawn we felt our way out of the snug cove into the larger bay beyond, there to zigzag through the anchored freighters. Michael was tense. By a series of carefully checked GPS positions and bearings from the lights ashore, he guided SEA QUEST through the waterway towards the open sea. He knew the smallest mistake could run us aground or worse.

Because global positioning satellite (GPS) fixes are more accurate than all but the very latest charts, we constantly try to relate the position of a known geographical marker, such as our mooring place in the harbor, to the chart. The difference between the latitude and longitude of the charted berth and the GPS reading usually gives us a discrepancy. It might be a distance like .2 of a mile, but we have seen inaccuracies on charts of more than a mile. Blind dependence on the little black box continues to bring many yachts to grief. Unless a skipper is exceedingly accurate in his calculations and then in his application of the figures, he may discover that his plotted course takes him straight through an island or onto a rock.

When the last light-beacon finally slid past, I breathed a hearty sigh of relief. Michael hauled up the double-reefed main and set the staysail. Sea conditions seemed favorable enough. In the early dawn we sighted Tokuno Shima. By noon, it was in our wake. Oki-no-Erabu now lay 30 miles to the south. Michael hanked on the heavy red jib and shook out a reef from the main.

Soon SEA QUEST surged up and sleighed down waves that had grown to 16 feet and more. Why were the seas suddenly so large? Careful examination of the chart showed a relatively shallow bank extending many miles north of the island. It lay at the junction of the East China Sea and the Pacific Ocean, over which the warm Kuroshio (Black Current) begins to divide to head north from the tropics to flow around both sides of Japan. Though the bank must always be somewhat rough, it was especially hazardous now with swells from typhoon Keith rolling in from the east.

The wind whistling through the rigging changed pitch to a higher octave. Its gusts nearly overpowered the reefed main. We plowed through the hissing seas at eight knots, almost hull speed. Tuning into the Guam weather report, I heard a toneless computer-generated voice give the current position of the typhoon: 17.8° N and 134.8° E. The typhoon had a 35-mile diameter eye with winds blowing at 115 knots, gusting to 140 and was presently located 600 miles to the east. It was a worry, but we had pressing concerns closer to home. At a certain point, a boat with too much sail just works harder, but goes no faster. By reducing sail, the speed drops just a little but the motion gets a whole lot easier. We worked together to get sail off. Under headsails alone we continued at a more comfortable six knots. Oki-no-Erabu drew closer.

High spray indicated Tina-Ko's artificial harbor located halfway down the length of the island, a narrow slot set between two parallel sea walls. To reach the entrance we had to plunge directly towards the foaming beach. A break in the right-hand wall gave a last minute escape into the sheltered harbor. We surveyed the narrow slot while riding high the crest of a big swell. The sight was daunting. A white tower on the land served as a bearing marker. Just off the beach rocks emerged from breaking surf. Adrenaline pumped in my ears; my hands shook, my courage ebbed; there was no room for error.

"Michael, you take the wheel. If we get a heavy wave under our rudder I may not be able to bring SEA QUEST around fast enough."

"OK. Hold on tight."

Trusting Michael to get it right, my nervousness abated somewhat. Two big rollers swept under us and broke against the rocks. Gunning the engine, the boat rode in on their tail. Michael spun the helm hard over. SEA QUEST leaned like a racer and seemed to struggle to make the turn into the narrow entrance before the next breaker grabbed her stern. Then SEA QUEST was deposited into the sheltered calm.

Oki-no-Erabu, a raised limestone island surrounded only by a narrow fringe of reef has no natural harbors. Tina-Ko's shelter is a dynamited and dredged hole in the reef shelf buttressed by concrete. On the other side of the island at Wadamari, there is a bigger manmade harbor, but it has a longer approach through the reef and, under present conditions, would have been impossible to enter.

Two hours earlier when SEA QUEST was still sailing off the northern end of the island, the owners of a coffee shop had sighted us. The yacht was the object of such intense speculation that finally, unable to contain their curiosity, the couple closed their shop to drive half the length of the island to watch us enter Tina-Ko. They knew something we did not. The Okinawa to Wadamari ferry had been canceled due to the heavy swell! If the ferries dared not venture here, how could we? Yamamoto-San, owner of Amigo Dive Shop, also arrived to gawk at us, and stayed to strike up a generous friendship. In his wheezing van with his hyperactive, half-grown black Labrador sharing the wooden back seat, we toured the island with him the next day.

Oki-no-Erabu is a 20-mile-long, guitar-shaped island. Sea-sculpted limestone has formed islets along the eastern coast that invites swimmers to play among them. Where the cliffs rear high there are great blowholes and other favorite places, we were solemnly informed, from which suicides (leaving their shoes behind) leap to the foaming seas below. Away from Oki-no-Erabu's

55

windswept shore farmers live in homes tucked into sheltered gullies and valleys for protection against the annual parade of typhoons. By contrast, the homes of mainland retirees are perched on exposed positions of stunning beauty, but frightening vulnerability.

The fertile limestone soils are Oki-no-Erabu's primary wealth. Flowers are cultivated; the early-season blooms packed off to the mainland are a major source of income, though sugarcane and a spluttering tourist industry also play their parts.

Oki-no-Erabu's main draw for visitors is an extensive system of caverns. In the subterranean passages, crystal walls and galleries of stalactites decorate a winding waterway. Most romantic and tragic is a shrine erected a mile into the caverns for the skeletons of an ancient couple wearing strings of neolithic Chinese beads who may have became lost in the maze.

Yamamoto-San took us to a luxurious *onsen*, the very last we would enjoy in Japan. Afterwards we sat down to a meal of local fish specialties, washed down with beer, and frequently interrupted by toasts of *sho-chu*, a distilled version of sake that is fortified with the spirits of sugar cane and sweet potato.

The following day, my birthday, dawned clearer than Michael's head. Though the breeze had moderated, the ocean swell in the harbor entrance was big enough to daunt a sailor. The ferries were still not running, but Michael felt confident he could take SEA QUEST out. We waved good-bye to our well-wishers who stood on the seawall to watch us leave.

By noon the strong breeze had died away. We watched Yoron Shima slide by to port. By 5:00 PM the northernmost tip of Okinawa, Cape Hedo Misaki, was in sight. We rolled through the tide rip off the cape as the blood-red sun peeked low through the clouds. At Jinama-Ko, small fishing craft lined the waterfront but the deep-water jetty was empty. Our anchor dragged halfway across the dredged harbor before finally catching on a ledge.

At 6:45 AM, a series of announcements from a public address system awakened us. They continued at five-minute intervals for the next half-hour, absolutely guaranteeing that we did not fall back asleep. Government loudspeakers are the bane of Japanese towns not only in the islands but on the mainland as well. Few citizens have anything good to say about them but accept their big-brother presence with impotent resignation. The 5:00 PM announcements, like an informal curfew, serve notice for children to go home. On the positive side, the loud speakers can quickly warn people, in case of *tsunami* emergencies, to head for higher ground.

In this hamlet the broadcast did not bother the local fishermen, because they were already up and away in their boats. Near us, an old woman wearing a white headscarf tidied fishing gear. Non-stop traffic appeared and disappeared through tunnels cut into the rugged terrain on a fast through-road that separated the village homes from the waterfront. The heavy clay roof tiles set with thick cement for typhoon protection were typical of Okinawa. Newer two story homes had flat roofs, big solar water heaters and breezy porches facing the sea.

The Ryukyu Islanders, who include Okinawans, are different from the mainland Japanese who treat them as inferiors. They are a robust people: broad faced, swarthy, possessing an exuberant love for color, rhythm and music. Their aboriginal dialect contains words and tonal sounds strange to Japanese ears.

Miki and I had hatched a plan. I wished to fly to California to see family there. Miki, keen to see Los Angeles, would go with me. Michael would stay behind to finish tasks our rush to leave Wakayama had not left time for. Having used Miki's cell phone to book our flight we were now sailing on a deadline. We had time for only an overnight stop at Jinama-Ko.

Impassively the fishermen watched SEA QUEST pass out the narrow channel next morning. Typhoon Keith had veered away to vent its fury in the North Pacific east of Tokyo, but over our heads a delicate web of mackerel cloud fanned out across the sky.

We had invested in some new fishing gear. A skipping plane beat a rhythm behind us, trailed by a few plastic squids. Though we had trailed the lure for 60 miles already without a bite, as we approached the Gulf of Ie Shima we ran through a hungry school of bonito and picked up two at once.

We rounded Cape Zanpa and swept past towering resort hotels overlooking the coast. Michael scanned the shore with binoculars. With yet another hand-drawn map and an aerial photo cut from a cruising magazine, Michael attempted to lo-cate Kadena Yacht Harbor. Military planes and sleek jets circled in the distance, and then dropped out of sight. "We must be close," Michael said. "They will be landing at the U.S. Air Force base." Then he spotted a mast behind the land. A towhead American youth in an army boat whipped out through a chan-nel, circled and then ducked back. We followed him into Kadena Marina.

American GIs had for many years informally used the bay's facilities for a yacht club and recreation area. Though the bay has room for less than a dozen yachts, we were made welcome on a vacant mooring. The showers were icy cold, a shocking disappointment to us, but friendly Americans offered us the use of their own quarters on the base for showers. Japanese yachts are not welcome at Kadena but are obliged to use Gino Wan Yacht Harbor five miles away, a bit of ethnic separation that I found disturbing because it reflected an atti-tude that seemed all too evident among the base personnel we subsequently met.

By recent count 1.4 million people inhabit Okinawa, an is-land only 45-mile-long and 13-mile-wide at its broadest point. Major towns are located at every bend of the coastline. With dense housing confined to zoned urban areas, there is still room for rugged mountains, farmland, pristine beaches, large resorts and the sprawling U.S. military base. On this narrow island, nearly everything faces the warm surrounding seas. Though it is still north of the tropics, the Kuroshio current gives Okinawa a balmy semi-tropical climate.

Okinawa was nearly obliterated during World War II. As the gateway to Japan through which the Allied forces invaded, tens of thousands of Japanese soldiers made desperate last stands here. Their commanders hoped to prove that the cost to the Allies of invading mainland Japan would be too great to contemplate. Ordinary people, mainly women and children, misguided by the propaganda machine, feared torture and mu-tilation at the hands of a demonized enemy. By the thousands, they committed mass suicide. Okinawa was the theater of war where young American soldiers grew up fast, if they survived at all, where all too many men from both sides died during the rout of the Imperial Forces from their last bastion.

On this narrow, hilly land of snaking roads and high-density urban areas, the snarl of traffic was unavoidable. Our American friends took us on a long drive. We had the impression that every building was new and much was built shoddily. Postwar reconstruction had been fast and cheap. There was a conspicuous absence of structures we had come to expect in Japan. The grand municipal buildings along with all the old shrines and temples are gone. Okinawa Castle had been rebuilt from scratch. Only the venerable family tombs built into protected hillsides like Oki-no-Erabu's farmhouses survived the bombing.

Viewing the scarred remains of what must have once been a fascinating island in the company of U.S. military personnel was a thoroughly alienating experience. Our American friends were hospitable and generous, but showed little appreciation for the subtleties of Eastern culture. It was not their ignorance that really made us sad, but Okinawa's bombed-out heart. Yet, perhaps it had to be. As the Japanese Imperial Army was forced back from their overseas territories, the Allies learned the sad truth that the mainland Japanese population, thoroughly indoctrinated by Imperial propaganda about the vicious treatment they could expect in the hands of the enemy, would truly fight to the last breath. It was the intransigence of the Japanese High Command that eventually forced the U.S. decision to drop atomic bombs on Hiroshima and Nagasaki.

The Japanese High Command in Tokyo sacrificed Okinawa to the cause of mainland Japan, and Okinawans know it. For fifty years, the Japanese government has continued to sacrifice Okinawans by allowing an American military base on the island (away from the Japanese heartland). Chain-link fences and "Keep Out" signs surround much valuable farmland—while resident foreigners treat Okinawans with contempt. Frequent rapes of local schoolgirls by U.S. military personnel who, because of military jurisdiction cannot be tried in local courts, continue to create festering resentment.

With so much destroyed, Okinawan traditional artifacts are now packaged and sold from a "cultural center," a cobbled-together village of working artisans. Only far away, among the small island groups that stretch away towards Taiwan, we were told, does the aboriginal culture still flourish much as always. We might never see these islands, for our plan was now to take leave from the Land of the Rising Sun and sail on through the troubled waters of the Taiwan Straits.

5

Far East Passage

Squalls and strong winds lashed Okinawa. We hated to set off in such weather, but our allotted time was over. A visit to the navy meteorological office informed us that the present 25-knot northerly was the result of an occluded frontal system. "It will soon moderate," we were assured. Our course was westward and the wind abeam. In fact, for early December it was not all that bad. Despite the gloomy skies and fully expecting seasickness to take its toll, we decided to head off into the lumpy ocean.

We had an extra crewmember, his sea-bag already stowed beneath the cabin table. Jack, who was rebuilding a 36-foot look-alike to SEA QUEST, had struck up a friendship with Michael. He and his wife Jan, both employees on the base, had

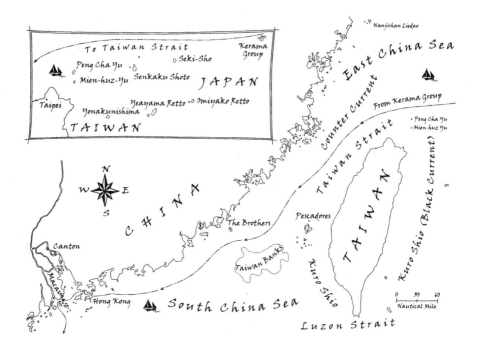

made him welcome during Miki and my absence, and greatly assisted his projects by taking him along to the base woodworking shop. Jack suddenly seized on the idea of earning his offshore stripes on a passage to Hong Kong. He asked to come along. Expecting a beam wind and a relatively easy passage, we agreed. His jolly company would be welcome.

Although the sight of surf over the bar of Kadena Harbor was not especially reassuring, we got underway. As the bow plunged into the first of the breaking waves I called out, "Hold on tight in case we touch bottom!" SEA QUEST saucily tossed a fan of white spray high into the air and plowed straight through to the open water. Under Okinawa's protected lee Michael and Jack hauled up the sails. Then SEA QUEST danced to the rhythm of the 12-foot swells that rolled in from the northwest.

Once the early excitement of departure was behind us, seasickness set in. I chewed a dry piece of bread and swallowed a second Bonine tablet to settle my stomach, my usual remedy. Michael was napping on the cockpit seat. Then I noticed the staysail slowly working its way down the inner forestay. The fitting for the halyard block high on the mast had broken.

We considered what we should do. One of the several groups of smaller Japanese islands south of Okinawa, the Keramas, lay only 12 miles away. There in a lee somewhere, we could haul Michael aloft to make the repair. As we approached the islands the wind intensified to 35 knots, blowing spume like sleeting snow. Shelter was now our first concern. The block could wait.

Details on our small-scale chart were obscure. We ran in close to skirt offshore rocks made visible only by the seas breaking over them. In the lee of Tokasiki Shima, one of the larger islands, an area of light colored water appeared dead ahead. Had we not noticed the shoal we might have grounded in the heavy seas. Inlets that looked like possible havens were all barricaded by shallow bars. Anxious, wet and tired we eventually rounded into the Kerama's only harbor and moored alongside an empty wharf.

We had already completed our final clearance from Japan in Okinawa. We wondered what complications our presence on Zamami Shima might create with the authorities. A police officer wandered by in the afternoon and we rather casually mentioned that we were sheltering from the storm. We need not have worried. He was more interested in the nationality of our female crewmember than in our present legal status. In the light of our experience at Nomoura-Ko, we now recognized that the official was on the lookout for smuggled Chinese and Koreans. Once he discovered Miki was Japanese, he lost interest in us.

Early the next morning after setting a double-reefed main and jib we motored past the breakwaters. Outside, the surf leapt and clawed furiously at the towering rocky peaks and the northwest wind sang in SEA QUEST's rigging to the tune of 25 to 35 knots. Should we just go? According to the weather forecast conditions would improve. This wind would give us a good fast run across to the north end of Taiwan. However, a glance at Jack and Miki gave us the answer. To them, the sight of the heaving ocean was plainly terrifying. Throwing the helm hard to starboard, SEA QUEST balanced for a long moment atop a massive swell, then turned to flee again into the safety of sheltered waters to wait out another day.

Abandoned on a restaurant chair at Zamami's seaside village was a newspaper weather map that showed a low hovering over China. The realization hardened our determination to leave as soon as possible, before the next depression arrived, regardless of how uncomfortable it might be.

The forced layover had given us the chance to catch up on our sleep; all of us were now more fit to face the 900-mile passage to Hong Kong. Eve-of-departure parties, even without alcohol, take their toll. Jack had rather optimistically brought *mal de mer* tablets for only three days, but in reality he needed some serious medication. I pressed a Scopoderm patch behind his ear and Miki dosed up from her own kit. But by noon, both of them were again laid low.

We had deliberated long and hard about which route to take to Hong Kong. Should we sail through the Taiwan Straits or take the alternate route to the east and south of Taiwan? It was thought to be safer sailing to the east of Taiwan, well away from any involvement with mainland China. But the Kuroshio runs up that coast at three knots or more. At a speed of five knots through the water against that adverse current meant we would perhaps average about two knots over the ground. If the current was stronger than anticipated we might not successfully buck it. We had also heard that the prevailing northerly winds set up wind-against-sea conditions that can be tough.

Another weaker stream of the Kuroshio runs up the Taiwan side of the Straits, with a countercurrent running towards the south near the coast of China. Could we hitch a ride on its back? What were the chances, if we ventured through the Taiwan Straits, that we would become prey to pirates or be dragged in as a pawn in the hostilities between the two Chinas?

The Okinawa-based U.S. military adviser reassured us. All was calm now, he told us. No incidents had been recently reported. So, lured by the promise of a quiescent political situation and an easier passage we now headed on westward towards the Straits.

The Kerama Islands had already dipped below the horizon in our wake when the throbbing rotors of a hovering helicopter jerked us from our reverie. It was the Japanese Defense Force buzzing us! Michael leapt aft to pull our New Zealand flag out straight. The helicopter crew studied it for a moment or two, then with a wave they flew off again.

Sayonara, Land of the Rising Sun. *Sayonara*, Japan.

We ran free under wet clouds on a bleak heaving sea. The wind was steadily veering to the north, indicating an improvement. From time to time a heavy wave kicked against the hull with such force that spray tossed high into the air dumped a solid shroud of water over the pilothouse. Although the cockpit was saturated our inert crew hardly noticed until I urged Jack and Miki to retire below. Though Michael and I tried to keep each other company with a bit of cheerful chit-chat we eventually retreated into silence, huddling like unhappy wet cats, waiting for the misery to be over.

We crossed over the 100-fathom continental shelf off the northern tip of Taiwan in the wee hours of the third morning. An adverse current had added 30 miles since we left the Kerama Islands. By midnight the wind became gentler. Michael shook out the reefed mizzen and we glided silently across the quiet waters. A full moon cast enchantment over the silky seas. My spirits lifted.

The lighthouse of Peng Chia Hsu Island sent a staccato beam into the night. We caught our first sight of the Taiwanese fishing fleet. It appeared our nice weather would not hold for long. Another front of dark cloud massed to windward. The first gusts pushed SEA QUEST over hard on her beam-ends and rattled the mizzen wildly, awakening me with the racket. I stumbled on deck. "I guess I dropped the reef from the mizzen a little too soon," Michael groaned.

By lunchtime SEA QUEST was well into the Taiwan Straits, neatly equidistant from the shores of both antagonists. A 150-foot steel vessel rushed headlong towards us, swept past our bow with little more than a scale of rust between us, and then circled round as if to come alongside. A shouting gaggle of fishermen waved from amid piles of nets. What was going on? Were these Chinese pirates intent on boarding us?

"They seem friendly. One of them has a camera," I reassured Michael. We waved back.

These rust-stained high-prowed trawlers towed large seine nets when they fished. But when their nets were stowed, they charged dangerously across our bow, their crew cheering before circling off. It was only later in Hong Kong that we learned that the superstitious fishermen were trying to shake their bad luck off on us!

It nearly worked. In the deceptive darkness just before dawn, after a long weary night of dodging lights, with Michael off watch and the rest of our crew below snoozing comfortably in their bunks, I was alone on deck. A maneuvering boat changed course to steer directly towards us. My fatigued brain assumed the vessel to be another curiosity seeker. Only when a strobe nearly blinded me did I realize with alarm that the ship was still trawling. I paid off just under her bow and then fell away to starboard with the help of the engine that Michael had instinctively flown up into the cockpit to start. I felt pretty dumb and also very embarrassed. Jack, who had not yet even stood a watch, happened to arrive on deck about the same time as the trawler approached and realized, even before I did, the seriousness of the situation.

Now we were again alone. The seas had emptied of fishing boats. The water around us had assumed a remarkable shade I had never before encountered, the color the French call *eau de Chine*. We had picked up a favorable two-knot countercurrent and SEA QUEST raced along on its back all the way to the Pescadores Islands before again meeting with the Kuroshio, which was setting north against us at two knots. We made good progress in a following wind. Late in the afternoon the sky slowly brightened at the western horizon. It was the first real break in the weather we had seen for six days. That night after the moon had climbed above the retreating trough, the sky cleared at last.

Miki and Jack had both improved with the weather and now, like hungry nestlings, ate all the food I could provide although they were still too groggy to help. On our fifth night we sailed through a fleet of fishing boats, all on different courses. It was like threading through a maze. Several boats shone their lights on us. When this happened, Michael would rake a powerful beam across our sails a few times, figuring it better to illuminate the yacht than to have lunatics charge over for another close encounter.

To avoid overfalls at the southern end of the Taiwan Straits we were forced to venture close to the Chinese coast. We had once heard a frightening story of a yacht impounded by gunboats after it had inadvertently entered China's waters. The narrowest part of the Straits lay between the shallow Taiwan Banks and the Chinese mainland, cloaked in thick haze. Although we tried not to venture too close, the shoal water and offshore Taiwan banks that extend across most of the Straits at this point spelled problems. Not the depth—it was all deep enough to sail over— but the banks develop vicious overfalls like rapids on a river. They are huge steep seas that can capsize even a large boat like SEA QUEST. In the early hours of the morning, the gap between the shoals and us narrowed. Though only 12-mile offshore, we saw no sign of either land or gunboats.

The next morning, with the sea like glass and the shoals behind us, Miki finally emerged to sit through the morning watch.

"This sailing I like," she said. "Very nice!"

"But Miki, we are not sailing. We are motoring!"

A fresh caught mahi-mahi heralded our arrival into southern latitudes. We had just crossed the Tropic of Cancer. Two strange craft caught our attention. Above lofty vermilion and green-painted transoms floated the fan-shaped bamboo sails of genuine working Chinese junks. We had scarcely believed that such vessels still existed.

The sun became hot and we gratefully absorbed the warmth. The invisible Chinese coastline lay only 15 miles off, choked under a smoggy pall. We figured we were probably safe enough here in the shipping lanes. Despite heavy seas and the pelting rain having scoured the decks and the rigging over the past few days, a thick oily film covered SEA QUEST.

When a light breeze finally set in we broke out the bright geniker, the first time we had used that sail since I had flayed my hand on the runaway sheet six weeks ago. It attracted ships. Chinese crews hung out over the sides of rusting vessels to get a better look, waving and even taking snapshots. We no doubt appeared as strange to them as the exotic junks had been to us.

Towards evening, the wind died. We drifted along with stationary fishing craft. Fifteen miles off China's unseen coast we heard a low rumble—like the drone of an approaching ship. However, the sound did not come from a ship, but from the Chinese nation, abuzz with the sound of millions of people working! That night, dolphins appeared bathed in living phosphorescence to usher us into the South China Sea. When they disappeared, we became enveloped in pea-soup smog. Container ships closed on us at an alarming rate, passing us only minutes after first appearing in the gloom.

Seven days after our departure from Okinawa, SEA QUEST joined the stream of ocean-going vessels feeding into the narrow Tathong Channel to Hong Kong. All of us were on deck to celebrate. The sun's early rays touched each of the surrounding peaks in turn before disappearing into shadowed valleys. Then we rounded Tung Lung Island where the glittering fantasia of Hong Kong itself spread before us. The thick haze had caused the sun to appear both magnified and blood-red, and threw a crimson light over the harbor's jostling coastal tramps, barges, trawlers, ferries, sampans, junks, and gleaming cruise ships. The majority of the vessels were rusting, flaking unpainted hulks, yet the exotic little teak sampans were rubbed and varnished to a high polish. Chinese sightseeing vessels decorated with gilded carved dragons crossed close under the bows of others with silk-caparisoned pavilions perched high above red-lacquered hulls.

We had arrived.

6

Into the Dragon's Mouth

The quarantine area was crowded so we squeezed in next to a coastal freighter and radioed the authorities. They arrived in a pilot boat longer than our yacht. After Michael had filled out the required paper work he borrowed a cell phone from the Customs officer to call our daughter. Marina was now living in Hong Kong with her husband and their year-old daughter. Formalities accomplished and permission received to proceed to the Royal Hong Kong Yacht Club, we set off in a snapping breeze. A tow-headed figure we would know anywhere stood joyfully waving from the waterfront promenade. It was Marina, camera ready to record us tacking smartly through the narrowest and busiest shipping lane in the world.

Once set apart on its own tiny island, the venerable Royal Hong Kong Yacht Club is now joined to the city by a causeway

China

To Canton

Pearl River Estuary

New Territories

Kowloon

Shekye

Hebe Haven

N

Lantua I.

Hong Kong

Macau

Fuel Barge

Taipa

Coloane

South China Sea

0   10

Nautical Mile

Hong Kong & Macau

that forms a malodorous cove, protected behind a breakwater against the heavy wakes of passing vessels. Double rows of moored yachts share the crowded bay with a community of sampan boat people living next to a sewage-filled city outfall. Raw sewage actually floats around the yachts' waterlines, providing employment for generations of coolies who earn their living cleaning it off. The foul odor gave new meaning to the name "Hong Kong" whose English translation is "Fragrant Harbor." But we learned that in teeming Hong Kong, unsavory surroundings are often blithely ignored.

We had chosen the yacht club as our base because of its proximity to the cross channel ferry to Kowloon where we could visit our daughter daily. Cheaper mooring in cleaner conditions is available at lovely Hebe Haven, we later learned, in the less congested outreaches of the New Territories. In the very heart of Hong Kong, we were here within easy reach of everything both good and bad that the city represented. Clogged traffic, throngs of fascinating people, double-decker tramcars, and classy boutiques. Within walking distance were narrow alleyways with fascinating stalls, underground supermarkets, cinemas, restaurants and block-sized shopping centers, not to speak of the hundreds of handkerchief-sized family-owned shops stocked with strange smelling foods and medicinal herbs. Further away, on the steep lower slopes of Victoria Peak were dimly lit emporiums holding immense collections of porcelain and antiques. At night huge commercial buildings bedecked in gay Christmas motifs illuminated our moorings.

A few days after our arrival Jack had flown back to Okinawa. Though sorry to have been disabled by seasickness, he insisted that he had learned a lot from his offshore experience. Michael consoled him. "It sure was no picnic, Jack, not for any of us. But now you know what you might expect if you actually do any long-distance cruising."

"Yeah," replied Jack. "I think for now I will just stick to short trips out to the Keramas until I get my sea legs!"

The busy city, the noise, the pollution, the fetid waters and the various tasks we needed to accomplish in Hong Kong exhausted Michael and me both physically and mentally. Nevertheless, between frequent visits to our daughter and her family, we re-upholstered our main cabin settee, fitted a new carpet, and topped up our provisions from local supermarkets. We also bought a laptop computer, about which we knew nothing. In the months ahead, learning to operate it without technical help would force us into a steep and reluctant learning curve. Of course, in between chores we had taken time to see the sights.

The Chinese, whose homes are often exceptionally small, live mostly on the streets. Throngs of chattering people jostled for fresh produce or dried foods, discount clothes and inexpensive jade, or sat at rough benches playing mah-jongg. Of course with a yachtsman's practical bent we searched the town for halogen lights, switches, and Teflon for repairing our windvane steering. The shopping opportunities Hong Kong offered to Miki were just too good to ignore. Each day after long forays she would come home laden with bulging bags. The crisis came when her bunk became so full she could no longer sleep in it. "If you buy more clothes, Miki, you just have to pack up some of your other stuff to send home," I insisted.

One Sunday we were surprised to find the downtown streets and squares crowded with thousands of Filipinos. It was as though a huge flock of migrating birds had suddenly alighted. One hundred twenty thousand Filipinos, nearly all of them women, work in Hong Kong as live-in domestic servants and sleep on their employers' kitchen floor. As Catholics, they have Sunday off. With no home and little money to spend, they congregate like flocks of noisy starlings.

About six months before our arrival, the sun had set on the British Empire in Hong Kong. Marina and Mark, who had seen the colony through the transition, said that, outwardly at least, little had changed. It was not the least bit apparent to us that this city-state was finally under the thumb of the most powerful communist country in the world. It was just "business as usual."

Just before our departure we took Mizzen, the ship's cat, to have a rabies shot and a microchip ID inserted under her skin, the first step towards taking her into New Zealand where quarantine laws strictly control the importing of pets. With proper papers, we were told she would spend less time in quarantine. As the months passed, we were to discover that this first step was only the beginning of a drawn-out, hugely expensive saga.

Our month in Hong Kong flew by until one day, in a spanking January breeze, we again tacked up the narrow waters of Victoria Harbor past hundreds of anchored ships to leave our precious family, granddaughter Lucia, and Hong Kong behind us.

West of Hong Kong is the island of Cheun Lau. Its harbors teem with fishing boats packed side by side like rafts in long rows. Near the breakwater of one of these bays, we found several fuel barges at anchor. One displayed a Caltex sign. We pulled alongside and filled at a fraction of the cost of Hong Kong.

We anchored overnight just inside the western tip of Lantau Island at Fan Lau Tung Wan. Though the sandy cove was beautiful and far removed from the noise of the teeming city, we rolled heavily in the wake of ships that plied to and from the Pearl River Delta and Canton in the heart of mainland China.

In Hong Kong we had the good fortune to meet a couple who were there to take possession of their new yacht, the GRAY GULL. They lived in the Portuguese colony of Macau, only an hour away by jet-hydrofoil ferry. In Hong Kong stories circulated about Macau of Triad murders at gambling casinos, where local gang members and tourists in the line of fire were indiscriminately gunned down. We were naturally curious to hear first-hand of the place.

"If you stay away from the casinos, it's safe enough," they said. "Come and visit us and we will show you around."

The territory of Macau is made up of the original island, now a peninsula of the mainland connected by two high bridges and a long causeway to the islands of Taipa and Coloane. SEA QUEST was almost under the first bridge when a police launch roared up and repeatedly signaled us to stop. Confused, Michael and I glanced at each other.

"We'll round up on the other side of the bridge. We can't stop here," said Michael.

We coasted beneath the highest span. The police prevented us from going further. Rounding up to lower our sails, we

dropped anchor. The launch circled. We could hear voices calling several times over the radio to their base. One of the officers
shouted out to us in hesitant English.

"Yachts must get permission before arriving. You have no
permission. You cannot enter!"

Normally the only yachts that Macau authorities see arrive
in an annual regatta from Hong Kong with a group entry permit organized in advance. As politely as we could while shouting, we explained the facts the way we saw them.

"A yacht in transit is like an ocean-going ship. We do not
need to notify the port authorities in advance!"

Eventually they took our point, relented and provided us
with a police escort while warning us not to stray to the Chinese
side of the channel.

Damp bone-chilling winds whistled down from China's vast
interior. The warm humid Christmas conditions had given way
to the winter monsoon. The temperature plunged 15 degrees in
half an hour.

As we moved up the estuary, we noticed a new airport built
on reclaimed land. The Chinese hoped the airport would draw
enough visitors to pull Macau from the semi-obscurity that, despite the introduction of legalized gambling and prostitution, it
had suffered during the waning years of Portuguese rule. Ranks
of apartment and office blocks crowded one shore; elegant
Portuguese-style villas, presided over by a crumbling cathedral,
were scattered along the other. Soon new construction will
block the gracious Portuguese homes from which the *Taipans* of
old enjoyed sweeping water views. At the time of our visit, 40
percent more land had already been added to Macau by reclamation and the job seemed to have only just started.

We rounded into a narrow channel, officially the border between China and Macau. It was choked with heavy barge, ferry
and junk trawler traffic. A Chinese gunboat advanced on us,
shadowing both our escort and ourselves before finally giving a
friendly wave and steaming off. We had considered the Taiwan
Straits to be restricted enough. Yet here we had a free nation
and a totalitarian one staring each other down across a mere
ditch.

Rounding another bend a nineteenth-century panorama of

squat masonry warehouses, bum boats, fishing nets, and motorized junks alongside ancient stone wharves, opened before us. The police forbade us entry to their tiny inner harbor of Doca Don Carlos, but indicated a place amid uprooted hyacinths for us to anchor.

During the great era of Portuguese exploration, Portuguese fishermen secretly settled the island of Macau in 1555. With the permission of the Emperor of China, the first tiny settlements were eventually consolidated and Portugal was left with a virtual monopoly on trade between the Orient and Europe. The *Taipans*, who were the European masters of commerce, were required to leave Canton after each winter trading season. In order to remain close, they made Macau their summer residence. After the Anglo-Chinese War in 1841, new ports were opened to foreigners along the China coast and the British settled Hong Kong, 60 miles away on the opposite side of the Pearl River Delta. The monopoly was broken. Macau declined in economic importance. The final nail in its coffin was the Portuguese decision to give Macau back to China in 1999.

Landing at Doca Don Carlos we headed into the old town and lost ourselves in the winding maze-like streets. From the bustling sidewalks, the air was redolent of barbecued meats and mouthwatering ducks dripping with fat. We lost our appetites, though, when we stumbled into the fresh produce market where every kind of wiggling, squawking, gulping, breathing creature was for sale. Fish, eels, tortoises, snakes, lake turtles, clams, squids, crabs, mussels, pigs, goats, chickens, ducks and even pigeons. In fact the only pigeons we saw in Macau sat disconsolately caged. To Michael and I, the public butchering of the animals seemed to be unnecessarily cruel. Miki gasped at the sight, and, horrified, she made a rush for the nearest exit.

The next day Jon and Cherie, our friends from Hong Kong, met us and took us to explore old Macau. Solid, Portuguese-style masonry buildings with shuttered windows, wrought iron grilles, arches, half columns, pastel-painted plaster and decorative tiles have contributed to a fine architectural legacy standing in stark contrast to the city's modern shoddy fabrications and higgledy-piggledy oriental street stalls.

The old city is a treasure hoard of gold jewelry, sparkling

gems and fine jades for which there appeared to be no lack of customers. We wandered under covered arches, narrow alleys and up winding steps to shopping streets that converged on a plaza cobbled in black and white stone where a fountain splashed. Portuguese children, watched over by a Chinese amah, chased round the plaza, their happy squeals ricocheting off the surrounding buildings. Off a side street, the magnificent São Domingo Church, built in the early seventeenth century, was resplendent in fresh yellow and white paint.

The most famous of Macau's churches was St. Paul's, designed by an Italian master builder. Today, only a great ruined façade and the grand staircase remain. "The greatest monument to Christianity in all the Eastern lands" was built between 1602 and 1637 with the help of local craftsmen and Japanese Catholics who had been exiled from Nagasaki by Japan's Tokugawa Shogun. He feared their allegiance was to the Pope and not to him. Adjoining St. Paul's was the first western college in the Far East, where missionaries learned to speak and write Chinese so they might infiltrate the Ming Court in Peking as astronomers and mathematicians.

Jesuits from Macau masterminded several duplicitous political missions in both China and Japan, and over time made strong enemies. Hard-pressed to maintain a flow of converts, the Jesuits allowed the Chinese to continue their custom of ancestor worship, the same ploy Buddhists had used earlier. They might as well have made a pact with the devil. The controversy over this course of action, a practice also used in both Micronesia and Melanesia, eventually split the church in Rome causing the Jesuits to be expelled from Macau and their great church and college to be used as a military barracks! The fabulously rich interiors full of treasures given by European aristocrats were destroyed in 1835 by a kitchen fire that burnt everything to the ground. The carved and colonnaded façade, its niches filled with statues of the Virgin and the Saints, are all that now remains.

We went into one of the city's coffee shops to shelter from the cold and drizzle outside, warming ourselves with liqueur-laced cappuccinos and European pastries. Then we hiked up to the oldest lighthouse on the Chinese coast. It is part of the Guia fortifications, originally built in 1638 to repel the covetous Dutch after they discovered Portugal's most jealously guarded secret: Macau was, in fact, Marco Polo's fabled and fabulous Cathay!

The next day we were relaxing below when a noise like machine gun fire caused us to leap to the decks. Though the Chinese shoreside showed no signs of warfare, on the Macau side smoke billowed from the precincts of the red-walled shrine of the A-Ma goddess. Another volley followed. Firecrackers had been set off.

This temple and the story of its founding date to the sixteenth century. A-Ma, the story goes, was a penniless young girl looking for passage home. At Canton she begged each of the rich merchants for passage on their junks, but was refused. A poor fisherman invited her to join him on his sampan. Along the way a furious storm arose, with winds so terrible that every ship but the one on which A-Ma had taken passage was wrecked. Once ashore in Macau she disappeared forever, but the rich merchants, in recognition of her divinity and ability to provide safe passage for boats, built this shrine for her in the very place she stepped ashore.

Cherie waved at us from the quayside and Michael jumped into the dinghy to fetch her to the boat. With a steaming cup of coffee in her hand, she explained that firecrackers were set off in shrines all over the city at the completion of building projects. This was happening several times a day since, fueled by enormous gambling proceeds, the Macau construction industry was booming. Speculators hoped that wealthy Chinese from the prosperous belt of southern industrial cities would buy these million dollar apartments after the handover in 1999. But prices were high, Cherie went on to say. Their spacious three-bedroom apartment cost the princely sum of US $8,000 per month. "And it's a steal," commented Cherie, "compared to those on the view side of Taipa where most expats live in one-bedroom apartments with kitchens the size of closets!"

We crossed the bridge from Macau to Taipa and then over a newly reclaimed area that would soon join Taipa to Coloane. We strolled through Coloane's historic village of mud buildings.

Entire streets were washed with a single pastel color to create narrow lanes of blue, pink, yellow, or green. A glazed tile inscribed with the street name was set into each corner house. Vermilion painted shrines seemed strange neighbors in this Old European village atmosphere, where they were tucked in between the houses.

A large fishermen's shrine was dug into a steep hillside for protection, we were told, against malevolent dragons. Figures of carp and other lucky symbols decorated the heavy tiled roof. Inside was a large carved panorama of the Heavenly Realms and a whalebone dragon-boat. Chinese lit joss sticks of incense or dropped coins in the box. Nobody paid attention to us.

The Chinese are pragmatists. Taoist beliefs allow them to pay homage to any god they think will assist them. It is the quality of individual actions and the respect paid to the many gods and to their ancestors' spirits, they believe, that affects life both today and in the hereafter. At funerals they burn little paper models of furniture, television sets, and money to insure that the recently departed are comfortable while they wait for reincarnation and God's final judgment. In a city dominated by large Catholic churches, it is fascinating to note that outside nearly every shop is a tiny well-tended shrine where incense and firecrackers are lit to bring luck and scare off evil spirits. The life of the average Chinese is a daily devotion to an almost tangible spirit world.

Each night we met up with a circle of Jon and Cherie's friends who gathered at local restaurants to enjoy traditional Portuguese food. With them, we shared thick soups, bread puddings, steaming clams in savory sauces, grilled cod and a multitude of rice dishes, with dry, full-bodied, hearty, or sweet wines to accent each dish. A couple we met this way, a Portuguese architect and his Swiss-born wife, told us they had always wanted to cruise incognito in Macau's coastal waters. So they built a local-style fishing junk. This high-powered junk, although outwardly identical to other working junks, was luxurious, having polished teak decks and an expansive lounge with magnificently carved Chinese panels decorating the stateroom doors. The junk carried ten times the fresh water of SEA

QUEST and a big generator, so hot showers were no luxury aboard this unusual boat. Not a drop of oil smeared the engine room's immaculate white paint, a fact that staggered the local ship owners. These stupid foreign devils, they must have thought. What is the purpose of such perfection?

When sirens wailed close by and a ship's horn repeatedly blasted, I rushed on deck. Upstream a ship was on fire, with billowing black smoke. A couple of people seemed to be swimming nearby. The mooring was cut and the ship drifted free, passing us close by while a fireboat and a large fire-fighting tug chased her. The crew had fled. Soon the water around the ship had turned white with foam and the tug's firefighting equipment had the licking flames under control.

At this time Michael and Miki were in town, happily scouting around. Michael returned, lugging a heavy sack of Portuguese wine. With a wide grin, he described the several lurid propositions that ladies-of-ill-repute had made to him. Off alone on the streets, he soon discovered he was legally fair game.

We took ourselves off to the maritime museum where we learned something our Western education had conveniently skipped over. A fifteenth-century Chinese navigator was, without question, one of the world's great navigators and should have been listed along with Leif Eriksson, Christopher Columbus, Magellan and Vasco de Gama in our school history lessons. Between 1405 and 1433, Admiral Cheng Ho commanded seven expeditions to East Africa, the Red Sea, Bengal, India, Ceylon, Java, Siam and Japan utilizing instruments and a rudimentary form of celestial navigation. Enormous fleets of great junks, up to 150 at a time, carried as many as 30,000 men on Admiral Ho's expeditions. By comparison, even a full century later, Portuguese navigators relied on jealously guarded piloting directions, secret courses, favorable currents and plain good luck.

7

The South China Sea

On the day of our departure from Macau, bundled in sweaters, padded jackets, scarves and mittens, we looked more like Michelin men with red noses than yachtsmen. To escort us, not just one, but two police launches arrived. While we dragged our anchor from the river mud, they idled nearby. We turned downstream to begin our journey across the South China Sea, renowned in the old days for its opium traders, pirate junks, and racing tea clippers. Just the name "South China Sea" conjured up in our minds Joseph Conrad's great sea stories.

Yesterday's fog had cleared. The low hills on the nearby Chinese coast stood sharply outlined against a backdrop of smog hanging over inland industrial areas. Pollution had so dirtied our boat that even the normally white baggywrinkle on the shrouds, there to protect the sails against chaff, had turned a grimy, oily gray.

As we swept down the estuary close astern of our escort, we hugged the Portuguese shore, careful not to stray into Chinese territorial waters while at the same time keeping a wary eye on ship traffic. Near the bridge our escort rounded up. The crew stepped from their heated cabins into the bitter 45° F chill to wave us a brief farewell. Did they think we were mad to sail out on these winter seas?

We set our course south-southeast into the muddy red waters flowing from the great Pearl River Delta. By afternoon, 20 miles offshore, we were surrounded by some of the most desolate, windswept islands we had ever set eyes on. Immigration authorities had been unable to advise us officially if we could take a short cut through them. Our Portuguese friends said that it was safe if we did not stop. We passed unchallenged.

Michael and I felt dispirited. When the weather had abruptly turned cold, I had caught a chill that dragged me down. Conditions at sea were tough. Miki had retired to her bunk. On a broad reach we surged through the inky blackness, the moon and stars obscured by heavy overcast. Only the dimly lit, crazily swinging compass radiated a tiny pool of light and warmth, but its dizzy glow confused my tired eyes. In such rough conditions, just eating requires tenacity, not to speak of cooking. Fortunately our prepared meals needed only heating. A good freezer is worth its weight in seasick tablets.

Miki was prostrate and wanted nothing: not attention, not sympathy, and certainly not food. She must have wished for the nightmare of being aboard this awful boat to stop, but she had burnt her bridges. When she had made paper darts of marriage proposals her parents were infuriated. The last straw came when Miki quit her prestigious job, something no sensible young person ever does in Japan. They knew that she would more than likely never be considered for an equivalent position again. Having made her stand at home, there was no turning back. She dreamed of a new life in New Zealand, unrestricted by the need to conform to the traditional Japanese role for women. She dreamed of finding a partner for her life's adventures—not just a breadwinner. Although going to New Zealand by boat had seemed pretty crazy, to now admit failure and turn back would bring shame. She could not go back, and at the same time she was afraid to go forward.

After just two days at sea the air temperature rose rapidly. Michael and I shrugged off our sweaters. We each had a bottle of water from which we frequently drank long drafts. We were aware of the ever-present danger of dehydration when crossing from winter temperate regions to the tropics. Crews are known to become irritable and argumentative, as well as lethargic. Miki worried us for just this reason. Not only did she refuse to drink the water we gave her, but she remained bundled up. When we poked our heads into her cabin to wish her a good morning, she would turn away grumpily without speaking.

The sea conditions settled. SEA QUEST soared along on a broad reach, her speed occasionally reaching eight knots. Michael and I settled back to enjoy the ride. But below, Miki still lay in her dismal bunk wrapped in all her winter layers, refusing to talk or drink. She had eaten nothing but perhaps some candies from her own little bag of treats and was apparently sleeping around the clock. The situation was becoming serious.

"Why don't you take off some clothing?" I urged Miki on the fourth day. "Michael and I have been wearing shorts and T-shirts for the last couple of days."

"I cold," she mumbled.

"Miki, you must drink some water."

She refused.

I felt too weary myself, just off from the 4:00 to 7:00 AM watch to act the part of tender nursemaid. Miki had no interest, it seemed, in helping herself. Why should I insist? I lay down in my bunk and closed my eyes. Rest, however, eluded me. Instead a frightening vision welled into my consciousness: Miki, her face etched with deep circles under her eyes, lay in a white-sheeted hospital bed, a drip in her arm. . . . Alarmed, I leapt from my bunk and fumbled in the refrigerator. I knew that she must drink liquids or her organs might fail. I forced the can of juice into her unwilling hand.

"Miki, you *must* wake up and drink." She pushed me away without bothering to answer. I was getting exasperated. "Do you want to end up in hospital?" Blankly she stared. "*Anata-wa byoin ikitai*?" I reverted to Japanese to get my point across. Still she stared. Holding the full water bottle up in front of her face, the same water she had been urged to drink the previous days but had not touched, I raged. "You must drink this!" With no response but a fixed gaze, I cast about for some other way to reach her. Then deliberately I unscrewed the lid and splashed a few drops across her face. At last I got a reaction. First incredulous surprise, then dark fury! Her eyes seemed to narrow and harden. In a soap-opera-like gesture she reached a hand up to wipe away the offending liquid.

"This has gone on long enough! Now sit up, Miki. Take this juice and drink it while I watch you," I demanded. Though she drank the juice, she pushed away the water. I could not think what to do next. "Michael, you come and talk to Miki!" I stalked off.

"We can't be polite any more, Miki," I overheard Michael say firmly. "We are very serious. You must drink this water and take off some of these clothes. In fact, I want you to get out of your bunk right now and come on deck to get some fresh air." He let down the lee-cloth and unceremoniously pulled her from the bunk. In the cockpit he rigged up another lee-cloth and wedged her into the seat with a cushion, placing a freshly re-filled water bottle into her hand. "Now start drinking and don't stop until it's all finished."

I pulled some medical books down from of the shelf and leafed through them. What had I read about dehydration? I found a reference. *Severe dehydration can lead to shock and death.* Plac-ing the open book in her lap I was glad to see her read the page, hesitate, and then pushing the book away, begin to drink.

Both Michael and I also showed varying symptoms of heat exhaustion such as dark urine, irritability, restlessness, and re-curring headaches, which of course made it even more difficult to care for someone else. Fortunately our own high water intake had kept the symptoms to a minimum. With Miki up in the cockpit, we fed her a lunch of deliberately over-salted chicken noodles and a Tylenol tablet to bring down the raging headache that she had long suffered in stoic silence. Had she let us know how she felt we might have been able to help her earlier. With the liquid, salty soup, fresh air and some painkillers she soon began to make a recovery.

Michael, with a happy grin, pointed to the east as I came on deck on our fifth day at sea. "Look over there!" Squinting against the glare, I stared at a low smudge on the horizon.

"That's Luzon and the coast off Subic Bay."

Subic Bay had until recently, been the home of the large American Far East naval base. Since the U.S. military had left, yachts had begun to use the harbor as a convenient port of entry, finding it cleaner and safer than Manila where yachtsmen are often robbed. Some yachts stay on there to do extensive re-fits, taking advantage of Subic Bay's underused workshop facil-ities and cheap labor, but others avoid the port as corrupt officials there often charge ten times the legal entry fees.

As the sun reached its zenith the wind veered to the east. We worked our way to windward towards Verde Passage winding between Luzon and Mindoro Islands. We continued to sail southeastward through the rest of the day and into the night. Lighthouses were visible from which to take bearings to confirm our apparent GPS position. Extensive shoals lay ahead and to the east. After careful calculations we made a tack at midnight. When we had passed shoals we tacked again onto a course which by morning delivered us to Mindoro Island's north coast.

We made a series of short tacks against the heading wind, very close to shore, where we could point higher in the calmer waters. Filipinos waved and watched us sail almost to their doorstep before we again tacked smartly away. Every beach and habitable foreshore along the rugged coast was home to a fisherman and his family. Thatched houses dotted the coastline and brightly painted outrigger canoes were drawn up high under the coconuts. Small ferryboats, also hugging the coast, chugged past. Miki at last seemed to enjoy herself, hauling in the sheets or dangling her legs over the high side. Her illness, Michael and I surmised, not for the first time, was at least half fear. "When she gets over her fear she will be fine," we reassured one another. I went below to catch up on some sleep.

The Philippines is a huge archipelago of hundreds of islands, large and small, offering a wealth of interesting cruising. Because we still had to make our way across Micronesia before the start of the next typhoon season in June we had only a month to spare. After resting at Puerto Galera where we would have time to become fully acclimatized to the tropics, we would head along the south coast of Luzon to the San Bernadino Straits into the Philippine Sea and the wide stretches of the North Pacific beyond.

Puerto Galera is on Mindoro, not Mindanao. The former is a fun-loving Catholic island only a three-hour bus and ferry ride from Manila, with a picturesque port as haven for cruisers. The latter is a Muslim stronghold for separatist rebels and pirates lying well to the south of our planned course.

By the time we neared Puerto Galera's Manila Passage, the sun was already dipping near the horizon. Just inside the narrow entrance Michael announced he was going below to radio the yacht club.

"But I don't know my way in and our chart is not very clear," I protested.

"It's a clear run around this headland," he said as he disappeared below decks.

Lush hills rolled down to the mangrove-clothed shorelines or gave way to stretches of powdery sand. In the far distance a church dominated the higher ground and below it buildings crowded along a waterfront. On a hill, in line with a cluster of moored yachts stood a prominent orange and white-painted tower. I steered for the tower and let Michael know my heading.

By radio, Michael raised the yacht club manager and mentioned that we were steering for the orange beacon. The manager made no comment, but engaged instead in an interminable three-way conversation about which mooring to use. While they argued, the sun set. SEA QUEST penetrated the unknown reaches of the bay. Miki kept watch but I felt uneasy. I called out, "Michael, there is shoal water to port but I can see *nothing* ahead. Get off the radio, please. I need you to look out!"

Robbed of its sunlight, the bright water became darkly opaque. There was a steady 15 fathoms under our keel, but then the depth finder began rapidly to scroll. I'd been half expecting it to shoal. The moored yachts ahead looked to be in shallow water. But glancing again at the instrument, the reading at first made no sense. *Only two fathoms?* I shoved the throttle into reverse. The blip on the screen trembled. Then with a shudder and a crunching bang we collided with solid coral.

Running aground is the quick way, if all else fails, to get the skipper on deck. He looked up from the chart table—incredulous! Dropping the mike he leapt two steps at a time into the cockpit. Surveying the scene, he quickly surmised SEA QUEST was now drawing about a foot less than usual and was lying with just a slight list. He returned to the radio to sign off.

"We don't need a mooring. We're aground."

Rubber dinghies and launches dashed out from shore. Men with Australian and British accents jumped aboard SEA QUEST's now exceptionally high rails. They all offered advice. Some milled about on the foredeck. Others investigated the depth under the stern. Michael quickly hoisted the mainsail and pulled it in tight, hoping there was enough wind to roll SEA QUEST far enough on her beam to float her. But with nightfall the wind had died off. One of the men in a large inflatable took a long line attached to the spinnaker halyard. Michael wanted the driver to put tension on it to rock SEA QUEST. The man, however, did not quite understand. Someone arrived with a tide table. High tide was due in only two hours time. More than likely it would give us the water we needed to float.

We bid all the helpful men good night and got dinner started. SEA QUEST has a heavy, flat, 18" wide box keel. Sitting on a coral shelf for an hour or two would do her no harm. By the time we had finished eating a good dinner on a strangely tilting table, the keel was bumping ever so gently. Fifteen minutes later we reversed SEA QUEST and hauled in the stern anchor Michael had placed in deeper water.

Gingerly we felt our way around in the dark, unfamiliar harbor until we found a clear place to anchor. Disgracing ourselves on a coral shelf was not how we had planned to mark our arrival in the Philippines. There was slight compensation for the mishap when our would-be rescuers acknowledged that already this year several other yachts had hit that reef. The true channel, we later learned, curved around the mid-bay reef to starboard.

Manila

Philippine Sea

Luzon

Lubang Is.

Puerto
Galera

Marinduque

Catanduanes

S. Bernardino Str.

Mindoro

Sibuyan

Burias

Bulan

Port
Palapag

Masbate

Samar

Sea

Panay

Sulu Sea

Cebu

Leyte

Negros

Bohol

N

W   E

S

Mindanao

Central
Philippines

0   50

Nautical Mile

8

Rich Land, Big Smiles and Poor People: The Philippines

Like Japan and New Zealand, the Philippine archipelago sits astride the infamous Ring of Fire. Here are more than 7,000 islands, some with elevations exceeding 9,000 feet. Luzon in the north and Mindanao to the south are the biggest. Between them lie Mindoro, Masbate, Samar, Panay, Leyte, Cebu, Negros, Bohol, and to the west, Palawan. The active volcanoes remind the visitor of the archipelago's comparative youth. Its population is polyglot, and its official language is Tagalog, based on the Malay dialect. Indigenous tribal people still inhabit many upland regions. Chinese, Arab and Indian traders have frequented the Philippine islands for the past thousand years.

Ferdinand Magellan discovered the Philippines in 1521. The Spanish ruled for several hundred years until they ceded their colony to the Americans as spoils of the Spanish-American War in 1898. After years of military scuffles it became a self-governing Commonwealth in 1935. The Japanese wrestled the archipelago from General MacArthur during the Pacific War. On his retreat General MacArthur, uttered his famous declaration: "I shall return!"

And he did. He liberated not just the Philippines, but the entire southwest Pacific. In 1946 the country became an independent republic. Today, about 80 percent of the Philippine population is Catholic. Mindanao in the south has a sizable Muslim population and it has become infamous for its Muslim separatist movement, a refuge for terrorists. Many foreigners often assume that the terrorism in Minadanao covers all of the peaceful Philippine archipelago, which is like imagining that the Chicago gangsters of the 1920s threatened the entire United States.

When daylight lit up the bay we moved SEA QUEST from our

hasty anchorage to a mooring amongst the other yachts. Cocks crowed. Dogs barked. The town was awakening. On the fore-shore, fighting cocks, in cages placed on the wet sand while the tide was out, preened their feathers. Houses and restaurants leaned out over the water. Graceful 30-foot-long *bancas*, local motorized double-outrigger canoes, crammed the bulkhead. Everything in sight, buses, trucks, motorcycle taxis, and ferries, was painted in exuberant primary colors. Travelers, locals, tourists and backpackers on the inter-island ferry from Manila alighted among the hustling tricycle-taxi drivers. Budget tourists were heading for accommodation at small beach resorts set on shimmering white sand beaches north and south of Puerto Galera.

We pushed our way through the bustle to the tree-shaded waterfront, admiring the fancy lettering, the religious tassels and racing stripes that adorned motorcycles and sidecars. A sweep of attractive harbor stretched before us with SEA QUEST tucked in amongst a dozen other yachts. A handful of Hong Kong yachtsmen keep their boats in Puerto Galera year round. Others arrive at the end of the monsoon to take advantage of Mindoro's proximity to good cruising grounds. Long-distance cruisers appreciate the relative safety of the port where they can hire a boat-sitter and fly off for a visit home. Half hidden by mangroves was the yacht club where inexpensive meals were served. Bush poles marked a narrow boat channel through shallows to a pontoon accessible only by dinghy.

A *banca*, as delicate as a dragonfly, skimmed across the lagoon balanced on its curved and tapering outrigger supports. It slowed and the pilot shut down its direct-drive engine. The tender vessel was paddled into the crush of others already alongside. The skipper tipped up one outrigger over another to lie across its neighbors like an embrace. Two laughing schoolgirls, residents of some remoter part of the bay, disembarked from the craft.

Tourists from the morning ferry browsed along the colorful shops or sat in the many outdoor cafes. Sandwich-board menus propped on the pavement in front of each announced the specials of the day: calamari, fish soup, chicken *adobo*, sauté pork and fries.

We walked up over the hill that dominated the town, past shops jammed with cheap clothing, heading for the post office. Along the way we passed the Catholic church where a banner proclaimed: "Parochial Church. An Evangelizing Community, A Witnessing Community." The postmaster lolled asleep in his chair while his assistants handed bundles of mail through the grilled barrier for customers to leaf through. We were conspicuously ignored. After a long wait I thrust a handful of letters through the barred window, waved them vigorously and loudly inquired, "Do you sell stamps?" One of the girls took them, checked their weights with a practiced hand, for no scale was within sight, chose appropriate stamps and after wetting them in a sponge-pot, glued them to the envelopes.

The circuitous road linked the ferry wharf to the market a mile away. Two-storied wooden houses with louvered jalousies and wrought iron work stood half-hidden in riotous clumps of banana and flowering shrubs. A young mother and her daughter tended a small roadside barbecue-fire on which they grilled fragrant sticks of marinated chicken-bits. We were soon licking sauce from our chins as we continued to amble. Some buildings were thatched. Others had balconies imaginatively constructed from polished, natural-grown twigs. Motorcycle taxis slowed to inquire if we wanted a ride and then, at our refusal, sped past with a racket and blue smoke.

The Filipinos of Mindoro have attractive lithe bodies, ageless olive skin that never wrinkles, and lustrous wavy black hair. It is not surprising that pensioners, mostly from Germany and Australia, come to live out their declining years in a place where their money goes far and young women are eager to become their wives. Common here is the sight of an aging foreigner with a brown-skinned toddler at his knee and a beautiful and apparently spoiled wife nearby. His pension will continue to support his offspring and his wife, if she refrains from getting remarried, after he dies. It is not such a bad deal, Filipinos believe, in a hardscrabble country where opportunities for wealth are few.

A few Mangyan tribal people, recognizable by their light build and makeshift rags, come to the towns from their high mountain homes. Though these people sometime labor for cash on construction sites, we were told they remain too free-spirited to adapt to the discipline of paying jobs. The Philippines suffers from unchecked logging that has degraded the aboriginal wilderness environment where traditionally the tribal people hunted or farmed small plots. These hill people are inexorably being forced into city slums.

On our earlier voyage north to Japan as we passed through the Solomon Islands, we saw first hand the damage uncontrolled logging can cause—and the devastating consequences for villagers. After the chief allowed the land to be clear felled, heavy seasonal rains washed out the exposed topsoil to spread fine silt over reef corals causing them to die, and with them the fish and shellfish populations that supplied the villagers with daily protein.

The covered market, where tropical fruits in excessive abundance spilled onto the road, threw us into happy confusion. Ripe pineapples, papaya streaked with yellow, tart limes, bananas, plantain and green coconut stood in small mountains. We spotted our favorite, golden mangoes, and in anticipation of a gluttonous feast, bought as many of the scented fruit as the three of us could carry.

Wednesday was butchering day, so I got to market early. It took a strong stomach to buy what I needed, so Miki did not come along. I saw no cuts I recognized, just lumps of flesh. Though chicken could be bought any day, by afternoon flies swarmed making the de-feathered birds look as though they were covered with a beaded rug. It was best to shop before the flies woke up.

Puerto Galera had a shoemaker and a tailor, a shop specializing in made-to-order frilly satin communion dresses and a scattering of small hardware shops, a telephone booth, several hole-in-the-wall pharmacies, three "dentists" to pull teeth, and even a tiny jewelry shop. Inside the only supermarket dusty shelving sagged under a load of canned goods and dry stores. A row of large chest-freezers contained ham, bacon, frozen butter and local ice cream. Fuji Instant Print was the most modern shop in town, but its automatic processing machine was regularly engulfed in clouds of dust from the busy road outside.

No one was the least concerned about us wandering through town before having officially entered the country, and no one could tell us when the proper official might arrive. It is not hard to understand why some cruisers never bother to check into the Philippines at all.

One day we found that the officer had arrived on his weekly visit from Manila.

"You have come from Hong Kong. Chinese must have visas," he warned us, sternly eyeing Miki.

"But Miki is Japanese," we assured him. As for us, SEA QUEST is New Zealand registered. We needed no special visas. The officer gave us a one-month stay.

"And where will you clear out?" he asked.

"Somewhere near the San Bernadino Passage."

"There is no port there. You will have to sail on to Samar."

We considered the implications.

"Why don't I just give you your clearance now?" he suggested. We were quick to take up the offer.

Though we had planned to rest at Puerto Galera for two weeks, we stayed almost a month. My cold developed into bronchitis. Miki had to go to Manila to visit a proper dentist.

Miki's mentor and our mutual friend from Wakayama arrived to stay with us aboard SEA QUEST, along with a couple of Miki's girlfriends. It was an opportunity for Miki to talk freely with sympathetic compatriots of her difficulty adjusting to shipboard life. She obviously found life aboard testing. Our isolation at sea, the need to learn seagoing skills, the tedium of passages and long watches, all made life aboard tough. So did fitting in with strangers whose basic life philosophy was different. There were many subtle cultural issues too. One day Michael wanted Miki to help repair some sail slides and was explaining how it all worked. She refused to assist, saying that in Japan the "master" does not explain or even try to show how something is done. Instead, a student just looks on until he or she fully understands it, and then does it.

After a couple of days in a rented beach house Miki returned. She seemed to have turned some corner in her mind, becoming suddenly a more open and willing hand on the boat. We knew that life aboard and our expectations were hard on her. Japanese girls are taught to be timid. Sometimes we felt like ogres for forcing Miki to even meet our demands halfway.

Miki had never swum in water over her head but now began to practice. Soon she was persuaded to forgo her float. New friends gave her a snorkel and within days she was bewitched by the wonders of the underwater world. With all of us healthy and happy again it was time to pull up anchor.

Despite Puerto Galera's charms it was a relief to leave. Swinging free off the tail end of a delightful tropical island in the Baco group eighteen miles from Puerto Galera, our time was our own and our surroundings seemed fresh and new again. As the sun neared the horizon the water darkened to cobalt while the palm trees lit up like flames. An outrigger canoe, so loaded with a cargo of hooting and waving school children that only a tiny sliver of hull remained above water, clattered along—giving us the impression that its occupants were skimming across the calm sea on their bottoms. We laughed out loud as the crammed small craft disappeared into the distance. Children seem so happy in the tropics. They sing and they shout. I wonder if they are not better adjusted than the confused, oftentimes spoiled kids of our big cities, nursed on TV rather than breast milk, who struggle to find a sense of self in a toxic, violent, virtual-reality culture.

The next morning we rose early and worked as a team to get the sails up and the boat underway. Astern, the Calapan car ferry carrying a red-blinking light approached. Sailing canoes with tiny triangular sails made from bed sheets ranged across the channel. One motorized canoe drew near, then cut behind us entangling his propeller in our trolling line. When he finally got disentangled he would be richer by the price of several nice lures.

Late afternoon found us tacking close to Marinduque Island. We were looking for water shallow enough to anchor yet sufficiently far from the beach to give us a good sleep on a windward shore. Near a pretty scattering of huts called Buena Vista, we found anchorage in 40 feet. Scores of fishing canoes were drawn up on the shore and in the shallows, larger ones were moored. But as soon as dusk fell a noisy disco reared to life, neon lights flashed and mega-decibel noise drowned out our gentle music below decks.

Beneath the ragged contours and deep cinder valleys of an extinct volcano we rounded the southern end of Marinduque Island. We set our course for Burias Island across the Sibuyan Sea, a 50-mile stretch of open water. From a float Michael noticed a flag waving. A canoe stood near another flag. A boat motored slowly towards us to draw us away from the net they had strung between the two. We waved our grateful acknowledgment.

Then, a couple of miles further on Michael exclaimed, "Ah, hell!" He threw the engine out of gear and jammed on the shaft brake. We coasted.

"What is it?" I asked in consternation.

"One of those bloody nets—with no flags!"

Men, whose heads were swathed in scarves against the heat of the sun, sat unmoving in a canoe a couple of hundred yards away. Behind SEA QUEST their net trailed out in a wide "V." Waving met no response. We dropped our mainsail to stop the boat dragging the net further. Only when we hollered did the canoe begin motoring our way. Michael directed the fishermen to unhook the undamaged net from our rudder.

"You caught a very big fish," Michael joked, pointing to SEA QUEST, not certain his English was understood, "We are sorry, but there are no flags. We could not see the net." The men just looked, shrugged their shoulders and smiled halfheartedly.

Although the water was thousands of feet deep, we began to sight anchored bamboo rafts designed to attract fish into their shade. A yacht, recently arrived from Belau, had unwisely attempted to navigate through this sea by night. It collided with something that seriously damaged the fiberglass hull. At first they thought it might have been a log. In hindsight they realized it was more than likely one these fish-attracting rafts.

In the late afternoon we approached the northern end of 40-mile-long Burias Island where we rounded a headland of weathered limestone into the lee of Busin Islet. While we circled the serene cove to find a place to drop our hook a grinning young man in a yellow canoe paddled out. Before the anchor was down he was seated comfortably on the poop without so much as a "by your leave." We forgave his forwardness, saying to each other, "This is their bay." Politely Michael asked the lad about the village. "Haraban Bye Bye, village name," he

informed us. We did not know if we understood correctly because the young man spoke almost no English. We left him on
deck when we went for a swim.

Now that both air and sea had become delightfully warm,
our evening swim was a ritual. Two-in-one shampoo works well
in salt water. We soaped down before diving into the sea in a
frothy ring of bubbles. On deck we rinsed the seawater off with
sun-warmed fresh water.

A voice called out, "Good morning, good morning." It was still
dark outside. Miki, who was sleeping topside, pulled the sheet
up over her face and ignored the voice. Villagers often assume
we keep the same early hours they do. On this particular morning we were not at all anxious to meet anyone. Michael and I
had been vomiting through the night in a reaction to salmonella
poisoning from Puerto Galera eggs. So it was with a groan that
Michael heaved himself from the bunk when we heard the clatter of someone climbing aboard.

A wide-eyed expectant-looking child and a deeply weathered man clung to SEA QUEST's rail. The man spoke English and
his expression of resigned sadness touched Michael. They carried on a polite conversation until I came on deck to take over.

"What is that noise?" the man asked.

"Our generator. We run it every day for a little while to keep
our refrigerator and freezer cold and to make electricity. Does
your village have electricity?"

"No."

"I heard stereo music last night. How is that run?"

"By battery," he answered.

"Why doesn't the village all get together and buy a generator?

"We are too poor, no money for generator."

Changing the topic I asked, "What's happening on the
beach?" There were mounds of sand heaped up and people
working.

"They sell sand. Ten pesos a bucket. To make cement."

He went on to say that although there was an elementary
school in the village few could afford to send their children

there and none of the fishermen were rich enough to own a motorized *banca* canoe.

With a sudden shift he said brightly, "My son he say, 'maybe
they give us some money!' "

I was momentarily taken aback.

"So," I teased the little boy, "you think this is a golden yacht
tinkling with coins, do you?" The father rapidly translated to
his son. "But we don't make a habit of giving money to people."

"For cake," said Papa, by way of explanation.

"Oh . . . well, I just might have something."

Below, I found a stash of butterscotch to which I added a
couple of sticks of chewing gum. The candy was received
gravely by the father and with a grin by the child.

Emboldened then, the father said, "I want to paint my
canoe but have no brush paint."

"Brush paint? I don't understand. Do you mean paint
brush?"

The father nodded, "Yes, paint brush and paint. I have no
brush, only coconut fiber."

The canoe hanging astern was already painted in pale green.
Perhaps he had another canoe ashore.

"I have no paint for wood," I said, "only steel, but I will
give you a paintbrush."

Now with paintbrush and candy in hand, the man realized
that there was not much more to be got from me, so he bid
good-bye and was off. I did not blame him for attempting to
rattle our rigging for goodies. Our boat undoubtedly represented more wealth than the collective assets of the whole village put together. Like in a fairy tale, the man and the boy had
naively imagined for one shimmering minute that we might
make their dreams come true.

Though less primitive than most of the Melanesian islanders
in the South Pacific, the Filipinos seemed psychologically im-
poverished. Perhaps they suffer more from living in a semi-
developed country where the television watched by many offers
a window into the lives of the very rich, and well-stocked shops
overflowing with attractive goods remain out of reach for the
often uneducated majority. They are an energetic and vital

people, handsome and warm with an astounding capacity to seize opportunities but impotent under the yoke of national policies formulated by rich landowning families who exploit the poor. Corruption is rife. Politicians routinely buy votes by distributing pesos to every voting family in a district. Democracy, although written into the constitution, remains unrealized.

Though Michael still felt ill, the Burias Pass contained few hazards. Luzon's coast and the beautiful Mayon Volcano remained visible until we rounded Cabarian Point. That day we managed only 26 nautical miles which took us across the entrance to huge Sorsogon Bay. By dusk we found our way barred by scores of men in canoes, setting long nets lit by floating lights. Each time we attempted to close the coast northwest of the Donsol River along a nameless expanse of coconut-fringed shoreline, a tiny boat would whiz up to guide us around still more nets or a larger boat would flash a warning strobe. The fishermen displayed a high degree of collective organization. Eventually we anchored. After darkness fell the lights on the nets made the sea look as though all the stars had dropped into it to form an immense fairy ring.

Just to the south was Bulan, the last town of any size that we would visit in the Philippines. Conspicuous under tin-roofed sheds was a large market. The bloated carcasses of fish floated off the beach along with the stench of rotting flesh and other unpleasant odors. We pulled our dinghy up between fishermen unloading their catch. Troops of children and a few adults gathered to stare at us. An excited butcher ran out. He pushed a large tray of gray meaty mounds under my nose. Reeling back I exclaimed, "No meat, no meat!" I was shocked by my own emphatic reaction. At that moment I felt only disgust for the sordid, smelly place and particularly for the unhygienic meat. Without haggling, in the first vegetable stall we came to, I bought nearly all we needed. The old woman serving us could not stop grinning.

Shopping in that steamy heat was discouraging. It was only after we discovered a fragrant bakery where we ate fresh banana bread that we felt strong enough to look for the gas station. There, the owner's friendly wife assured us that the 80 gallons of diesel we needed would be delivered to the dock by lunchtime.

Half an hour later we maneuvered the boat as close alongside as we could. There was a 10-foot gap to bridge between the old rotten pilings and the new concrete pier. Michael swung the fuel on the end of a halyard across the gap while a ragtag collection of young men enjoyed the spectacle of Miki and me grappling with the slippery plastic barrels.

Though SEA QUEST was anchored a long way from shore determined little boys on the beach collected all the littered Styrofoam they could find into copra sacks for flotation and swam out. Joining the little boys in their game, Michael tossed a partially filled balloon to the children, then followed it into the water with a big splash. The youngsters took turns performing flips from the slippery deck and afterwards we welcomed them aboard to share the novelty of shampooing their hair. With the little boys gone and the heat diminished, we again headed ashore to join the throngs enjoying the pleasant cool of the evening walking the streets of Bulan.

We admired the latticed timberwork and ornate wrought iron, now nearly rusted away, of fine old townhouses. No doubt these grand homes had been built in times of much greater hope and prosperity than today. Modern construction is of no architectural merit, just the same ubiquitous concrete and tin seen everywhere in the tropics. Saturday was clean-up day. In the dusty side streets, children and women set alight the little heaps of leaves, twigs and litter that they had swept into piles.

Bulan sits near the southernmost tip of Luzon, a tip we had to round to pass through the San Bernadino Strait and on to Balicuatro Islands off Samar's northern coast. Torturous currents roar through these straits: when the tides on the South China Sea are high they are low on the Philippine Sea side. To avoid strong rips, whirlpools, and overfalls we delayed our departure from Bulan until 9:30 AM, but we still had a fast trip. When, in mid-afternoon, we approached Balicuatro's emerald and turquoise enchantment the light was good enough to make out the offshore reefs extending far beyond the islands. We possessed a detailed chart of the bay but decided against anchoring near the village. Instead we dropped the hook close to a low mangrove island. Even cruisers need a day off now and again.

The next day the wind was blowing at 20 knots from the northeast. We wondered if these were the tradewinds that we needed to get us to Belau. Soon the cumulus clouds began billowing. We set a reefed main and jib. Outside the shelter of Balicuatro, squalls and strong currents swept us to leeward. It was obvious we could not make the 38 miles to Batag Island in daylight. We sheltered behind an unnamed spur of islets and reef off Catarman on the big island of Samar.

Then catastrophe struck. The generator had stopped soon after we had set off from Balicuatro. Michael checked it after we anchored, expecting a clogged filter. But as he stripped and tested the motor he began to worry. When broken bits of hardened steel from the fuel injector pump fell into his hand, Michael's fears were realized. Though we could make electricity from our main engine, we needed the 7-hp Kubota to run the compressor for the freezer. Our frozen food supply was now at stake. He had to get the motor operating.

We carried no spare fuel pump. This was the Philippines where there are few phones and even fewer fax machines: we could not send out for a new part. Michael rolled the shattered pieces in his hand. "If only I could glue this all together."

"Glue," I interjected. "That piece would collapse in an instant, wouldn't it? Doesn't it move?"

"It rotates to adjust the amount of fuel each time the plunger is pushed inside," he explained.

Michael pulled out a box of white Marine-Tex, a grade designed for plastic not for metal, but it was all we had.

He made a jig on which to precisely reconstruct the shattered pieces. Applying a coating of Marine-Tex to the broken edges he formed a collar around them while making certain the pump return spring would still fit without having its movement obstructed. He laid it out to harden. Next morning he trimmed and dressed the repair, re-assembled the fuel pump, and primed the system. The engine only stuttered along. "What's going on?" he muttered as he disassembled the pump once more. "The Marine-Tex has held but the copper washer has split."

From scrap, he set out to make a new one. The job had

taken all day and on the final re-assembly the Marine-Tex cracked. Thirty-six hours had passed. The freezer's temperature was steadily rising and the contents would not be safe much longer.

Over a quick meal Michael, suddenly inspired, said, "I'll reinforce it with sail twine!" This time he layered the Marine-Tex over the twine. Nothing more could be done until it had hardened off, a wait of at least 12 more hours. By late the following afternoon, after sanding and burnishing his handiwork, he re-assembled the part.

"The Boat Angel has surely taught you a thing or two dismantling and putting together that engine," I quipped. We like to think that an angel looks after SEA QUEST who forces us from time to time to tackle jobs we've ignored.

He started the generator and for exactly one hour and five minutes it worked. When it sputtered to a stop, a collective groan rose from the three of us. Michael was at wit's end. The freezer thermometer hovered at above zero.

Michael dived back into the engine room. Fifteen minutes later the engine roared to life. Michael straightened as he came out. I saw a broad grin spread across his face. "It only was out of fuel. So much was spilled every time I worked on it, the tank had run dry!"

The day before we had quit our rolling anchorage to sail 24 miles to Port Palapag while the part was curing. Our small-scale chart showed a cleft between mainland and island. Was it a short cut into the huge bay beyond? As we rounded up to drop our sails two fast-moving *bancas* passed us, their passengers raising a loud cheer. We were uncertain about entering the narrow pass, but the *banca* skipper vigorously waved us on.

The entire population of a seaside village seemed to have come to watch the passengers arrive. Untidy children jostled each other on a concrete pier. Like a mother hen brooding over her chicks the white-washed façade of a Spanish-style village church brooded over the village. The rays of the late afternoon's sun gilded it too, the only gold these fishermen were ever likely to possess. We did not try to stop and only narrowly avoided grounding when the channel closely skirted a sand bar before it gave way to the peaceful bay beyond.

In the morning, if the mended part still held and our food remained frozen, we planned to set sail for Belau, the first of the thinly scattered Caroline Islands that span Micronesia across 2,000 miles of ocean.

We were barely out of bed the next morning when a young man's cheery voice hailed us. Holding aloft a small tuna he called out in good English, "You want to buy this fish for five dollars?" He paddled nearer; I threw him a line.

"Yes," was my reply, "but how much in pesos? I have pesos."

"How much you want to give me?"

"One hundred pesos?" I ventured.

"Sure, anything you say. It's the only one I caught and I want you to have it."

"What is the name of this place?" I asked.

"Cahayagan Island," he said.

"Where is Port Palapag?"

"It is here. It is not really a port, just a fishing village," he replied with a grin.

"Does the village have vegetables or fruit to sell?"

"The village has nothing, only fish. The market is at Catarman, 25 miles away. You want fruit. I'll see what I can find."

Other *bancas* arrived, filled with young people. A few girls approached in a friendly and sociable manner, speaking English.

"How do you know English so well?"

"We study four years in school."

"Only four years! Do you watch TV a lot?"

"No. We only have a generator at night, so we see a little then, but only some of it is in English."

"So how do you learn?" I asked puzzled.

"We read novels."

Turning to Miki who desperately wanted to improve, I commented, "Well, there's your ticket!"

The young people were very curious about her, wanting to be introduced and to exchange addresses. Two youths asked if they could write to her.

When Miki would not reply, I joked, "Only if you want to join Miki's 'Broken Hearts Club'."

The fish seller came back with his boat loaded down with a

stem of fat bananas, a huge hand of plantain, some coconuts and two perfect papayas.

Ecstatic I asked, "How much for all this?"

"No money," he said. "It's OK."

"I will give you something for your fuel and a gift for the village." He seemed pleased. From the lazarette I pulled a big wrapped bundle containing all the discarded cushion covers from the settee that we had recovered in Hong Kong, much of the beautiful reversible tapestry still as lovely as the day it was woven. I knew clever hands would find good use for the unusual fabric. I also pressed into his hand another hundred pesos. Then we toasted the kindness of these people with a couple of drinking coconuts.

Confident at last that our generator was working, we agreed it was time to push off from the Philippines. After a good lunch, the mainsail was hoisted and the anchor raised. With a last wave towards the now deserted shoreline we set our course to round the reef that clawed to seaward from Batag Island, past an abandoned lighthouse, a relic perhaps of the time when the Japanese held the country. As we sailed by, natives dove into the curling surf to search for shellfish while nearby, fishermen in canoes rode the ocean swell. They barely glanced our way.

9

In the Wake of the Polynesians:
Passage to Belau

It was March 6, the day that in 1521 Ferdinand Magellan first set eyes on Guam, and introduced Western civilization to this part of the globe. Magellan's fleet and starving men arrived from the east, 99 days after discovering a passage that would become known as the Straits of Magellan. We were striking out instead from the west, from the closely clustered archipelagos of Southeast Asia, in the wake of the earliest seafarers in this region who made the same passage more than 3,000 years ago.

Our crossing of Micronesia towards the east would prove to be a challenging windward passage, even in our modern yacht. It gave us pause to imagine the hardships endured by the proto-Polynesians in open canoes. On reflection it seemed inconceivable that they had wandered blind into the Carolines. More likely, we thought, they learned of the existence and perhaps even the location of particular islands from returning survivors of accidental voyages. Later because of over population, defeat in war, or simply the ambitions of a young headman, expeditions were mounted fully prepared with the plants and animals necessary to the group's continued survival. Today, hardly a sea-

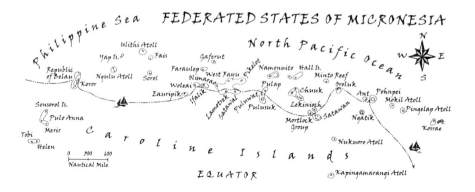

son goes by when fishermen from the Philippines are not swept out to Belau or the Yapese atolls. There are also old stories of disoriented Caroline islanders arriving on the southern coast of Samar, only to discover long-lost relatives already settled there!

Although we planned to hop from island to island, as the early settlers must have done three thousand years ago, our ultimate intention was to sail into the eye of the prevailing winds due east 2,500 miles to Pohnpei.

This might be another good time to question our sanity if not our common sense. Had a speedy return to New Zealand been our sole objective we could have considered going south around Papua New Guinea, then along Australia's east coast. Even then we would eventually have to face crossing the Tasman Sea, a notoriously difficult passage. By sailing east across Micronesia we would have the opportunity to explore seldom visited atolls. With seasonal westerly winds expected to pick up, now was the best time of the year. With the decision made we set ourselves to the task.

Belau, known before Independence as Palau, lay just over 650 miles from the Philippines. Five days out in fluky winds, SEA QUEST still drifted haphazardly. We made little progress in our search for favorable winds or the Equatorial Counter Current while the coastal currents of Samar seemed to suck us closer. Though motoring gave us a sense of progress, we had neither the resources nor the will to motor all the way to Belau. But when we shut down the engine, we again drifted aimlessly.

The three days of strong northeasterly winds we had experienced while nursing our generator back to life had evidently been an exception. This year's El Niño had upset the normal tradewind pattern. Day after day of windless travel-brochure perfection followed. Nothing hinted at change.

Then we felt a stirring. The breeze kicked the ocean to life. A pod of porpoise leapt in the moon-shadowed seas. When a terrified flying fish, flapping furiously, landed in my shirt collar to shed his scales across my shoulder in a silvery ribbon of light, I yelped in surprise.

Michael had risen early to take star sights and now we stood together watching the sun's first rays streak the eastern horizon.

"We are losing our wind again," Michael remarked.

"Yes," I replied with resignation. "Never enough wind—and when it comes it's always on the nose."

Unleashed from its nighttime shroud, the sun beat down relentlessly. Michael and I sheltered in the doghouse. Miki, silent and morose, sat day after day in a sort of stupor, exposed to the elements, burning the color of dark mahogany. She had been aboard almost five months. Although she had made her final decision in the Philippines to continue the voyage, she was still fighting some inner demon. Michael and I could only hope she would find a way to adjust.

As the days continued windless we became concerned over our diminishing stock of oil. It was necessary to top up the crankcase of our old engine after every ten hours of use. Heat, motion and the utter peacefulness lulled us to sleep. Almost imperceptibly the wind increased; little waves chattered in growing excitement, a few noisily slapped against the hull. The boat heeled, the wake hissed. Awakening to a freshness that had been absent before, we found ourselves amid whitecaps.

Another tiny cross was placed in a string of others marching across the plotting sheet. A discrepancy between the logged distance and the charted distance indicated for the first time some vestigial current in our favor. Was this the elusive Equatorial Counter Current we had sailed to 5° south to find? Now our course improved by the hour with the track chart showing a slow curve toward the east.

Although the wind fluctuated our progress remained steady. The constellations marched by in a steady progression while SEA QUEST appeared to move hardly a jot. To port the Pole Star slid closer to the horizon, its light dimming as we neared the Equator. To starboard the Southern Cross cartwheeled ever higher and blazed brighter.

At dawn on the eighth day Michael shook me awake. "We must make an emergency repair," he said.

A nut had fallen from the masthead block requiring that Miki and I man the winch to haul Michael aloft. He would have to replace the nut as SEA QUEST heeled on the wind. Should we round-up and shake the pin loose, we would loose the halyard as well.

Miki and I performed our part without error. Michael ar-

104

rived back on deck with only a few bumps and minor scratches from the wild ride at the masthead.

"The sea may look flat," he said "but up there it's gyrating like hell."

Nearing Belau, sea life abounded. Dolphin ripped into a school of tuna. Tropicbirds, trailing long tail plumage, wheeled and chirped. A gentle black noddy, a white blaze upon its dusky forehead, fluttered to rest on the furled mizzen. Then at dawn of the tenth day Belau's 600-foot hilltops finally came into range.

From the spreaders, Michael scanned the horizon. A conspicuous wreck on one side and a beacon to the north signaled Toagel Mlungui Pass, the entrance through the reef. As we neared, the vivid turquoise lagoon came into view behind a line of shimmering breakers. We ran forward to drop the genoa while the engine ticked away in readiness for strong or unpredictable currents. Inside the lagoon markers picked out the 18-mile channel to Koror, Belau's main town.

"The rhumb-line course was 650 miles but we actually sailed 960 miles," Michael informed us after checking the log. "We never got the break we were hoping for."

Over his shoulder, Miki and I studied the erratic lines tracking across the chart from Samar in the Philippines to Belau.

"What can we expect for the next leg?" I mused.

"That's difficult to judge. If winds continue light and easterly it's going to be slow going," he answered.

A sudden strong gust heeled SEA QUEST sharply, sending sunscreen and cameras scuttling across the deck. Where the open lagoon narrowed the wind swept down in fierce williwaws. We rounded into the port at Koror where a container wharf, the Shell Oil facility, and a beachside hotel spread out before us. Michael radioed Port Control.

"Tie up to the main wharf," the voice instructed.

The concrete wharf looked ready to murder SEA QUEST! The only unoccupied dock was a wall of rough concrete. Just one huge truck tire served as fender. On the dock, a uniformed figure stepped out to wave us in impatiently. Despite the gusting onshore wind, I eased SEA QUEST into the gap between fuel barge and rafted fishing boats. By luck as much as by good judgement we scrunched against the single truck tire.

The Customs officer made a show of searching SEA QUEST by opening a few cupboards and staring fixedly at the paneling. "We get a lot of drugs here," he explained.

Once cleared we were directed to anchor among the pretty nearby Rock Islands.

10

Belau: Stone Heads and Ancient Secrets

The Rock Islands are nature's masterpiece. Clusters of these fairy-tale islets lie within a barrier reef that surrounds most of Belau's main islands. Formed by a cataclysm that thrust the old seabed 200 feet higher, the coral petrified to limestone. Time, wind and weather have carved what was once an undersea reef into a maze of stunning mushroom-shaped Rock Islands intersected by a tangle of navigable channels. The scenic clusters of islands, Belau's near perfect climate and an undersea world of unparalleled bio-diversity in a lagoon as clear as spring water—any cruiser would feel in heaven.

From our anchorage we followed a channel artificially dug during the war to an inner harbor crowded now with small dive and charter boats. The Marina Hotel serves as gathering place. Over a beer, locals Richard and Rita made us feel welcome. Former cruisers, their two eldest daughters now had interesting jobs as skippers of live-aboard dive ships. When Richard discovered we needed to track down generator parts he kindly offered the use of telephone, fax and email in his law office.

From Marina Hotel it is a dusty mile to the main street. We studied faces as we walked. Belau's present population is a kaleidoscope of Malay and Melanesian spliced into strong Polynesian stock. Archeologists say Belau may have been occupied as much as 4,500 years ago by seafarers whose mainland ancestors sailed and paddled their vessels out of Indochina, although carbon dated artifacts so far only go back to about 1,000 BC.

When we dropped in at his office, Richard explained a bit about Belau, known as Palau until Independence in 1994. "Despite the western trappings, Belauans live by the old rules. Their income and free time are completely absorbed in obligatory support of their extended families." He went on. "The culture is traditionally matrilineal. Property is passed down through the

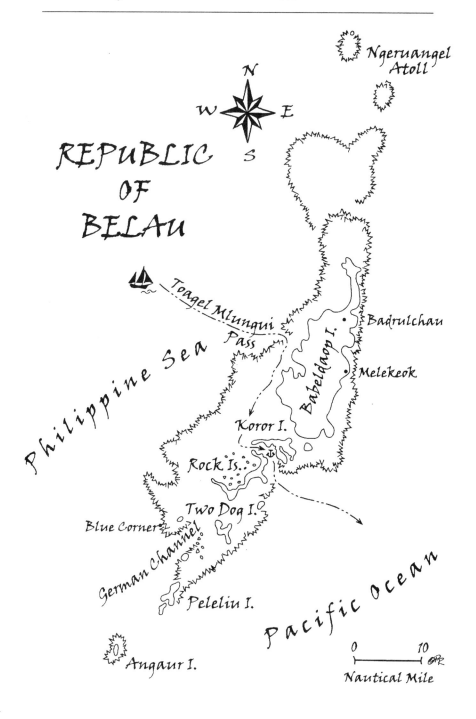

Ngeruangel Atoll

REPUBLIC OF BELAU

N
W E
S

Toagel Mlunqui Pass

Philippine Sea

Badrulchau

Babeldaop I.

Melekeok

Koror I.

Rock Is.

Two Dog I.

Blue Corner

German Channel

Peleliu I.

Pacific Ocean

Angaur I.

0   10
Nautical Mile

daughters, and it's the elder women who are responsible for choosing the male chiefs."

Today the country has just over 15,000 inhabitants and a cumbersome government. It is divided into 16 states; each with its own legislature, court and local government bodies. One state has only 200 people. Since World War II when Belau was liberated from the Japanese, the citizens have grown fat in government office jobs that pay well but demand little. The top-heavy bureaucratic structure seems to be an attempt to put as many of the population on U.S. subsidized payrolls as possible. However, the people of Belau rejected America's proposal to replace the U.S. base at Subic Bay in the Philippines with a new one here. They voted instead to become "nuclear free." It appears their ready stream of aid money may be drying up. Should that happen, today's comfortable prosperity may change. Locals so scorn any sort of menial or heavy work, that Chinese and Filipino labor, representing 25% of the total population, is imported for construction and road building projects.

At a concrete meeting house, we stopped to take a photograph of the unusual architecture. Traditional high-pitched South Sea Islands *bai* once graced every village. Unmarried girls lived in these men's houses as concubines. We are told the men treated the girls well, bestowing upon them valuable custom money. Understandably, this archaic sexual custom has died out, but the Belauan "money" is still treasured today.

Jeff, a young scuba diving instructor, had come to pay homage to Belau, a Mecca for serious divers from around the world. In return for a week's passage aboard SEA QUEST, he agreed to show us the dive sites and coach Miki, who only began to *swim* in the Philippines, to scuba dive.

Our first night out, SEA QUEST was snugly anchored in a Rock Island cove so narrow we tied our lines to shore. We lay between verdant islets set like bright jewels in the turquoise waters. In overhanging branches tropicbirds fed their squawking young. By day we wandered the narrow passages among islands that looked very similar to each other, taking care not to become lost.

Leaving that cluster of Rock Islands, we crossed a broad

expanse of open lagoon. Miki kept a sharp eye out for hazardous shoals and scattered coral heads. At the south end of the lagoon we anchored near a bright sand spit adjoining a jungle-clad island.

The Indochina-Malay region was the cradle of marine fauna. As one moves east across the Pacific the different species become less abundant. Belau, located at the perimeter of the Philippine Sea in the convergence of three nutrient-rich ocean currents, enjoys the highest concentration of sea life in the Pacific. There are some 1,500 species of tropical fish and 700 different types of coral and anemones, twice the diversity of Hawaii.

As for diving, Belau has it all. Wall dives, drift dives, and manta stations. Cave dives, shafts, tunnels, underwater caverns with stalactites, and even World War II wrecks. With Jeff's assistance we planned to have a go of at least a handful.

When the sun was high enough, we entered the narrow German Channel, a shortcut through the reef cut a century before by colonial phosphate miners. It took us from the inner lagoon to a bight of water where the barrier reef bends inward to form a broad bay. Along its walls dive-boat moorings are screwed into the coral below.

Michael stayed at the helm while Miki, Jeff and I leapt overboard at Ngemelis Wall. Slowly we dropped 60 feet while the wall plunged out of sight below us. A dozen sleek gray reef and white-tip sharks patrolled nearby. On seeing these so close, Miki froze in fear. Jeff took a grip on her so she would not dart away in panic.

Late the next afternoon we picked up a mooring at the Blue Corner, a notorious diving spot. There were no other boats in sight. It was Miki's and my turn to keep watch. Jeff and Michael slid beneath the sea's glittering surface in a place known for its schools of shark and barracuda. With Miki and I their only backup, they could afford little risk. Half an hour later the galley alarm went off. Their time was up. Although I never ceased scanning the reef through the glare with binoculars, after the first five minutes I had seen no trace of bubbles.

I signaled Miki to drop the mooring. A school of frightened fish broke the surface; the strong current dragged at SEA QUEST.

Miki at the start of the voyage from Wakayama

Michael helping to carry a *mikoshi* from the shrine

Monks climbing
steps at Kompira-san

Baby-blessing at Shinto
shrine. Mother and
baby are wrapped in
traditional cape

SEA QUEST docked at Huis ten Bosch. In the foreground, Michael holding the cat

Shinto shrines at the site of a large Buddhist temple near Nara

Seto Naikai older style fishing boats

SEA QUEST tucked among fishing boats at Hagata-Ko

Michael and Tere at Okinawa's Chinese garden

Miki and Tere with friend visiting Buddhist temple

Miki and Tere on moon bridge in Chinese garden, Okinawa

Macau's main Portuguese-style plaza

Hong Kong sampan, seller of hot grilled lunches to other boats

Miki and Tere beside turquoise sea and eroded limestone islets on
Oki-no-Erabu

Macau's oldest lighthouse built by the Portuguese and the first lighthouse along the coast of China

Miki and Tere in marketplace, Bulan, Philippines

Philippine children with Miki

Tere teaching Miki a "rolling hitch" knot.

Miki and her scuba diving instructor, Jeff, climbing aboard SEA QUEST in Belau

Philippine banca visiting alongside SEA QUEST

Miki keeping watch through the German Channel

Traditional Belau men's house, or bai, Babeldaop Island

Klidm, carved stone heads and 37 foundation stones of unknown origin on Badrulchau

SEA QUEST among rock islands near Two Dog Island

Miki with Japanese World War II cannon in a Babeldaop fortification

Miki at Shinto shrine for Japanese soldiers outside a cave on Peleliu, Belau

Sᴇᴀ Qᴜᴇsᴛ entering Koror's inner harbor, Belau

Miki with island girls in house, Eauripik

Young man guides SEA QUEST to shelf on which to anchor outside of Eauripik reef

Eauripik canoe house where Michael meets with the chief

Tere, Miki and friends wading across reef on Eauripik

Miki being transported out to SEA QUEST, Eauripik

It was past the deadline—and still no sign of them. The seconds dragged slowly as anxiously I circled the boat. Then two black blobs appeared against the glare. Under my breath I swore *I'll never let Michael out of my sight again!*

Jeff was ecstatic as he climbed aboard, but Michael was quiet. Privately he said later, "The current was so strong it nearly ripped the mask from my face. Without our reef hooks we would have been swept to sea." He paused and continued. "Next time I'd prefer something a little less traumatic."

At the southern extreme of Belau's lagoon lies Peleliu Island. We just managed to squeeze into landlocked Beck's Harbor at high tide, but once inside, apart from sand flies, it was a perfect anchorage.

Peleliu was the site of the infamous "Forgotten Battle" of World War II that claimed the lives of more than 14,000 Japanese and American men. From atop Bloody Nose Ridge, we overlooked the killing zone. Here the marines had the job of prying the suicidal Japanese out of the 600 manmade caves they had built into the limestone escarpment. Although the Japanese Central Command knew by that stage that the war was lost, their men were ordered to fight to the death.

A loud blast shook the ground. We leapt involuntarily. One of the thousands of live bombs still strewn in the rugged hills had spontaneously exploded, a common experience here. The shock connected us across the intervening years to the rusting helmets, artillery pieces, canteens and cooking pots still littering the cave entrances.

Today Peleliu is better known in some circles for its local strain of cannabis. Young tourists sporting tattoos and navel rings come here intent only on sun and fun.

We returned to Belau's main town of Koror to pick up the vital replacement generator part that our son, Conrad, had air freighted from the States. Then, at the invitation of a Japanese construction manager Miki had met casually, we roamed northern Babeldaob, the largest island of the Belau group. At Melekeiok the community has rebuilt a traditional high-peaked *bai* meeting house.

We continued on to Badrulchau. Thirty-seven monoliths stand on this ancient site. Stone pillars weighing up to five tons stand in a double row. They are oriented north and south and notched to take floor joists. The building must have been huge. It was built at a time when 30,000 people, twice the population of today, inhabited the island. Sweeping views made the site a great lookout. Weathered stone faces, *klidm*, carved from five-ton basalt blocks look out across the landscape. Pottery shards indicate the stone faces were there by the first century BC, if not before.

Klidm are hidden all over Babeldaob, but most were defaced when the Japanese tried to introduce the Shinto religion. Some *klidm* are reminiscent of Easter Island carvings, others remind us of those found in Vanuatu. Indeed, they are probably all related. After all, it was their relatives who continued on to settle the Pacific at the time when Europeans were still in the Dark Ages.

The time to strike out across Micronesia was drawing near. But how would we fill our nearly empty 400-gallon water tanks? The country was in the grip of a drought so severe that even the island's biggest waterfalls had dried up. Water was rationed. Would we be forced to purchase desalinated water from one of the hotels for a dollar a gallon? John, owner of the charter yacht ECLIPSE, came to our rescue by offering his berth for a few days while he was out on charter.

"The water is turned on for about an hour in the morning and an hour at night. You can fill up then," he suggested.

The water, however, did not flow. Desperate or unscrupulous people had broken into the supply pipe nearer its source, siphoning off what little there was. A week passed. John was due back tomorrow.

I happened to look up and noticed a dark cloud to the east.

"Michael!" I shouted. "I think it's going to rain!" Emerging from below he stared at the cloud only a moment before leaping into action.

"Let's get the awning hoses rigged—fast."

By the time the first drops fell, we were ready. Water gurgled cheerily into the tanks as the downpour intensified. Miki helped me haul out all our dirty laundry. Laughing together, we set to work scrubbing bedding, towels and clothes. Though I kept glancing at the sky, the downpour held steady. Down and down it came while we, like joyful children with wet hair and clothes plastered to our bodies, sloshed back and forth across the now muddy lawn carrying armloads of clean clothes. At the moment when SEA QUEST's tanks began to overflow and the laundry was completed, the rain abruptly stopped. There was nothing to hold us back now. It was time to head to sea.

11

The Mythic South Seas:
Eauripik Atoll

Subjected to fickle winds, our course continued to be erratic. Not only did the wind toy with us but so did the ocean current, tugging us to the north, then west and finally towards the east.

On the eighth day sweeping squalls bore down bringing 35-knot easterly winds and life-giving rains. SEA QUEST labored with sail and sometimes engine to windward. Though Miki was now taking night watches in calm weather, tonight was her first solo in stronger conditions. She had to frequently adjust the wheel. If Miki did not make the boat fall off the wind, the sails would go aback, jibing the boat onto the other tack. From our bunk below where we dozed fitfully, Michael and I could hear frustrated cries as she courageously struggled to perform her duty.

We were voyaging through a stretch of ocean containing 15 scattered atolls that are today part of the Federated States of Micronesia's Yap State. Although these islands extend eastward 600 miles they contain only about seven square miles of land. Yap Out Islands are culturally and linguistically different from

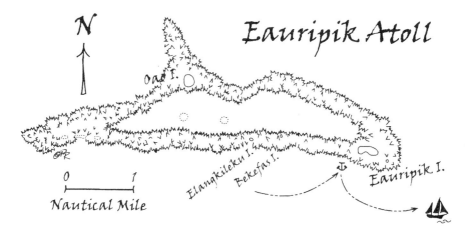

Yap, remnants of an empire that may once have included all of the Caroline Islands, possibly even Pohnpei—an area of ocean larger than the U.S. mainland. In times past islanders gave tribute to Yap, whose magicians could unleash typhoon or drought on the islands if displeased.

The islands of the Western Carolines were part of trading circuits that reached as far as the Northern Marianas. On their forays for the turmeric they used ceremonially, they witnessed the arrival of the Spaniards in Guam—and the cruelty imposed on that island's people. This cruelty caused the Carolinians to suspend voyages for many years until their desire to obtain metal to make tools made them overcome caution and resume their trips. The Yapese, who went to Babeldaob to quarry calciferous limestone, and the people of Belau kept each other informed about early European incursions. When Vilalobos, an early Spanish explorer, landed on Yap and Fais in 1543, he was astonished to be given the Castilian greeting, "¡Buenos dias, marineros!"

Our GPS failed on our tenth day as we neared Eauripik Atoll. Despite cloudy skies Michael was able to take several sextant sights. We hoped to spot tiny Eauripik, but knew we might sail right past. The atoll reef is just five miles long with less than a tenth of a square mile of land. It was 3:30 PM when Michael sang out "Land ho!" What a forlorn speck Eauripik seemed, like drifting flotsam. Gradually the distant blur turned into a coconut-clad island, the gold and browns of its broad reef exposed by low tide.

Suddenly our VHF radio crackled to life.

"Yacht, this is Eauripik Island," a husky voice said. "Do you want to rest here awhile?"

Captain Cook, addressed like this, could not have been more astounded.

"SEA QUEST back to shore. Hello! Yes, we would like very much to stop overnight," Michael hastily replied, "but there is no pass into the lagoon."

"Shore back. The boys will show you where the government passenger boat anchors."

Two men appeared on the drying reef carrying a small outrigger canoe and launched it into the surf. Rounding into the island's lee we let the mainsail flutter into its nest of jack lines. The canoe bumped alongside. A young man wearing a loincloth climbed aboard and introduced himself as David. His companion struck off by canoe into the distance.

"Follow him," David instructed.

Where the reef indented slightly, we let go the anchor. The depth sounder read five fathoms on the coral shelf, but as we pulled back on the chain the indicator slid off the scale. It was unnerving. We double-checked that the anchor held. Though tenuous, this was the best and *only* anchorage at Eauripik.

"As long as the wind is from the northeast it is safe here," David assured us.

Soon five more outriggers bobbed in the rolling swells behind SEA QUEST and brown faces radiating warm smiles crowded into the cockpit to sip lemon drinks.

"I'm in the military but home on leave for a month," David said by way of introduction. Many of the young people, he told us, were away at high school or working for wages on big islands like Saipan or Chuuk. "Relatives send back money so people here can buy things they need." Eauripik, he explained, had a population numbering less than 100 people.

There were so many strangers aboard I began to get nervous. Everyone seemed so pleasant, so happy and so helpful I had let my guard down. Our first intimations of what was to come occurred when Michael decided to take a quick swim to check the anchor. His flippers and mask had disappeared along with one of the boys who earlier had borrowed his gear to "find you some fish." The boys aboard reassured us. "It was taken by mistake. You will get it back in the morning."

The island's fiberglass longboat was sent to fetch us to shore next morning. The calm weather conditions gave us the confidence to leave SEA QUEST at her precarious anchorage. After dragging the longboat across the shallow shelf, we found ourselves in a lagoon so bright it perfectly matched the men's turquoise loincloths. Exotic high peaked roofs were shaded by a canopy of lush vegetation. On the edge of an ancient platform of cut coral blocks supporting the men's house, young boys dangled their legs. When we hove into view, they leapt up to run along the narrow shore shouting excitedly.

We approached the main canoe shed. Chief Louis, 50-year-old and rheumy-eyed, sat amongst the wood chips. The authoritative power wielded by a high chief on these Out Islands was far from democratic. We squatted respectfully. Michael pushed a 20-pound bag of rice forward as a gift, an act we would repeat at each island we visited. The chief spoke indirectly to Michael through a second person, not because he lacked a command of English, but to emphasize his position.

"Naturally you are aware," he said, "of the fees that the government of Yap have decreed must be paid by all visiting yachts?"

Because we had not visited Yap, which lies a few hundred miles north of Belau, we were ignorant of these new fees.

"Vessels must pay a $25 anchoring fee and $20 each to land!" Silence fell while we digested this.

"We are very sorry," said Michael, "but we cannot pay these fees. We do not have so much money." Again silence fell.

"This is the new policy," said the chief.

"I appreciate that the government may have suggested this fee, but if every island wanted money we could not afford to go anywhere!"

"This is the policy." Another long silence.

We seemed to have reached a stalemate. I decided to risk a word.

"On Lamotrek Michael did many small repairs for people and they did not charge us any money." We had visited Lamotrek three years earlier.

"What did you do on Lamotrek?"

Michael considered for a moment. "Well, for instance, I drilled holes in steel to make spears."

"Can you do some grinding for us? Can you help us repair some fiberglass?"

"Sure," said Michael.

"OK then. You can stay. And now you can look around the island. The boy will take you."

While the chief had parlayed with Michael, women gathered at a distance to peer curiously at us. Michael and I approached the nearest ones, who gravely shook our hands. The women were garbed about the waist in sarongs of heavy hand-woven cotton they called *dhur.* As we walked along the village paths, friendly people seated in the doorways of their small homes waved to us.

A gregarious woman with a big smile invited us into her house, built as narrow as a ship with rounded ends like those in Tonga. Enormous butts of breadfruit wood supported beams and rafters lashed neatly together with coconut-fiber twine. Thick palm mats cushioned the floor of packed coral rubble while finely woven pandanus mats, tucked during daytime in the rafters, were used for sleeping. Between the doorways hung a net-covered baby's cradle, which gently stirred in the cross-breeze.

Back on the path, a group of passing men stopped to talk. One offered to fetch us coconuts to drink. While we waited Michael asked how the island had fared during the war. A man, about 40, answered. When the Japanese occupied the island, he explained, they indoctrinated the people about American "barbarity."

After the Japanese withdrew American reconnaissance planes flew over the atoll. Because of their fear of Americans, they thought to outwit them. Even though the Japanese were gone, they strung up a Japanese flag to show that real soldiers defended the island. Their action backfired. The American pilots, thinking the atoll a last holdout of the Japanese, dropped incendiary bombs, killing several people.

"All the strong young men were in Belau during the occupation," he said. There under forced labor they nearly starved, but being naturally endowed with the so-called "thrifty gene," they all came home.

Eauripik was one of the last outposts of paganism, but that was about to change. The Catholic Bishop of Micronesia was arriving in a fortnight to baptize a majority of the population. Only the chief and a handful of others would refrain. A large thatched building named St. Mark's Catholic Church now took pride of place, but the real heart of the atoll still lay half-buried in a mound.

Two young women had joined our guide. "Do you want to see the place of the goddess?" Shyly we were led away from the well-beaten path to a slight rise overlooking a large well-tended taro pit. The girl pointed to a black rock, the size and shape of a head and said: "This is our goddess stone."

How long had the islanders paid homage to the forces of nature on which their survival depended, those forces of which they were so intrinsically a part? Was it for a hundred, five hundred or a thousand years? That black basaltic stone representing *Hoosh,* a faceless but potent power, came from elsewhere, probably an original homeland far to the west.

Stripping a palm leaf from a nearby tree the younger woman split it with her thumbnail and then drew it out into a circle. Handing it to me she gestured that I should place it with the leis. "Don't touch the stone," she cautioned gently.

Kneeling amid the forest litter I lay the wreath.

We walked on through mixed groves of breadfruit and coconut past thatched homes, nearly all perched atop impressive foundations. "Can you tell me about all the stonework I see?" I asked the young women. The girl carrying a plump baby recounted a story.

> Long ago a powerful soothsayer predicted a monster typhoon. He said it would cause violent surf to crash across the atoll. Everyone would die. The prediction scared everyone so much they made a plan and set to work to cut stone from the reef to build a platform of cut coral blocks raised to the height of three men. The finished platform was of sufficient size to contain the whole of the island's population. Hardly had they finished when the foreseen typhoon struck. The tower saved all the people. Later, when the danger seemed past, it was taken down and used to build individual house platforms.

The tale may be true. Had the priest and others who had an affinity with nature recognized odd weather patterns and the hotter than usual sea temperatures that might cause threatening climatic conditions?

Half a century or more of interference and handouts has psychologically weakened today's out islanders. Although government intervention has prevented starvation after typhoon devastation or drought, it has also eroded their natural resilience and self-reliance. Foreign and church influences have undermined traditions that once insured survival and were the cement of the community. Traditional medicine, fishing skills, respect for taboos that ensured against the depletion of resources are just some of the customs lost.

Today the children are packed off to schools to study a foreign curriculum. The adolescent years are often spent learning computer skills in off-island boarding schools. Every day spent away from home learning Western subjects is a day less spent absorbing the old lore. Of course total self-sufficiency *is* a pipe dream. Even these remote islanders are now dependent on having some of their children living and working abroad. Are they better or worse off? I wonder.

Micronesia's main exploitable resource is the vast area of sea it encompasses over which the government can grant fishing licenses. Who will benefit? The people of the remote atolls, or the big chiefs of the larger islands? Will the trade-off of self-sufficiency for Western-style education turn out to be vital to an island economy based on the fragile ecology of their reef, or will it do little more than enable islanders to fill in application forms for social welfare?

Hens and their peeping broods scattered before us in alarm as we continued on. Fat dogs and puppies, unaware of their ultimate fate, lay basking happily in dust and sun. Pigs near the sandy beach dug themselves cool pits to lie in. The cooking sheds sat apart from the houses, more like camps than kitchens. Blackened cook pots, heaps of green and ripe coconut and the flesh of clam or fish buzzing with flies, marked the places of preparation.

Island cuisine is often rough-and-ready but on this island it was more basic than most. Heavy-set women attested to the high consumption of coconut oil. The nutritious taro patches are small, the seasonal breadfruit scarce. The thin soil is able to support only a scattering of lime, banana and papaya trees. On Eauripik coconut is used as cool drink, flavoring, oil, cream, snack, baby food, chicken feed, dog food, desert, alcoholic beverage, sweet syrup and candy!

Despite many economic and social changes, not to mention frequent off-island travel, the population still clings to many old customs. Males and females maintain strict segregation after puberty. Women always show deference to men and are never permitted in fishing canoes; the canoe sheds, fishing nets and men's houses are off-limits. The women farm taro, weave, cook and attend to the babies. Apart from a few teachers, men fish, help sometimes in the taro patch, build canoes and twist coconut fibers into rope as they while away the long afternoons drinking coconut-toddy.

A noisy group of little boys just let out of primary school ran up and reached endearingly to take our hands. With strong white teeth, they tore chunks from the soft outer husk of the young coconuts they were eating, generously offering us bits to chew.

On the island's windward side beneath tall breadfruit trees stood the women's house, built on a low foundation of neatly cut stone. Harnessed to back-strap looms like those still used in Indonesia, a dozen or so women worked threads into many-hued two-yard long sarongs. A younger woman was winding a new warp of bright colors onto a pegged board. Unlike the cotton wraps they wore, these were made from natural and dyed banana fibers with a luster like raw silk. With some restraint, the women muttered words of welcome. Perhaps this area was off-limits for Michael, for hardly had we been there five minutes when a tall lad approached. Michael was to go with the young man to work with his grinder on knives, axes and spear points in the men's house. Michael's tour of the island was over.

Miki and I enjoyed watching the quiet industry of the weavers. A young woman with a toddler called us over, inviting us to share her mat and bringing us hot food to eat. She introduced herself in exceptionally good English.

"I am Manuela. I was in Vancouver for five years with my brother," then added, "I liked it better there than here!"

"But Eauripik seems like paradise."

"No. Here we are restricted. There I had choices."

"How are you restricted?"

"We girls cannot go where we want. We must always show respect to the men. We cannot even visit your boat." The last prohibition seemed to rankle the most. After observing the easy relationship between sexes in Vancouver, I could well understand her frustration.

"Will you sell the banana-fiber sarongs?" I asked, changing the subject.

"No. These *dhur* are for presentations to the bishop. But we weave all the time," she continued. "Sri Lanka traders in Yap supply us with the cotton thread and then buy all we can make."

Several of the younger girls left their work to gather near us. Miki picked up a small leaf basket someone had dropped, expressing her admiration.

"Perhaps the girls will show you how to weave one."

At once a palm frond was cut, split and sectioned. The simple-looking basket turned out to be complicated enough that an older woman was called from her weaving to patiently demonstrate the finer points of its construction. While we plaited we talked.

"Are any of you married?" Though one was nursing her baby, they all shook their heads. "Aren't there enough eligible men on the island?" I teased. "I've noticed a few good-looking guys."

"We are all related," one said resignedly. "We must go to the other islands to find husbands not of our own clan."

Over-population of the atoll and the fear of inbreeding had created an ongoing crisis. In the calm summer weather, people travel by canoe or government vessel between the scattered islands, for trade, for visits and to look for spouses. Some travel to Saipan, Chuuk and Guam and never return. Occasionally a foreign fisherman sheltering nearby from a storm may be especially well received on the island, a help to the gene pool.

"Would you like to shower?" Manuela asked unexpectedly.

Leading us behind a woodshed the women helped us tie on borrowed *dhur*, but neither Miki nor I cared to go topless. We would allow our skimpy shirts to get wet. We were led towards the beach.

"What is this?" wailed Miki. "Where is the *shower*?"

The sun was low now, the sky tinged with sunset. Several women immersed themselves in the sandy shallows in a scene reminiscent of a Gauguin painting. Barefoot we picked our way across sharp coral and soft bodies of sea cucumbers. I lowered myself into water still warm from the sun's blazing heat. Young children, attended by their mothers, splashed quietly around us. When we rose to leave the evening breeze raised goose bumps on our wetted skin. Miki and I were escorted to a cistern beside which two buckets of well water awaited us. I had already guessed this might be the outcome, but Miki moaned with genuine disappointment.

We should not have been so surprised. Actually the islanders bathed in a manner similar to ours on SEA QUEST. We kept a barrel on deck from which we could rinse ourselves free of salt after our daily swim in a minimum of fresh water.

Because the evening was peaceful and the tide still too low to use the launch to return to SEA QUEST, we were urged to stay for the dancing—a practice session for the approaching visit by the Bishop of Micronesia. Miki and I were led to a house where we were fed cold taro and boiled fish. Michael was engaged in the men's house in the serious business of drinking *tuba*, the islander's coconut beer.

After dark the three of us were led to a clearing. Flaring palm leaves from which wild sparks whirled up into the surrounding breadfruit trees illuminated a double-row of male dancers. In a complicated variation of a classical war dance the men rhythmically wielded sticks. They needed more practice before the bishop's arrival.

Manuela glided up beside me to whisper. "You want to see the women dancing?"

Michael, overhearing, was not about to be left behind. "I'm coming too."

"The men will be angry because we've taken you," Manuela stated diplomatically. He came anyway.

To Miki and me Manuela said, "We have *dhur* for you, a gift. Will you wear them?"

Dressed in striped *dhur* like the others now we followed our guides across the island on darkened paths to the women's place where another palm frond fire blazed.

Twenty-five bare breasted women stood in a line whose ends disappeared in the flickering shadows. The strong voice of a song-mistress led the chant. The chants faltered, as women craned to see and follow the leader's routines, but then gained momentum. Pubescent girls, their breasts just tiny buds, stood at the end of the dancing line, slim and delicate as reeds. They were a contrast to the full-grown women who were running to fat on their diet of coconut. Though heavy bodied, no Eauripik woman was obese. They were too well muscled. Planting and harvesting taro, long excursions on the reefs to haul back heavy loads of clam, turtle and octopus, the continuous need to gather firewood, cut and grate coconut and move around heavy cauldrons of food prevented both laziness and obesity.

The palm frond fire replenished by small boys suddenly flared, etching each handsome and sweating face against the darkness. I felt mesmerized by the repetition of the simple dance movements. In the flickering light, past and future merged. These women formed a living bridge across time. Their courage and skills, their social organization had enabled them to exist for generations upon this scrap of land only inches from the restless, clawing sea. If the scientists who predict global warming are correct, the seas will inexorably rise. One day in the not too distant future, a typhoon may overwhelm this island, drowning everyone. Brave survivors of time and challenge will have become victims to global warming and Western greed. Already they say that they have never had so many typhoons each year, and the temperatures have never felt so warm. I had to remind myself that only 6% of the world's population consume 60% of its resources.

The next morning canoes bumped alongside early, stirring us out of bed. David had brought reef fish and was returning Michael's snorkeling gear. A young man wanted to trade several octopuses for fishhooks. Before long David was scaling fish astern while Tino, a 30-year-old, was leafing through photo albums. Another young man helped Miki boil, clean, and then fry the octopus with garlic and onion. Two other teenagers roamed about and then lay down on Miki's bed while she, in the galley nearby, kept an eye on them.

Next morning, though, Miki was miserable. "What's wrong?"

"I have sad story. Look," she said pointing forward. "Gone my ring and my watch." For a moment, until he recalled all the activity the day before, Michael was incredulous.

"Is that everything?"

"Yes, I find after you go to bed. No more gone."

We started a thorough check ourselves: chart table, doghouse, cameras, and deck locker. We discovered Miki's facemask in the doghouse prompting us to check further. My fins, my dive knife and other small things were also gone. We headed ashore to consult with the chief.

Meetings were called, discussions held. Michael was taken to a house to eat and then called to sit for more discussions. "What exactly *were* the items stolen?" the chief sternly asked through his second. "Is this list all of them? What exactly do they look like?"

The thieving boys kept out of sight and offered no apologies, but eventually all the items on the list were returned—except those things we had yet to discover!

Despite the blatant stealing, we were convinced that most Eauripik islanders were decent people, and Chief Louis was a good man too. Thievery, remarked on by the earliest mariners, has always been part of the Micronesian culture. Strangers are always considered fair game. Despite this incident, I felt a sisterly warmth towards Manuela in particular, and empathized with her frustration over the restrictions she had grown to resent after her brief sampling of emancipated womanhood in Vancouver. The simple island lifestyle elicited in me a deep response. In the company of these women weaving together, some part of me felt like a drooping cut flower placed suddenly into water. I was not naïve enough, however, to believe that I could live happily-ever-after confined on a narrow shelf of land restricted by rigid custom and an almost changeless routine.

We said our farewells. An outrigger canoe waited to transport us one-by-one from the edge of the reef to SEA QUEST, now rolling heavily in the sea swell. With Manuela and her friend we waded 100 yards, the girl carrying a stem of green bananas, the island's present to us. Garlanded with fragrant leis, I was the last to be taken up in the canoe. I could not help but cast looks backward at the two silent young women standing knee-deep on the reef. They longed for my freedom. I longed for their lives of ordered simplicity.

12

Ifalik and the Bishop

Imagine for a moment a place where people never have to sweep the floor, find a parking space, get stuck in traffic, shop at the supermarket, wash clothes, answer telephones, wear shoes, keep accounts, license the dog, pay taxes and insurance bills. This is Ifalik in a nutshell. The island is large enough to support extensive taro patches, copious coconuts and a productive reef. It is unique for its reliance on a working fleet of sailing canoes. By decree of the chief there are no generators, videos or motor-powered launches. Sailing canoes serve even as transport to Woleai, the government center, 25 miles away; but they are primarily used to bring in the daily catch of fish from the ocean outside the lagoon.

After entering an obstacle course of scattered coral heads, SEA QUEST swung peacefully at anchor in the placid lagoon, the atoll's islets offering welcome protection.

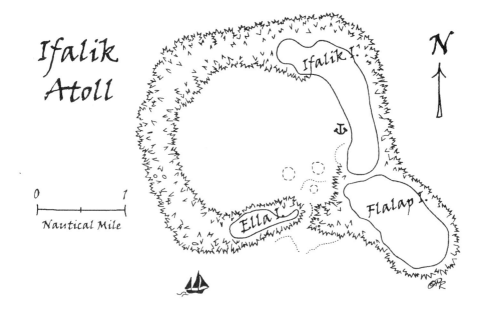

Ifalik
Atoll

Ifalik I.

Ella I.

Flalap I.

N

0   1
Nautical Mile

Chief Francis looked heavily marked by time and weather. From cataract-glazed eyes, he surveyed us after we had crossed the islet with a guide to find him. He seemed to have reinterpreted the policy. "You have to pay $65 every day," he told us.

"That is too much money for us," we replied instantly.

"You must talk to the other chiefs then. I am old now. They make the decisions."

Chief Pekalimar, the second in command, was a vigorous, domineering man in his mid 60s. Under clan carvings of dolphin, turtle, lizard and a three-foot representation of male genitals in his canoe shed, he reiterated the new policy. We said we could not pay this much but would be happy to be of assistance, in anyway we could.

Eventually Chief Pekalimar agreed. "We understand. You will do things for us. You can stay."

Ifalik Atoll is spread across two adjacent islands and a third on the far side of the near-perfectly circular lagoon. Its half-square mile of land area supports around 500 people. A path runs the length of the two inhabited islands, only recently divided by the terrifying fury of a super typhoon. A thousand years had turned the barefoot trodden path into an avenue overarched by palm trees and breadfruit. Ambling in its dappled shade we were met by the curious gaze of women working near their homes and friendly men, each one stopping to greet us.

The single red loincloth, sign of a high-ranking individual, and a handful of blue ones caught the breeze where young men, now dozing in the shadows of the shed, had hung them to dry after their morning swim. Other young men worked under the watchful eye of a master builder, in a sea of fragrant wood chips, fashioning a new canoe from the trunk of a breadfruit tree using sharp-bladed adzes.

An older man took up pulp as fine as silk that had earlier been stripped from the husks of greenish coconuts soaked for a week in sea water. Thrusting a bundle of the fiber between his thighs he drew out the threads, twisting them and spinning by hand, adding wisps every inch or so until the twisted cord measured a couple of feet long. Another man sat down to help, picking up the lengths two at a time, rolling them on his thigh to make double-twisted twine. Hung over rafters or piled in heaps on the dirt floor, was the product of thousands of hours of labor that required no machinery or tool: only skilled hands.

Chief Pekalimar visited SEA QUEST in the afternoon. He had learned to read and write Japanese during the war, and despite the passage of years could still speak it. He ordered Miki around in rough Japanese.

"Bring me coffee. I want a light. More tobacco."

When he left, Chief Pekalimar issued an invitation that sounded like a command.

"Michael. You come with me to drink tuba."

On his return, Michael confessed that he was three sheets to the wind. "I just want to eat dinner and go to bed," he said.

That night the lagoon was like a millpond. While I lay beside Michael reading I became aware of an irritating noise coming from the windvane rudder, as though it was sawing back and forth. I rose, wrapped a sarong around me and stepped out on deck without bothering to pick up a torch. A dark head was just visible over the stern.

"What are you doing?" I demanded.

A young man dove into the water and swam beneath the boat. He came up gasping for air under the bowsprit. He was almost half way to the beach when the skipper burst into action. In almost a single motion he had the dinghy in the water and was aboard, starting the engine with one hand while pushing the plug into the drain-hole with the other. With only a two-horsepower outboard, the swimmer had the advantage, but as he neared shore after his long sprint, he rested on a coral head to catch his breath.

"What did you steal?"

"Nothing."

"I don't believe you! You came to steal. What did you take?"

Michael's anger primed by his Eauripik experience was beginning to build. He shone his light in the man's face. "Give me your mask and dive torch."

"No."

Michael brandished the oar. "You are not going anywhere until I get those things. I'll meet you tomorrow at the Chief's canoe shed. You can explain what you were doing on my boat and I'll hand them back to you." Seeing he had little option, the young man complied and Michael watched him disappear.

On returning to the boat he made a thorough check. "The fellow cut the self-steering cables for the windvane and took a block," he called out. Both ropes had been severed, but his thieving was interrupted before he could pull off the second block. Michael's temper came to a sudden boil. He put the conch horn to his lips and repeatedly began to blow. Then he again headed ashore.

"I need to find out who saw the man if I hope to get the gear back."

Two lights approached.

Miki and I sat in the darkness waiting. Miki repeated several times, "It's scary. I couldn't let my husband go ashore in the night like that."

Perhaps she was right. It was foolhardy. There were risks. Would the youth be tempted to dart from the shadows to attack Michael with the knife he carried? Time dragged on until I saw the small skiff detach itself from the darkness near shore to make its way back to SEA QUEST.

"The crippled old man who sleeps in the canoe shed knows who the boy is. Won't say though," explained Michael.

"Well, at least someone knows the young man's identity. It's a small island. The secret cannot be kept for long."

The next day kind people with worried expressions said that a few youths besmirched the island's reputation. The theft led to an endless round of discussions with Chief Pekalimar, who now seemed surly, but unlike in Eauripik, this incident was never satisfactorily resolved. The youth, people whispered, was of chiefly rank—he could not be publicly chastised.

One afternoon waiting for Michael to return from a conference with the chief I watched a schoolteacher clean out pots used for collecting sap from a cut coconut stem to make beer. "I guess your people have been making tuba for hundreds of years," I said.

"No. The chiefs have only allowed us to cut tuba here for about ten years, since the big typhoon when we had little to eat."

It surprised me that on an island as intent as Ifalik on keeping its traditions, the making of an alcoholic beverage had been encouraged. "What did people do before they had tuba to drink?"

"They got up early to fish and went to bed when the sun went down—and they went night fishing. No one does that any more because every afternoon they drink until they are drunk. If I drink all the tuba I make, I will sleep and be late for class."

Shades of regret colored his words. Tuba drinking appeared to be the source of growing domestic and social problems. Women had openly complained to me that the habit was leading to ruin. House repairs, canoe building and other important activities were often ignored. The health of the men was being undermined. Six recent deaths could be ascribed to excessive drinking.

We never tired of watching Ifalik's fleet of outrigger sailing canoes. In the first light of dawn, a half dozen 30-foot vessels would be launched into the dark waters along ramps of slippery palm fronds to skim effortlessly through the narrow channel to troll for tuna along the outer edge of the atoll reef. One late afternoon we intercepted them. With coconut ropes straining, the vessels raced towards us, each with six men spread out across the outrigger and the double-curved boom carrying the lateen sail arched high above them. Tacking is a strange maneuver. When the helmsman is ready to turn about, he eases the sheet to luff the sail. A crewmember lifts the sprit of the movable mast from its stem-head chock and passes it to the opposite end of the canoe. Canting the mast towards the new chock, the helmsman takes up his steering oar and moves aft with it. The crew hauls in the sheet, tightens the backstay and then climbs to the windward outrigger float that serves as counterweight to the straining canvas. The sail fills, the craft lifts away on the new tack. Unlike a conventional vessel the canoe never turns; it just reverses ends.

Only one mariner fully trained in the old skills remains on Ifalik. We searched out William the Navigator, now a grizzled old man. He had long ago been one of the last initiated into the seafaring art by Mau Piailug of Satawal, the most famous of contemporary Micronesian *palu* navigators. It distressed William to admit that the younger men on Ifalik had no interest in traditional navigation lore although they continue to go to sea in canoes. With the sound of the lagoon lapping behind us, William recounted a recent near tragedy.

A group returning from Woleai 25 miles away became lost. They thought at first that they had passed to the south of Ifalik. They headed northward to get their bearings on a shallow bank where they sometimes fished, but they could not find it. When they realized they had sailed into a region devoid of islands they fell into a deep gloom. For several weeks they sailed on, tacking south then north again. One of the schoolteachers aboard later told me that in his despair he was ready to throw himself overboard. The oldest man advised the men to take a grip on themselves. "Look for birds. Notice from where they come in the morning," he said, "then watch the direction they fly in the evening." There were few birds, and those they saw seemed to fly erratically, but birds eventually led the desperate men to tiny Eauripik. This bit of lore saved their lives. William felt rightly proud.

The island was now abuzz with anticipation for the upcoming visit of the Catholic Bishop of Micronesia. Word arrived that His Eminence was due the following day. To prepare for tomorrow's feast thirty men hauled out an enormous coconut-sennit net. Twenty canoes were launched, the big net straddling two of the largest. Only men and boys were allowed near for the nets were taboo to women. Michael joined them.

The net was spread out across the shallows with a bamboo fish trap attached at the apex. Men armed with sticks and palm fronds fanned out across the shallows to drive the frightened fish towards the trap. Soon the bamboo trap was filled to capacity. It took the strength of a dozen men to lift it from the water.

Fish were not the only victims. While most of the villagers were fishing other men grabbed a pig. There came a frantic squealing. Pigs are not easily dispatched. Miki and I held our ears for several minutes before silence again fell. As we had learned, the facts of the food chain are self-evident in the islands. Certainly the killing of animals was not for the squeamish. Far worse had been the horror of the turtle slaughter on Eauripik where men women and children all assisted in removing organs and eggs from the body of a still frantically moving turtle.

Now that the fish were caught and the pig and a few dogs slaughtered, the islanders were primed for a feast and the bishop's arrival. The islanders have unwittingly sealed their own fate by their mass conversion. Though on the one hand they profess to want to maintain their ancient customs, Chief Pekalimar explained to us, the church exerts continual pressure on people to shift their allegiance from clan and chief to the church authorities. Naturally, most of the chiefs remain pagan.

The Church and the chiefs are mutually exclusive. Though the newly converted islander feels a welcome sense of freedom from submission to his chief, in subtle ways the church's judgment against his formerly pagan way of life is an assault on his identity and self-respect. In truth, he feels like a child set adrift. Conservative societies assimilate new ideas very slowly. In Micronesia change brought about by war, occupation, religious conversion along with Western-style education and the lure of jobs away from home has all come too quickly. Instincts honed over millennia enabled the island chiefs to steer a safe, conservative course. Wise judgments helped keep people alive. The chief's native wisdom no longer prevails; thus the island becomes like a rudderless ship, the captain rendered impotent.

The Church brings with it not just new allegiances and the inexorable erosion of the chiefs' authority. It opens the door to a culture of greed and materialism, a scourge on a fragile atoll ecosystem, which is the reason why Ifalik's chief has, for the moment at least, banned modernity. Despite efforts to stem the tide of change, Ifalik and other oceanic societies show strong signs of fracture. Children no longer learn fishing, farming, food preservation and preparation skills, or herbal medicine and therapeutic massage practices. The navigation skills and lore are almost lost. Meanwhile the desire for consumer goods has grown, allegiance to chiefs has waned. Tuba consumption also takes its toll. With these factors in mind, and knowing that the margin for survival is tenuous, annihilation may be just around the corner.

The bishop's chartered fishing boat, a temporary shelter of canvas spread over its aft deck, had picked its way through the coral-studded channel. Not wishing to disturb the scheduled confessions and baptisms we had remained aboard SEA QUEST. Now young girls arrived in a canoe with leis and urged us to come to the beach. As we stepped ashore a man hurried up. "Some men from Lamotrek know you and want to meet again," he explained.

Manuel and William greeted us with smiles and handshakes. They had recognized SEA QUEST when they entered the lagoon. "Why are you here?" we asked curiously.

"We have come to take care of a little business."

The business was a funeral. William's brother had failed to return from sea after night fishing although he was part of a group of 30 men, all in small canoes. Twelve days later human remains washed up on Ifalik. Manuel and William had come to pay their last respects.

The sound of women singing drew us to the church. The bishop, splendidly attired in European-style purple surplice and miter flanked by his silken-robed assistants, looked rich and alien next to the tiny tin-roof church. Amando Samos, the first native Micronesian to be appointed a Catholic Bishop, had recently returned from the Vatican to take up his new duties. He broke away from his party to courteously greet us. It was his first trip around his diocese, he told us, as well as the first any bishop had made in the last 20 years. With a weary laugh he added, "It's likely to be another twenty before I do another trip in such a boat."

The bishop explained the way he saw the present situation.

"Things are changing whether the chiefs like it or not. At the moment, the chiefs on some of the islands still have all the power over the people. This is not a democracy. We cannot change things all at once. We take a small step at a time, allowing the old pagan customs and the church to live side by side. We know that in time the good of the church will spread to all the people."

Imagine the Catholic Church, the world's greatest authoritarian institution, using the "democracy" ideal to boost their argument!

Those who could not squeeze into the tiny church squinted through the steel louvers or squatted outside. Babies cried and were put to the breast. Chief Francis did not enter but sat with a group of older men. Though the pagan group resented the bishop, they kept a close eye on the ceremonies.

The mass over, the newly confirmed women and a lesser number of men, all bare-breasted and wearing newly woven white *dhur*, formed up into lines. Rhythmic clapping was joined with counter-clapping. People sang "We are happy, happy, happy!" The singing grew more heartfelt with each repetition. A circle of ecstatic women surrounded us. Scores of mothers, young girls, toddlers and rag-tag kids, shook our hands while all the time reciting "Peace be with you." I am not certain what *manna* they thought we possessed, or if they thought of us as Christian brothers and sisters, part of a larger world that they had just joined. Whatever the reason, their spontaneity was infectious.

Now preparations for dancing began. Mounds of blossoms, cut palm fronds and other greenery were collected, along with baskets of ribbons, artificial flowers and other decorations. Out of these materials, palm frond skirts, leaf collars, woven flower crowns, arm and ankle bands were constructed. Ifalik is the ultimate throwaway society; however, everything is biodegradable.

The 40 young women selected to dance were powdered with yellow turmeric along with Miki and me. Decorated with a lei made of herbs and heavily caked in yellow turmeric, I felt like a chicken about to be fried. On our flower bedecked foreheads was drawn a golden line. Vermilion spots were placed on our cheeks. Then the cooking pits were opened and the freshly woven palm-leaf baskets were filled and distributed to the heads of families. The men as a group ate in a big clearing under the tall coconut palms. When they had their fill, young boys delivered the remainder of the food to the waiting women.

The dances had been set to ancient chants, the catechist told us, the words altered for the occasion. No longer did the songs speak of ancient deeds of valor or hardships endured. Now they centered around the love of Jesus for his children and the community's gratitude towards the bishop. The bishop's eyes closed and his head sank deeply to his chest. Three weeks of voyaging, over-eating and *tuba* drinking had all taken their toll. A visiting priest, the worse for the tuba he'd drunk, shouted out, (in keen appreciation I'm sure), "Lay it on me, Baby!" The giggles almost stopped the dance. The bishop awoke with a start.

It was time to say farewell. We never did recover the block cut away from SEA QUEST's windvane rudder. Despite the unfortunate incident, we had felt privileged to witness the festivities arranged for the bishop's visit. We picked our way out through Ifalik's difficult channel and at 5:30 PM rounded up in the reef's lee to get the sails up. Behind us, the encircling lagoon remained as tranquil as it had through all the days of our stay. In the evening light, the sails of the returning fishing canoes shimmered like gold. Heavily laden with a wealth of silver fish, the crew stood up to wave vigorously, their craft making a silent passage past us.

Out of Ifalik's lee, a ferocious chop caused Michael to regret the many extra rounds of *tuba* he had imbibed on his last goodbye tour. Tonight's dinner would be skimpy or skipped.

13

Lamotrek and Atoll Politics

Soggy gray clouds filled the sky. Gusts clocked 40 knots and heavy seas blocked our way. With each swell, SEA QUEST shuddered and stopped dead. The cat sat in a puddle, her fluff reduced to strings of salty damp. An exhausted booby flew over the boat a few times, and then landed clumsily on the stern rail. Even when Michael brushed past to trim the windvane, he did not fly away, but only squawked grumpily.

Michael headed below to get some sleep but just past midnight leapt on deck again when the sails backed with a loud bang. The equatorial region was now highly active with thunderstorms. Like a bloodied but determined prizefighter SEA QUEST gathered herself after each knock down to stand for the next blow. I blessed her steel hull. Below decks, Miki cringed at the noise only an iron hull can produce, later admitting to nightmare visions of sailing to the bottom of the sea.

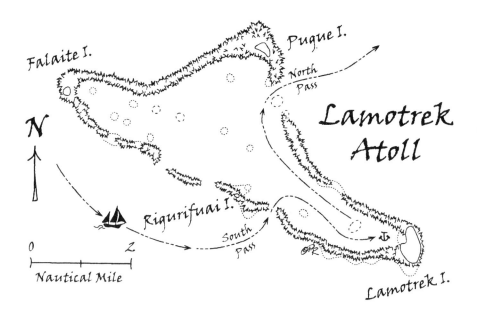

At dawn we sighted the Elato Group, 15 miles from Lamotrek. Passing south of the main island, Falipi, we entered the channel that bisects the group. Michael decided to get forty winks. I called Miki to help me keep watch as we neared the reefs surrounding Lamotrek lagoon. Then the engine died.

From his bunk below Michael sleepily demanded, "What's going on?"

I glanced at the cockpit gauges. "It's not overheated," I shouted back. "Maybe it's a fuel-block."

Since taking on dirty fuel in Belau, we had been constantly plagued with problems. Michael had already cleared the in-line filters of accumulated water several times.

We were now in the lee of Lamotrek's reef. While Michael sweated in the engine room, Miki and I sailed SEA QUEST along the reef's protected south edge. After bleeding the fuel system, Michael successfully restarted the engine. On deck again, he spotted South Passage, some two-and-a-half miles west of Lamotrek itself, visible in a break of the almost continuous curl of white surf. On the western side of the atoll lies Falaite. The main islet, Lamotrek is seven miles to the east. A wrecked fishing boat on the far side of the lagoon indicated the North Channel.

Ahead was a lush but low thicket of coconut palms. Eight years before, Lamotrek was all but destroyed by a powerful typhoon. Storms have always threatened the lives of atoll dwellers. In 1816 after a devastating typhoon that leveled the coconuts and filled the taro pits with salt water, 900 people from Lamotrek and adjacent islands had fled sure starvation in a fleet of 120 canoes. The fleet was caught in another gale. The great majority of the islanders perished.

The passage from Ifalik, a mere 116 miles, had taken two days of hard sailing. Children raced along the beach and men climbed into a brightly painted canoe to paddle out to welcome us. The radio grapevine had alerted our friend Joe, the island's medic, of our arrival. As we stepped ashore, Joe met us and whisked Michael off to the men's house.

A group of women preparing food looked up smiling as Miki and I approached. "How is your daughter Marina and her husband Mark? Where are they now? Who is with you this time? Will you eat?" Steaming taro lathered in rich coconut cream was presented to us on a big soft green leaf.

How amazing, I thought, that they still remember our names.

The women wove food baskets, mashed taro, grated coconut, gathered coconut husks, tended fires, and stirred pots. It was happy communal work.

Not far from the gathered women Katherine, Joe's wife, sat immobile, taking no part in the work. Her high rank set her apart. At her side was her cheerful retarded daughter, her head shaved. Was it to discourage lice or to scare off the boys?

Katherine invited us to share her mat. She spoke no English. At my queries she merely nodded or shook her head. Curious children stood by her giggling and staring, ignoring Katherine's admonishments. Though I reached out to them, they hung back, still regarding Miki and me as strangers. The silence grew.

A large woman hurried forward, reached out to me and pressed her nose to my face sniffing, the islander's embrace.

"Mary, come sit with us awhile," I implored, but knowing that Katherine might object.

"I must go home now to cook. Why not come with me?"

"Miki and I will go with Mary awhile," I said turning to Katherine, glad to find an excuse to walk somewhere.

"You remember our custom," Mary said. "When the men are in the canoe shed we do not walk on the path."

Indeed, I did remember. Her brother was now in the shed. I do not know how she knew he was there. Nevertheless, as custom required, bending deep from the waist in a low bow, she stumbled off the beaten path through the rough grass.

Frangipani trees and tobacco planted in neat circles of coral rubble surrounded Mary's house. We sat outside on a rough bench next to a table the size of an orange crate where she served us boiled land crabs, rice and twists of deep-fried dough hard enough to break our teeth on. Offering food to strangers comes naturally here.

Small children pulled apart the red crabs with their dirty fingers, dropping the shreds of flesh into the rice for us to fish out, or offering it to us directly. Two young men appeared and spoke to Mary, who was now skinning green breadfruit with a coconut shell. When Joe had discovered Miki and I no longer sat with his wife, he sent the youths to fetch us back. Why, I wondered? It was obvious, however, that he expected to be obeyed. We returned to Katherine's compound.

At 42, Katherine could barely walk on her arthritic legs. Bad knees seemed to be a common complaint. Were the painful symptoms an unhealthy reaction to introduced Western food, particularly quantities of white rice and sugar? Was it a symptom of diabetes? Most men and women here aged rapidly with little middle ground between young and old. The agility and strength required to harvest coconut, balance in canoes, and walk on reefs and a hundred other everyday chores essential to island life, were severely curtailed as the disease took its toll.

Like Mary, Katherine offered us delicacies, fatty chunks of turtle meat to be washed down with sweet coconut water. Joe had also sent a young man to translate for us, but the sullen boy distanced himself, resentful of having to leave the merry-making in the canoe shed. I soon tired and lapsed into silence. I was exhausted and ached for my bunk. Bad weather had robbed us of our sleep. Michael would be even worse off, I thought. The shadows lengthened to extinguish the last glimmers of daylight from the sky and lagoon. Inky blackness extended beyond the glow of Katherine's kerosene lantern.

It was bad manners for me to go to the canoe house so I was enormously relieved when Michael's pale form finally emerged from the shadows. My skipper and spouse stumbled and swayed, clearly inebriated. "Get me to the boat," he pleaded.

Later he explained that after all available *tuba* had been consumed, the group had begun drinking a lethal homemade brew of yeast, water and sugar.

A schoolteacher paddled out to SEA QUEST the next day. He mentioned that Lamotrek's High Chief was not a man but a woman. Veronica Laefaiyob, now living on Elato Island, was the oldest member of the highest of five clans, the Mengaulfashe. To her falls the duty of appointing the two sub-chiefs. A man from a common clan may marry into a chiefly clan but will have no rights or power to influence that clan's activities, although his son would one day. Like in Belau, land rights follow a matrilineal succession.

I mentioned to the schoolteacher the stress that seemed evident among the island men.

"Yes, It's very stressful here. At least we don't kill each other like in the old days! There were bad fights then. Today the chiefs work hard for peaceful relations."

He pointed out, however, that nepotism is rampant. A chief's relative would be appointed to one of the scarce government paid jobs, even if he was less qualified than someone else. Chiefs, though mostly acting responsibly, liked to reinforce their own positions, their wealth, and of course the importance of their clan. "The new headmaster is the chief's son," he went on to say. "All the other teachers have to follow his and his father's orders."

"But how can the chief interfere? Don't you just teach a curriculum set by the state?"

"Yes, we teach the curriculum, but if he wants anything from the school we must give it to him."

"You mean that the school property becomes a sort of extension of the chief's property?"

"Yes, that's it. In addition, those people who get their jobs by appointment don't put in an eight-hour day. They just do a couple of hours and then go fishing. And it's the same in Yap. People are paid to work in offices but they do no work—they just come in and sit for an hour or two or sleep at their desks. They go home early. Here I have to get up at 5:30 AM to cut my *tuba* and then again after school. It's a long day."

I wondered what he would think of life in New York City!

Michael became Mr. Fix-it. A broken outboard, some fiberglass repairs, rewiring a solar panel was all part of a day's work: the currency by which we made ourselves welcome. Late afternoons were spent whiling away the hours in the men's house. Aboard the boat, I cooked food for the next leg of the voyage, puzzling over just how to prepare the slimy turtle meat we had been given into something delectable—or if not delectable, at least edible. The turtle hunt was in full swing. A boat arrived from Satawal Atoll to collect some of the catch. Every day half-a-dozen turtles were brought to land. With motorized longboats they had now become easy pickings in mating and egg-laying season. Although we understood that the chiefs on their annual visit to Yap had agreed to cease taking mating and egg-laying turtles, at home they obviously found it politic to look the other way.

That afternoon when we walked ashore, seven more live turtles lay waiting on their backs for slaughter. Others were in various stages of dismemberment. Two young men lounged near a turtle shell from which they were removing green meat. I did not think it was our place, as guests on the island, to give a lecture on the morality of taking turtles, but I could not resist giving a dig.

"There has been a big catch, I see."

"Yeah," answered the man in the red T-shirt.

"On Eauripik they mentioned it was out of season and illegal."

There was a heavy silence. "Sometimes the fisheries patrol boat stops us."

"A fisheries boat way out here?" I said in astonishment.

"Yeah."

"But there is no fisheries boat here now." I stated.

A slow grin spread over the young man's face.

"Yeah."

The inter-island ship arrived early one morning bringing passengers and emergency supplies of rice and flour to the island. The long drought this year had soured the taro. People and plants survive on coral atolls only because rainwater seeps through the porous limestone surface to float as a lens of fresh water on the salt water below. The roots of taro set in their deep pits and shallow wells tap this limited supply. If too much water is drawn from the wells, or a drought is prolonged, the lens contracts and salt water is sucked in. One hundred and seventy-six bags of rice and ninety-one of flour were distributed around the lagoon. "All for free," an old man exclaimed. So it should be, I thought, if it is true that the world's rich industrial nations are primarily to blame for climate change and the human consequences to fragile ecosystems.

The time had come to leave the Yapese Out Islands, each of which had seemed to us unique in the world, each with its small cargo of survivors attempting to navigate increasingly strange and treacherous seas. We slowly got underway. Miki and Michael were still queasy from the latest bout of food poisoning after I had made a chocolate cake. Considering we had already suffered salmonella poisoning in the Philippines, presumably from raw egg, I should have had more sense than to allow them to lick the batter from the bowl.

Pohnpei was still 500 miles to the east and our will to beat to windward was weakening fast. Only the thought of the mail that would be lost if we did not show up kept us going. The men in the canoe house predicted that the squalls and wind we now had would give way to a westerly that might last a month. It seemed too good to be true.

14

Puluwat Atoll

The fabulous prediction of westerly winds had come to nothing. Thirty-six hours later, just 20 miles off Puluwat Atoll, we finally shut down the engine to drift quietly, waiting for the sun to rise high enough for us to see our landfall. Cautiously, coming from the southwest, we approached Puluwat's difficult channel, glad now for the glassy calm conditions. We could see every detail of the shoal reef over which we had to pass, as through a magnifying glass. Ahead, just to port, the surf curled. My heart beat faster. Michael stood aloft. Miki relayed his commands. I called out the soundings from my place at the helm. A stone's throw from the breaking surf, Michael signaled to abruptly swing to starboard threading a wall of reef on one hand, foaming coral

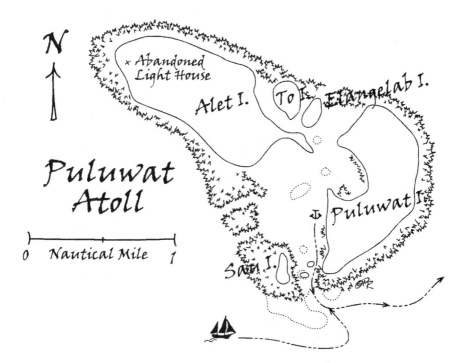

N

Abandoned
Light House

Alet I.

To Elangelab I.

Puluwat
Atoll

0 Nautical Mile 1

Puluwat I.

S   I.

heads on the other. The water continued to shoal. Worry gave way to relief as we sneaked past the last obstacle into the placid lagoon.

Puluwat is the quintessential Micronesian atoll lagoon. There is a special loveliness in the close-set arrangement of its verdant islands. The light has a rare quality. Breezes sweep unimpeded across the reef, the protection given by the narrow islands slender against buffeting angry seas and raging winds.

Puluwat consists of a community of about 800 souls, divided between two churches. The self-segregated Catholics live at one end, the Protestants at the other. Before visiting our friends it was our duty to pay our respects to Manebi, the senior chief. Puluwat and the atolls to the east are now part of the State of Chuuk in the Federated States of Micronesia. Tradition on this island is no longer very strict. The chief simply accepted our gift of a bag of rice and welcomed us without mentioning fees.

Young men swarmed nearby over a large canoe. Today, Chief Manebi explained, after three years of toil, the new boat was to be launched, ballasted, rigged and tested. Tomorrow there would be a feast. It was a big occasion for an island where sailing canoes are seldom used, replaced by a growing fleet of fiberglass launches whizzing noisily across the lagoon.

Our friend Monica waited under the palms with her family, embracing us when we stepped ashore as though we were lost children. We were disappointed to discover that they no longer lived in their breezy, deeply shaded, thatched canoe shed, but had proudly taken up residence in an unfinished concrete house, as hot inside as an oven.

During the Japanese occupation of Puluwat, Monica and her two sisters had been forced to take husbands from amongst the soldiers stationed there, thus joining 200,000 other "comfort women" serving the Imperial Japanese Forces. The older people and children were sent to tiny Pulap, 25 miles away. When the men were repatriated to Japan after the war, there were no tears. In Monica's words, "we were treated like slaves."

Most of the women with Japanese husbands became infected with syphilis, rendering them sterile. Monica adopted

144

children. Her sisters did likewise. One of Monica's eight children, Konce, a large woman with a ready smile and intelligent eyes, is the island's nurse and midwife.

Miki was shocked to hear Monica speak vulgar, uneducated Japanese. Only the roughest sort of men would speak this way—and never to a woman. It showed just how little respect they had for island women. Later the family visited SEA QUEST. For 72-year-old barefoot, bare-breasted Monica, the yacht was an entirely new world. She peered into cupboards and explored cabins, happily digging her bare toes into the pile of the carpet. She jerked back in fright at the cold of the refrigerator. Seeing a tap, Monica turned it on. Water gushed out. She quickly turned it off. Islanders do not waste water. Our gimbaled Primus stove that swings when the boat rolls mystified her. She most admired the luxurious double bunk in the aft cabin under the breezy hatch. In front of the bulkhead mirror Monica paused to do what every woman who catches sight of her own reflection does—she preened.

The canoe launching was over by the time we made it back to shore. Men already sated from too much *tuba* were still drinking. Still tender from his bout of salmonella, Michael had sworn off the stuff at least until he felt better. To stay out of temptation he sat with me near a cookhouse where women continued food preparations.

Delicate balls of mashed breadfruit swam in a bowl of coconut cream. Flies crawled over the uncovered food and buzzed around buckets of newly caught fish. A woman whisked at them in a desultory manner. It was obviously a hopeless task. As the women were scraping fish with huge knives and the tines of a large fork, iridescent scales flew off to adorn their bare skin like fancy sequins.

As she worked, Alicia carried on a monologue in excellent English.

"My sister-in-law would offer you some food but she is embarrassed by the flies."

"Thank you," I replied. "We enjoyed your breadfruit when we visited earlier." It had been freshly made then and delicious.

I was surprised she mentioned the flies. Island people usually ignored them although I found them a constant irritant.

"How do you tolerate the flies?" I asked out of curiosity. "We even battle them on the boat."

She paused to think and then answered ruefully, "I guess we are immune to them. They are just part of life. It must be all the trash that makes so many of them."

"How come you speak English so well?" I asked.

"I lived in Guam for ten years. When my nephew died six months ago, I came with the casket and am still here." She paused. "I was married but my ex has returned to Michigan, taking our three children with him."

For many weeks, men had been cutting and stockpiling materials. A new canoe shed was to be built and would be assembled in just one day. Every family on the island was expected to lend a hand. Four corner-posts of trimmed breadfruit wood had already been dropped into the deep holes, the earth tamped firmly down and the tops mortised to fit the long lintel beams.

When we arrived about noon, the basic structure was already in place. Tall gable ends supported a ridge beam which young men straddled while lashing roof poles securely with sennit twine. Beneath them, men maneuvered another pole, tossed a line up over the ridge, and then hauled the rafter into position. More than a hundred men squatted or lolled in the long grass. Laughing women, some wearing T-shirts, were busy preparing lunch. In the lagoon bobbed a small flotilla of canoes laden with woven roof-thatch and bulky coils of freshly made coconut cordage.

Progress, material goods, and a growing population have brought crowding and increased litter. Gone are the breezy thatched homes. On Puluwat, unlovely concrete dwellings elbow each other for space, sometimes separated by no more than an airless footpath. Tin cans, plastic combs, bottles and other slow-to-disintegrate rubbish just lie where they fall. Traditional islands have large pits set at intervals along the main paths and near houses where such trash is burned and buried, but I saw none of these on Puluwat. The authority of the chiefs has declined. Church leadership has not asserted itself, although Puluwat was one of the earliest Caroline Islands to become Christian in the late 1800s. The islanders are turning away from their sense of communality that was formerly the norm. At the same time, they are purchasing goods that are harder to dispose of when they wear out or break.

Changing living standards are bringing about heavy reliance on boat engines and generators, which in turn create problems. Just where does one dispose of two gallons of used sump-oil on a pristine and fragile coral atoll? The health and survival of an atoll dweller is dependent on the composition and fertility of the atoll itself. If oil or any other chemical contaminate were poured on the soil, it would immediately leach into the freshwater lens less than six feet below. Poured into the lagoon, the chemicals will inevitably cut a swath of death.

The dead calm of the past week gave way to moderate northeast winds. To take advantage of them, we cut our visit short. A tearful Monica piled layers of sweet-scented frangipani leis on us and had to be gently dissuaded from caking our bodies with coconut oil and turmeric. She waved until we were out of sight.

15

The Mortlock Group

Passing over Condor Banks hundreds of miles from land, in flat calm seas, was a unique experience. Just 12 fathoms under our keel the sandy bottom shimmered through sapphire water. Normally we would steer well clear of such a dangerous area. But the calm weather did not last. Our passage east-southeast, 283 miles to the Mortlock Group, would prove as hard going as the others. We had again sailed into the doldrums.

Some imagine the doldrums to be windless, but that is not

entirely so. Warm air rising at the Equator creates scattered low-pressure disturbances, rather like the bubbles that rise in water set to boil. The sky fills with cloud and squalls, each a semi-independent cell surrounded by an airless patch. Approaching one of these cells on port tack we saw rain ahead. The wind began to strengthen, temporarily improving our course. But it soon veered, then died away altogether, leaving us in a lumpy sea, unable to hold steady on any course. Frequently adjusting winches, dropping and then raising sail again, is exhausting work.

After 12 hours of this labor, the seas died away. We motored 50 miles directly east. By that time the Intertropical Convergence Zone (ITCZ), a modern name for the doldrums, had retreated. The northeast wind picked up to blow at 15 knots. Now SEA QUEST made easy progress towards the north end of Satawan Atoll.

The Mortlock Group includes half a dozen atolls stretching 180 miles southeast from Chuuk. Moch is a tiny islet on the outer perimeter of Satawan Atoll. *Motus*, strung like jade beads along the perimeter of the huge reef, enclose 382 square miles of lagoon. Atop the reef, a large factory ship, run aground a couple of years before, was now a rusting hulk. On our earlier visit to Satawan Island, the largest and most eastern on the atoll, we stumbled into a graveyard of abandoned Japanese tanks, still parked along what was once the military airfield.

With a spanking breeze under a picture-book sky we tacked in close to admire the islets while Michael scanned with binoculars to pick out where we could enter the lagoon between Moch and Aferene. On Moch, children began to holler and wave, running to keep pace as we sailed along a deep blue channel. Our zigzag course from Puluwat had taken us 99 hours and 423 miles.

Chief Johannes Robunda paddled up alongside SEA QUEST to introduce himself after we had dropped anchor to the east of the island. Unable to get from his tiny canoe to our boarding ladder, he promised to come back later. When he did return in his fiberglass launch he explained he was related through his wife to Amando Samos, the bishop we had met at Ifalik.

The chief had spent 15 years as a cook in Chuuk's schools and hospitals, returning home to take up his duties only after his father died. His childhood memories remained vivid. Moch escaped the war's heavy fighting, he said, "but not the occupation. The Japanese soldiers tried to keep all the food. We had to steal to live. We stole breadfruit, coconuts and bananas. They took all the fish we caught, so men would hang some on a string under the canoe, but often, by the time they got home, the fish had been taken by sharks."

Chief Robunda said that the island people were anxious to trade with us. People arrived in canoes bearing stems of coconuts and shells to trade for baby clothes and a baseball bat. When we arrived on the beach later, a large crowd met us and welcomed us with coconut drinks. Chief Johannes put us into the hands of a couple of young men. They escorted us beneath groves of breadfruit and palms that threw soft shadows across the broad path that encircled the island. We thought at first that the crumbling Protestant Church was abandoned because of great gaping holes in its rusted roof, but when we peeked inside a handful of worshippers smiled from their woven mats. Nearby we found the foundations of the original stone and concrete Catholic Church. It had been pulled down some years earlier but not yet been replaced. Meanwhile the Catholic congregation of 700 was accommodated in a temporary structure of wattle and thatch with a coral rubble floor.

The Christian missionaries' long-standing grip on the island is evident in the way the natives dress and live. Only recently have stringent religious prohibitions been relaxed. Women were now allowed to cook on Sunday, but there seemed to be little drinking. We saw no coconut trees tapped for *tuba*; no use of betelnut. Girls wearing Spanish combs in slicked-back hair joined the boys to gawk at us, but whenever I approached, even by myself, the girls retreated, giggling. Why was it that these girls, with bright dresses down to their ankles, were so much shier than their cousins on the other islands?

All the people were exceedingly handsome and slim. Women adorned their smocks with fancy lace-trim and machine appliqué. But the traditional back-strap weaving skills are lost. Only pandanus sleeping mats, crudely woven coconut fans and a few small canoes are still made. Even thatching skills have deteriorated. The canoe sheds we saw were covered with crudely bunched bundles of pandanus leaves, which not only let the rain in but also quickly rot.

Michael asked one of the youths, "Do the girls marry on the island or must they look elsewhere for husbands?"

"Most marry locally." Perhaps this explained the homogeneity of the features: oval face, narrow forehead, slightly flared nose, tipped oval eyes, straight black hair and relatively light skin.

Schoolteachers, all of them men, resting in the shade of a small shed invited us to join them. They shook our hands while shooing away children. They proudly pointed out that the entire community had pitched in to build the new two-story schoolhouse, now considered a model school. This high school, with a roll of 380, not only takes in local students, but also those from Lekinioch and Etal, neighboring atolls. These children, I reflected, knowing how much hard work went into construction, will have learned not only to value school buildings but perhaps even their education.

The path took us to a beach stained pink under sunset's crimson flares. Though the young girls and men had all fallen away during our long walk, a host of young boys still tagged along. Now, without firm adult supervision, they grew rude, mimicking us, teasing Miki and taunting each other in a manner noticeably less restrained than on traditional islands where boys assume early the dignified mantle of men-in-training.

We stayed several days at the peaceful anchorage, and explored the small islands, diving on coral as pristine as that of any five-star dive resort.

Each island in Micronesia lured us to linger longer than planned. May was gone. Although we had expected to be in Pohnpei by now, Lekinioch Atoll was just over the horizon. How could we resist visiting an anchorage which on a chart looked like the new moon? We tacked along the *motus* that fringed Lekinioch and in the lagoon entrance surprised a fisherman who seemed utterly astonished to see us. A large statue of Jesus Christ overlooked the channel. We dropped sail and motored towards a partially ruined jetty. "Welcome to Lekinioch" read a large painted sign.

Our old chart called the atoll Lukunor. However, the new constitutions for both the Republic of Belau and the Federated States of Micronesia had legislated pre-colonial forms of names for scores of places. Palau had become Belau; Ponape was now Pohnpei, Lukunor is Lekinioch and Truk is now Chuuk. Tremendous confusion will no doubt prevail for the next 20 years, or until we stop using old atlases and out-of-date charts.

Abraham, a 14-year-old, introducing himself as the "acting mayor," greeted us as we stepped on to the jetty. His brother, the real mayor, was presently off-island, he explained. "You are very welcome, very welcome," he intoned in a big-brother sort of voice. "You are free to walk anywhere. My cousin will escort you."

Children clamored to take our hands. Women, as colorful as bright flowers, with babes in their arms and toddlers clutching at their legs, stared from a distance. Dominating a grassy common was a large, new, concrete-block Catholic church. Opposite stood the crumbling original, converted now into a pigsty, its arched windows and doors barricaded with rusting wire.

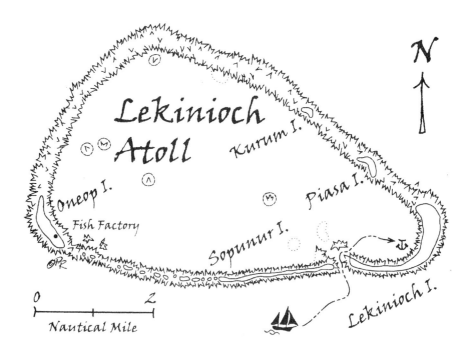

Sullen youth lolled on the grass, barely acknowledging our cheery greeting.

We stopped to gawk at one of the signs of financial prosperity. It was a fanciful new house built in Chuukese style. To the basic foursquare plan was added a breezy portico, gallery and a second-story open-air room reached by way of an elaborate staircase. Baroque arches, arabesques, and bright-hued multicolored paint characterized the architecture.

Other quaint buildings can be found in Lekinioch. German traders, the colonial masters before World War I, left a low house with a series of pretty columns and arches for windows. The Japanese took it over for their wartime headquarters and added inlaid shell patterns and *hiragana*-writing which Miki translated as commemorating an important visit to the island by a relative of Emperor Hirohito.

Today local men and women work at a Japanese-managed fish factory on the far side of the lagoon. Remittances from the 200 or so Lekinioch natives who have left the island, a full quarter of the population, also contribute to the island's prosperity. Although families continue to lead a subsistence lifestyle, growing their own food, the cash income allows them to purchase luxuries. Many women wore 22-carat gold jewelry. A more welcome sign of encroaching civilization were noticeably fewer flies.

An old Merchant Marine sailor paddled out to SEA QUEST, bringing with him shells to exchange for epoxy glue. He discovered Miki aboard, and wanted to practice his Japanese. Poor Miki! Everywhere she went she got an ear-full. The wartime Japanese were "mean," he said. They forced the islanders to produce food for the Satawan base where thousands of hungry troops were stationed.

Miki later told us that she was embarrassingly ignorant of anything Japan had done in the war. Neither her family nor her teachers had explained much about Japan's involvement.

"They know a lot—but they don't tell me!"

The old mariner, who had traveled widely, now lived with his wife in a house built by his German grandfather. Behind thick-plastered coral rubble walls and tiny shuttered windows, it was dark and cool inside. With its rustic furniture and heavy planked floors, the house reminded me of a settler's museum. Among his possessions was a Pfaff sewing machine. It dated back about 85 years, yet still worked. Unfortunately its old-style needles were now unavailable.

When Michael returned the machine, now adapted for modern needles, the mariner as a gesture of appreciation presented him with a triton shell. Back on SEA QUEST I doused it in a bucket of seawater. A nest of cockroaches swam out.

The wind was fair. It was time to set sail.

16

Oroluk: Terror in the Night

Two days out from Lekinioch darkly etched thunderheads and a blood-red sunrise seemed an ominous harbinger. Nervously Michael tucked a second reef into the main. Lightning flashed in an inky night sky. Rain bucketed down; the wind howled.

By dawn, the blow was over. Minto, a large but landless atoll, lay ahead, made visible by its harvest of wrecks just above the horizon. The illusion that the rusting, rotting hulks of trawlers and freighters were afloat disappeared when the limpid inner lagoon came into view along with the gaping holes in the vessels' sides. A pair of factory ships lay side by side, the second apparently wrecked while trying to save the first.

Frigate birds wheeled in the up-draughts. Boobies sat brooding upon the silent ships. It is likely most of the ships plowed into Minto Reef at night when visibility was poor. There

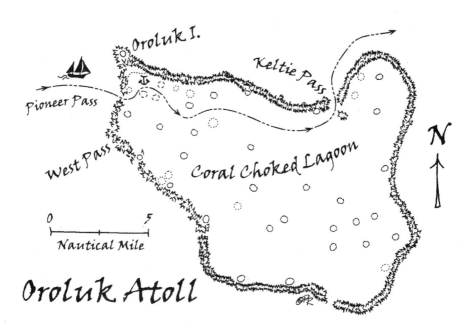

Oroluk I.

Keltie Pass

Pioneer Pass

West Pass

Coral Choked Lagoon

N

0   5

Nautical Mile

Oroluk Atoll

would be no warning for a blind ship approaching. The chart soundings recorded depths of over 2,000 fathoms only a few hundred feet offshore. Now the gloomy rusting hulks gave fair warning to mariners who might forget the awful truth of a moment's carelessness.

Sailing from under the atoll's lee, SEA QUEST's bow rose to meet the swell. Just then the equatorial sun, a moment before fiercely incandescent, dimmed. Dark rainsqualls drove before them spume and pale mist. The seas flattened under the sudden fury; raindrops like lead shot clattered to the deck in a seething hiss. We hastily shut the side curtains and closed the hatches. Moments later, the brief fury spent, the reef and its cargo of iron corpses had disappeared from sight.

As dawn broke SEA QUEST rolled from gunwale to gunwale. Jugs and bottles, pots and pans, tapes and books all made a racket below. We were again becalmed. A reputedly uninhabited island on the edge of a 17-mile reef, Oroluk, stood 148 miles northeast of Minto and 185 miles west of Pohnpei: somewhere just over the horizon. It seemed an inviting place to stop.

As I took over the watch, Michael said, "Motoring will stop this rolling around. We haven't far to go." With that he started up the engine, set our course and headed below to catch a few winks. To the east, rain clouds cast a gray pall across the sharply etched horizon. After the squall moved away, I detected a low blur. With binoculars, it resolved itself into land four miles off the starboard bow. I awakened Michael.

The island was not deserted. A thin plume of smoke drifted lazily from the canopy of coconut palms. Its submerged reef was extremely difficult to see in the light. Had it not been for a telltale current rippling the surface, we might have missed the narrow opening of Pioneer Pass. Cautiously we approached. Inside, extending from the island about a half a mile, was a shoal of clear sand. As the lagoon seemed very deep elsewhere, we anchored here in only three fathoms.

A scrape and bump alongside awoke us from a nap. A smiling woman, along with her nine-year-old daughter and teenage son, hailed us from a fiberglass launch. Miki was already on deck, exclaiming happily as they passed up baskets of cooked taro, coconut crab as red as Maine lobster, husked drinking coconuts and a ripening papaya. Last of all the boy lay a vermilion coral cod almost reverentially at our feet.

We helped the visitors aboard and offered them refreshments. The woman, a handsome Polynesian, introduced herself as Etelinda. The family had left Pohnpei's Kapingamarangi Village ten years previously, to take up life here on Oroluk, an island that at the turn of the last century had suffered a typhoon so devastating that it lost its people and half its dry land. These new settlers had worked very hard planting groves of breadfruit, banana and papaya.

"There were no taro pits either," she said. "These we had to dig."

Ten people, all related, now live on Oroluk, she said. Though typhoons sometimes still batter the island, they expressed contentment. A government supply ship stops by four times a year along with occasional fishing boats. HF radio had transformed their isolation and with the help of the marine patrol enabled them to protect the atoll from poachers who repeatedly raided the reef for baitfish.

By the time the group had left, the sun lay low. We snorkeled in the sparkling lagoon. In the afterglow of the sunset, with shampooed hair and bodies free of salt we were overcome by a marvelous lassitude. Before we succumbed, Miki and I hastened to prepare the rock cod for dinner. Just as we began to serve up, a ferocious squall laid SEA QUEST over, sending water glasses crashing to the sole.

Michael and I watched horrified as the wind speed needle crept past 40 knots and off the scale! Inky blackness enveloped the lagoon; rain pounded against the doghouse windows. The east wind funneled directly towards us down the 17-mile lagoon. On the outer edge of the shoal on which we were anchored, surf began to form. Michael switched on the engine. The unlit island was invisible. We seemed to float within a seething fishbowl. Grabbing the light, I shone the beam towards a curious discoloration in the dark water beside us, and even as I did so, it moved closer.

"Michael, we are dragging!" The closest coral head had been some 50 yards astern. The boat jarred slightly, then again harder. "We're grounding!"

157

I threw the idling engine into gear while Michael dashed forward to the anchor.

"Miki, turn off all the lights below!" Not understanding me, she switched on all the cockpit lights, temporarily blinding me. Then she understood. Like a smothering cloak, darkness descended.

I tried to steer to the east-southeast into the eye of the wind, away from the beach. SEA QUEST would not answer the helm. *Maybe the wind is pushing us sideways,* I thought, struggling hard to compensate as we violently pitched. The dinghy, lashed to the outside of the starboard stanchions, shook and crashed alarmingly, ready to self-destruct.

Ignoring the flailing skiff, Michael steadily worked in the chain.

"All clear!" he called out. "Just keep on a course of 120° slowly," he said as he stepped back to the cockpit. "I've got to get this dinghy secured or we'll loose it. Hold her steady."

The compass spun while I fought for control. When, in a flash of lightning I caught a glimpse of the island ahead—not astern, where it should be, I panicked. *We are being driven right up into the shallows!* I swung the wheel hard to port and screamed for Michael. Mercifully, he came straight aft.

"What the hell!" He grabbed the wheel from me and gunned the engine so hard I smelled burning oil. The depth sounder confirmed we had run out of water, but miraculously we did not ground. Perhaps the force of our turn coupled with the beam wind threw the boat over so far that SEA QUEST became considerably more shallow-drafted. Perhaps we ran off the edge of the bank. Michael positioned us beyond the sandbank's edge in deeper water before dropping the anchor and all 48 fathoms of chain, pulling back to be sure the anchor was snug. After some deliberation he decided to set a second anchor on nylon rode. Despite this, surf welled up beside us. We felt insecure.

We waited in the damp cockpit for another squall to pass. As soon as this squall was gone we would lift both anchors and move out into the main lagoon taking care to avoid a patch of coral we knew to be there. Finally, Michael went forward.

"We've lost an anchor!" he shouted back to me. "The rope has chaffed through. The line must have jumped off the roller."

Or maybe it had just parted under the strain, for the heavy snub-rope on the main anchor chain had also given way.

Tears ran unchecked down Miki's face while the anxious cat wove frantic circles. We planned our next move with the exactitude of a military campaign.

"The second anchor," I mused, "does it have a nylon rode or a polypropylene rope that floats?"

"Oh, no! I think it may float, and all we need now is a rope in the prop!"

With the high-powered spotlight, Michael searched around the boat but could not spot the floating rope. He grabbed the dinghy anchor and shackled an orange float to it. He then coached Miki how to drop it over the stern as a marker for the lost anchor. With Michael ready on the foredeck I eased the engine into gear to take the strain off the chain. The wheel felt strange under my hand. I spun it to port and then again to starboard.

"Michael! Stop!"

"What is wrong?" he yelled back exasperated.

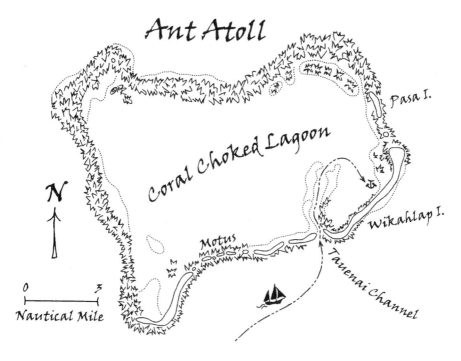

"The steering. She's not answering the helm!"

"I'll go below and check."

Nothing was amiss. *What the hell is it,* he said to himself. *Where's the break?*

He crawled into the engine room and began to unscrew the cover over the chain sprocket in the steering linkage. Something dug into his knee. He picked it up.

"The steel key!" he exclaimed. Seeing my puzzled look, he explained. "It locks the sprocket on the shaft."

Somehow, our frantic steering had caused the key to drop out. "Thank heavens you found it!"

"If it had rolled into the bilge, I might not have."

While he and Miki set to work reassembling the linkage, I went aft with a light to check the windvane rudder. I found it jammed hard to starboard. It had been forcibly skewed when SEA QUEST grounded against the coral.

Ha! I thought. This was why the helm did not answer earlier. The main rudder was fighting the windvane rudder to port and turning us in double-time to starboard.

With the key reinstalled and the windvane rudder straightened we raised our main anchor and placed the marker. In 12 fathoms we again dropped the main Bruce anchor along with 260 feet of chain and a prayer.

In the morning, Michael discovered that, when SEA QUEST hit the coral, the jolt had lifted the main rudder off its hinge so it now swung free of the lower gudgeon. The rudder had to be put right before we could sail. From the water, after having rigged lines, Michael directed Miki and me on the two cockpit winches to ease the rudder up enough so that he could lever it back into place. Fortunately the rudder shaft had not bent.

The family arrived to wish us a last farewell unaware of our lucky escape. More coconuts were handed aboard (fifty now cluttered the deck) along with several papayas. One gift was a large bottle of coconut syrup, which Michael soon discovered was perfect on his Sunday-morning pancakes. I reciprocated with a five-pound bag of flour, some canned goods and a jar of jam.

"Would you mind delivering these kerosene containers back to Pohnpei?" Etelinda asked. "They will be refilled by our relatives and returned on the next ship."

Etelinda had mentioned a coral islet adjacent to Keltie Pass at the opposite end of the lagoon as a possible anchorage. Had the weather been settled we might have spent several days diving near this sandy strand, occupied by a colony of blue-faced boobies, right out of Dr. Seuss, who watched us unafraid while sitting on pairs of blue eggs while gangly juveniles looked on. But on the horizon loomed another black squall, a sharp reminder that our idyllic daytime anchorage might become a nightmare after dark.

We made good progress for 24 hours on this, our last 172-mile passage beating to the east. Then Guam weather station reported a weak cyclonic disturbance directly south of us, an early herald for the new typhoon season. Pohnpei is generally free of serious typhoons. Although they breed in those turbulent latitudes typhoons rarely attain enough size to blow very strongly this close to the Equator. But it was into that disturbed area that we were now sailing.

Conditions deteriorated as we were overtaken time and time again by 35-knot squalls. Finally, sixty miles out of Pohnpei, the weather cleared once more. A jubilant school of short-nosed dolphins arrived to race near SEA QUEST, leaping and chasing each other, their underbellies blushing pink in the evening light.

By noon on the next day, Pohnpei's port of Kolonia still lay at least seven hours away. Ant Atoll was just nine miles from our present position. Although we were keen to arrive in Pohnpei—the end of our 2,500-mile sail east through Micronesia—prudence led us to stop overnight so that we could enter Pohnpei's Jokai Pass in good light on the morrow.

17

Pohnpei and Mysterious Nan Madol

Pohnpei's ancient volcanic land of cliffs and mist-covered mountains, like an emerging goddess, erupted from the sea. Beyond the mangrove-lined coast tortuous valleys wound into a steep uninhabited interior. Countless waterfalls dropped into hidden jungle pools. Pohnpei Island, crowned by 2,595-foot Mount Ngihneni, *The Tooth of the Spirit*, is about 20 miles in diameter and encompasses 140 square miles of land. The encircling reef is narrow; its lagoon so coral-choked that, even with local knowledge, navigation through its channels is hazardous.

As we were advancing rapidly along the coast under a brisk breeze, a towering fortress-like massif dominated our view. Beneath Sohek's Rock on the northern side of the island stretched spectacular Kolonia Harbor.

According to legend, the ancestors of Pohnpei's people sailed out of the south with the great navigator Sapikini from the fabled land of Eir. Seven men and nine women assisted by a divine wind met the octopus Litakita, who took them to a large submerged reef. They decided to build upon this reef. Calling upon heaven, they brought down large rocks with which to form an altar. The women filled the altar with soil from their native land. As the party watched, the island grew high upon the waves with the protective reef surrounding it. To mark the holy origins of the island they named it Pohnpei, "Upon an Altar."

Archeologists now believe that Sapikini and his kin most likely came from Samoa. Traditionally, groups traveling from Fiji, Tonga and Samoa included an equal number of women and men and carried with them the seeds and animals they needed to subsist in a new land. Were these travelers caught in an unexpected current, called in their myth the *octopus*? Were they overwhelmed by a cyclone that pushed them well to the north? Unable to see the stars and beset with squalls and violent weather in the thick haze of the doldrums, did they become disoriented?

In this immense ocean devoid of land they may have drifted for weeks and a number of them succumbed to exposure or starvation. They might even have passed over the same tantalizing shallows as we did; land only a few dozen feet below the keel but as out of reach as though it were leagues away.

Imagine the group's weary disbelief after being lost for many weeks when a mere smudge on the distant horizon grew into a mighty island, so high its peaks were lost in cloud. A celestial altar! The gift of Divine Providence! Upon touching shore would they not have fallen to their knees to bless the incredible land they had chanced upon—and perhaps carefully placed a

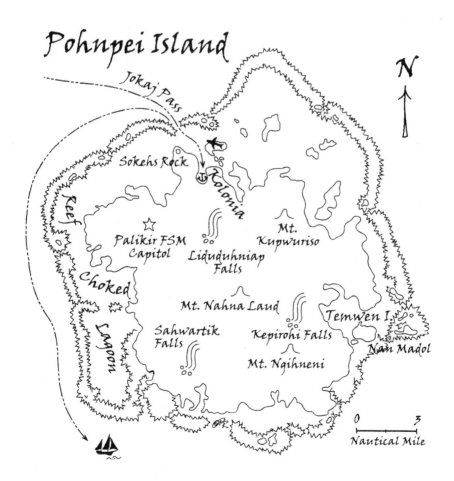

163

ballast stone from their original homeland so that they might be anchored to it?

The legend of Sapikini's accidental discovery also accounts for the origins of *kava*, now known as *sakau* on Pohnpei, a plant which is thought to have been indigenous to Samoa or Fiji.

It was mid-afternoon on a Friday when we dropped sail to enter the reef passage. Michael made a note in the log that we had sailed almost 4,000 miles in zigzag tacks to span the 2,500-mile distance from the San Bernadino Passage in the Philippines. Kolonia Harbor slices deep into the sheltering land under the escarpment of Sokeh's Rock. A causeway joins the commercial docks and the airport across several low islands.

Along the eastern shore, planted with coconut and breadfruit trees, appeared the picturesque thatched huts of Kapingamarangi. This village, Etelinda's former home, is occupied by the inhabitants of a small atoll of the same name 400 miles south of Pohnpei. The government resettled them here in the 1930s after a drought killed half the population on their home island.

The main channel into the harbor was well marked. Port Control directed us by radio to tie alongside a Taiwanese fishing boat rafted to others at the commercial dock. The harbormaster, then the local police, followed by Customs, Immigration and agricultural officers accompanied by various hangers-on, arrived in waves to squeeze into SEA QUEST's cockpit. Some traipsed below decks in their heavy boots. All were courteous, apologizing for the inconvenience of rafting up alongside smelly fishing boats.

Asked by Immigration to produce our Cruising Permit, which must be applied for well in advance, Michael could show them only a copy of our letter requesting it, dated months earlier. Although we had never received a reply, having the letter as proof that we *had* applied was sufficient. The clearing-in went smoothly, but for a clever sleight-of hand by the young agricultural officer who requested a $20 overtime charge. Had the officer's supervisor, a German, not dropped by afterwards to review our papers, we would never have known.

Only when the clearing-in process was completed and evening was almost upon us were we at last free to go. The harbor would be an exceptional anchorage but for the fact that it is haphazardly strewn with reef. As we entered the channel to the inner bay a rainsquall engulfed SEA QUEST. Unable to pick out the channel's outline in the fading light, our heavy keel ground on the coral. After pausing to let the squall pass, we continued to an anchorage kept naturally free of coral by the flow of a fresh water river. Its shores were littered with the wrecks of barges, workboats, a dredge and even a 40-foot yacht, all reminders of the ravages of past tropical storms.

Shaded by the mangrove's thick canopy, was a bar. Rumors, as the business is called, offers the use of their dinghy dock and a grubby shower for a small fee to visiting yachts. Not that there were many.

Like Koror in Belau, the streets of Kolonia are spread out. During pre-war times Kolonia housed a huge Asian population of Japanese and Koreans. Ruined premises and overgrown gaps attest to the former size of a town that also housed nine brothels. Another legacy of World War II was a forlorn group of rusting tanks in shoulder-high grass parked next to a supermarket.

Only one mail-packet awaited us at the Post Office, not the stacks of letters we had expected. Michael's mother numbered consecutively each bundle of forwarded mail. Where might be the missing packets, also addressed like this one to "General Delivery, Kolonia, F.S.M?"

"Maybe they have been sent to the *main* post office," the teller suggested.

"Where is that?"

"At Palikir."

Palikir, located a half-hour taxi ride away, is a new town designed to be the capital. It houses the government administrative center for the Federated States of Micronesia as well as the campus of the College of Micronesia. The staff insisted there was no mail awaiting us there either. Exasperated and unconvinced, Michael persuaded the postmaster that together they should forage around in the back room. To mutters of "most irregular," they entered a room where stacked boxes overflowed with letters marked "Return to Sender." Old postmarks indicated some had languished here for a year. An hour's search uncovered our missing packets.

Later we wandered around the town. Several small hotels overlook the harbor and there is a scattering of reputedly good restaurants, had our budget stretched to such luxuries. Kolonia's oldest ruins, dating back to 1886, are a legacy of the brief Spanish colonial period. Much of the old Spanish wall, once enclosing Fort Alphonse, still stands. All that remains of the Catholic Church, built in 1907 by the Germans, but deliberately torn down during the war by the Japanese, is the bell tower. Near the village of Kapingamarangi in an old German cemetery, is the grave of one of the island's early German administrators, Viktor Berg. He was felled by a mysterious illness and was hastily buried just one day after his curiosity led him to dig up some ancient graves at Nan Madol!

One of the surprising things about Kolonia is that most people here are buried in their own front yards. The whitewashed above-ground graves are turned into glass-walled mausoleums festooned with dazzling garlands of artificial flowers, each mausoleum more elaborate than the last.

Kolonia is a sleepy town. The once thriving pre-war Japanese export trade has been replaced by official aid from the U.S. government. There is little commerce in Pohnpei apart from the licensing of foreign fishing fleets from Taiwan, Korea, China and Japan. Corruption is rampant. The island's traditional clan heads, now having access to government money, buy longboats with powerful outboards, build themselves luxury homes and drive imported cars. Meanwhile basic public services like the hospital and dental surgery are understaffed and underfunded.

The aid money is unsupervised. Few Americans live on the island, apart from those employed at the College of Micronesia or members of the Peace Corps. Several countries, among them Japan and Australia, take a strategic and commercial interest in Micronesia. As a result, Pohnpei, the capital of the Federated States of Micronesia, plays host to many embassies.

Pohnpei is both geographically and culturally fascinating. Many of its traditions endure today despite the cultural onslaught of German, Japanese and American colonialism and the annihilation of more than half the population by smallpox or measles. Even today, the island's five chiefs, the *Nahnmwarkis*, retain a degree of supernatural power over their subjects. The

166

Pohnpeians, although converted to Christianity, assume that potent ancestral ghosts support the authority of these *Nahnmwarkis*. Should a chief's subject commit an affront, even if the transgressor and the chief himself remain unaware of the transgression, the ghost will seek retribution. Sickness follows, usually involving the subject's child. Invariably if a child falls ill, fingers point to the parents. Illness is unnatural, people believe. There must be a guilty party. To expiate the offense, confessions must be made and a feast paid for.

Most of Pohnpei's approximately 40,000 inhabitants live on the island's muddy shores. They live in extended family groups in primitive dwellings tucked amongst the roots of mangroves or perched on the lowermost slopes of jungle-covered mountains. High on the mountain slopes they conceal farm plots where enormous prized yams are grown, some so big they require six men to carry. Used as special tribute for the *Nahnmwarki*, the yams help buy the owner status in the island's elaborate hierarchy. Each Pohnpeian strives for a prestige title that will bring privilege and obligation within his or her matrilineal clan.

Education and financial independence have brought profound changes. A few take advantage of new commercial opportunities to escape from the burden of family and clan obligations and move to town. This nascent independence is seriously undermining the chiefs' autocratic power. Though Pohnpei's social complexities are intriguing, locals tell us it would take a lifetime to fully understand them. A more seductive attraction for the visitor is the ancient city of Nan Madol, which consists of mysterious megalithic, basalt-crystal ruins.

We headed out to Nan Madol, on the southeast corner of the island, in the back of a pickup truck. It was a typically hot and humid day, unrelieved yet by the usual afternoon downpour which mercifully cools things down. The two-hour ride took us along rutted roads surrounded by the lush vegetation of this rainy tropical Eden. Vines entwined telephone poles, shrouded trees, and swallowed up unsightly roadside litter and even abandoned cars. We bumped past haphazardly planted groves of breadfruit, guava, banana, betelnut and coconut. People waved from shanties made of concrete and tin.

The legend of Nan Madol states that two holy brothers,

Ohiosohpa and Ohiosihpa, sailed a fleet out of the west from *Katau Peidi*, the Place of the Sunset, bringing with them a sophisticated and alien culture, and a cult that revolved around a sacred ceremony involving an eel. Intriguing old tales of the Caroline Islands speak of the existence of a once-great empire that stretched across the breadth of Micronesia. Perhaps it was this empire that included the great stone cities on Pohnpei and Kosrae Island to the southeast, the massive stone "money" of Yap, the megalithic "Latte" stones of Tinian, Guam and Saipan. Perhaps the empire even embraced the megalithic ruins and terraced hillsides of Belau.

After the truck stopped at our destination, we hiked along a shaded jungle trail until we reached the edge of a narrow canal lined entirely in heavy polygonal stone. The high flaring walls of Nan Dowas, a structure that some call a fortress and others a temple, towered over our heads. At low tide, the silted canal was only knee deep. We waded across.

Dripping, Michael, Miki and I climbed the broad western steps to enter the massive portal into what was once the private

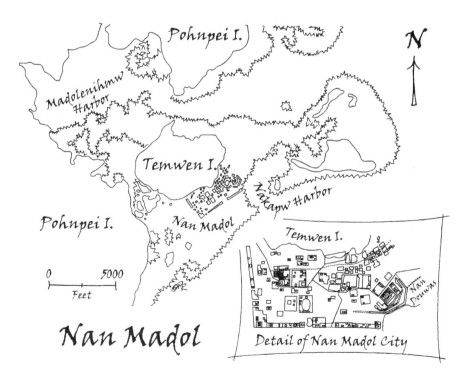

Nan Madol

Detail of Nan Madol City

domain of Pohnpei's ancient ruler, the *Saudeleur.* Intense heat radiated from the dark stones. Courses of closely fitted basalt logs rose 25 feet over our heads to form monumental, 12-foot thick walls. The broad corridor that led from the outer structure to the center was used by the *Saudeleur* himself. All other men were required to crawl on hands and knees through guarded low side entrances.

Located in the central courtyard is a semi-subterranean crypt. Bars of light penetrated columnar lintel stones and illuminated the mossy, cool interior. The crypt was not intended for permanent burial. The newly deceased *Saudeleur* was entombed there only long enough for his flesh to fall from his bones, after which his bones were washed, prepared and deposited in some permanent sacred place. Several other smaller crypts were located between the inner and outer walls as were underground cells, perhaps for prisoners awaiting sacrifice.

Apart from architecturally pleasing curves that lift the corners of the outer walls, soft touches are absent from this temple of massive stacked stone—unrelieved by gardens, sculptures, or plastered walls. The black-faceted rock seemed intimidating, but when the island's elite lived in high peaked thatched houses in Nan Madol's 200-acre spread of canals and raised islets, it must have been lovely indeed. The canals were clear then; the islets planted with flowers. The whole area was breezy and surrounded by white sand, reef and sparkling water set against a curtain of deep green mangrove.

Standing on the high outer walls we were astonished by the sheer magnitude of this megalithic site which, according to calculations, contains more rock than the Great Pyramid of Cheops. Mangroves have buried many of the islands, but at high tide in a dinghy or canoe it is possible to explore miles of cleverly laid foundations along imposing channels. Throughout the city hundreds of thousands of tons of the same strange layers of prismatic basalt logs were used to form solid wall perimeters for each islet, behind which was placed enormous volumes of closely packed coral rubble. To the southeast a massive sea wall forms a 30-foot thick rampart more than a mile long.

Nan Dowas was once known as the "Temple of the Dragon." Local legends say that the entire city was built with the help of dragons and a knowledgeable magician. By the time Pohnpei became ruled by the *Saudeleurs* around 1,200 AD, archeologists believe that the island's population had grown to at least 30,000 people. The new rulers centralized political control and set to work creating their megalithic constructions.

Archeological evidence indicates that about 2,000 years ago houses on stilts were built over the slightly submerged reef surface by the earliest inhabitants. Nine hundred years later, stilt houses gave way to islets artificially elevated with rubble. With the coming of the *Saudeleurs* the entire site was re-planned and laid out.

To the southwest was the residential area, Madol Pah, eventually to have 34 islets. To the northeast was the ritual ward, Madol Powe, with 58 islets including the mortuary compound, Nan Dowas. As a tribute to the new rulers the local people were forced to quarry the basalt stones, transport them and then build the massive seawalls and the foundations for the 93 islets. Construction probably continued well into the seventeenth century.

The *Saudeleur* dynasty lasted 500 years before their rule degenerated into cannibalism and was finally overthrown. It was defeated, so legend tells us, in 1628 when Isokelekel invaded with 333 men from Kosrae. Isokelekel became the first *Nahnmwarki* or High Chief in a hierarchy of lesser chiefs. Their descendants have to this day continued to rule each of Pohnpei's five districts. By the mid-nineteenth century when Europeans arrived, the complex had only recently been abandoned.

Many have questioned where the enormous volume of stone used in constructing Nan Madol came from. Possibly millions of tons were quarried from the opposite side of Pohnpei near Sokeh's Rock or alternatively from the colorfully named "Chicken Shit Mountain" in the west, both which have "Devil's Post Pile" formations. According to legend, the stones *floated* or *flew* into place. Many Pohnpeians still believe a baby dragon dug the canals and tunnels under the reef shelf while the mother dragon, directed by a knowledgeable magician, placed the big stones to form the many canal walls and foundations for countless other structures.

Although nothing certain is known of the ethnic origins of the two fabled brothers, Ohiosohpa and Ohiosihpa, their fleet,

170

or the era in which they came, one thing is obvious. The invaders were sophisticated masters of stonework—a skill undeveloped by the natives up to that time. They and their successors, the *Saudeleurs*, possessed consummate engineering skills and a great talent for organizing and forcing immense gangs of workmen to build this "Micronesian Venice." Archeologists imagine that these stones, many of them weighing up to fifteen tons, but a significant number approaching the size of the largest, a monster of 50 tons, were floated into the canals slung beneath a raft of bamboo. Apparently a crew from the television *Discovery Channel* tested this theory. After several failed attempts, the team succeeded in moving a small stone weighing only one ton.

The mysteries of Nan Madol do not end with these ruins. Beneath the waters of the adjacent bay there is said to lie submerged another even more ancient city whose square outlines can be faintly seen from the air and whose shallower areas divers have explored. Legend has it that this City of the Gods had already sunk beneath the sea long before the present people of Pohnpei arrived. When the brothers Ohiosohpa and Ohiosihpa searched for a suitable site on which to build their own religious center, they were told of its former existence and guided to its location.

Divers have photographed various underwater structures, including a row of upright columns as tall as 30 feet. Did they once support the huge residences of a ruling class as did the megalithic *Latte* stone pedestals and coral capstones that were left on Saipan and Tinian by the "spirits of the before-time people?"

These apparent traces of manmade structures, built after the end of the last ice age but before the sea level rose, bring to mind the undersea walls off Bimini in the Bahamas and others found off the Indian coast and at Yonaguni in the Ryukyu Islands of Japan. Archeology is unable yet to explain many baffling monuments and puzzling remains scattered throughout the oceans of the world that do not seem to fit conventional historical time frames. Add to this the technical difficulties involved in exploring undersea remains and archeology is truly out of its depth.

For 600 years from the time of the *Saudeleurs* through to the more recent *Nahnmwarki* chiefs, commoners brought daily food tribute to their priestly rulers. After the native population was ravaged by disease introduced by the earliest European whalers, the *Nahnmwarki* no longer had the clout to force the remaining commoners to provide enough tribute. They were forced to abandon their sacred city.

Before World War I, when Micronesia was still under the boot of the Kaiser, a German archeological team had with Teutonic thoroughness collected all the evidence they could find from Nan Madol. Unfortunately it was all lost when the ship taking the haul to Europe sank at sea. Nonetheless, various teams still work intermittently to draw back the curtain of time, most notably Steve Athens, Bill Ayres and others under the direction of Hawaii's Bishop Museum.

Now surrounded by a silence broken only by the shriek of a hidden bird, I stood overlooking the enigmatic sanctuary of Nan Dowas, reflecting that generations of Europeans have shared my fascination for this place and its mysteries. The natives of Pohnpei hold the ruins in awe, and will not venture near at night.

The afternoon sun was casting shadows across Nan Madol. It was time to be on our way. But first we made a stop at Kepirohi waterfall to swim amid its swirling currents under the delicate arcs of a hundred cascades. When we tired of struggling, we clung to ledges to allow the tumbling water to beat upon our backs. Eels, invisible up to that moment, emerged to fight for scraps left from our late lunch. Finally unable to delay longer, we climbed into the back of the pick-up for the long ride back to Kolonia.

Pohnpeians conceive their own history as falling into four successive eras: the Age of People, the Age of Saudeleur, the Age of Nahnmwarki, and the Age of Foreigners. Perhaps the locals themselves were only dimly aware that the Spaniard Alvaro de Saavedra sighted their island in 1528, because he did not land there. It was not until 67 years later in 1595 that Spain formally claimed legal ownership. In the 1800s Pohnpei became a popular stopover for Yankee whalers until in 1865 the Confederate

American warship, SHENANDOAH, swept through the Pacific ports to sink most of the 40-strong Union whaling fleet, four in Kolonia's harbor alone.

Protestant missionaries had been first on the scene in a race to convert natives; a fact which led to endless conflict after the Catholic Spanish administration arrived in 1885 to occupy the land. The by now firmly Protestant natives objected to attempts by Catholic priests to reconvert them! The last straw came after Spanish settlers, in a rather un-Christian move, attempted to use the natives as forced labor. Skirmishes developed. The Spanish governor was killed. In 1899 the Spaniards gave up the struggle and sold the Caroline Islands to the Germans, who were itching to develop a copra industry. Before long *their* attempt to use the natives for forced labor triggered a major revolt.

At the end of World War I, under a United Nations mandate the German administration was replaced by Japanese trusteeship. In recognition, perhaps, of the problems encountered by their predecessors, the Japanese bypassed local labor altogether. Instead they imported thousands of their own nationals along with Koreans and Okinawans to provide the skilled work force needed to establish a flourishing local economy based on copra, trochus shell, agriculture and seafood.

Pohnpeians, who continued to live in a subsistence economy, were soon outnumbered, accounting for only about a third of the total population, with less than ten percent in Kolonia. After the Japanese defeat in 1945, the entire Asian labor force was deported. The local economy collapsed and the U.S. government stepped in to administer the island as part of the United Nations Trust Territory of the Pacific Islands.

U.S. funds subsidized the Peace Corps, the setting up of development projects such as hospitals and clinics, institutes for learning, libraries and the like. Although America has been roundly criticized for not doing enough to develop the islands economically, the U.S. administration took up its duties in the region mainly to prevent a power vacuum in strategically located Micronesia. However, to grease the way and keep the locals happy it was politic to create a little material and financial dependency. With the end of the United Nations Trusteeship and moves towards independence, millions of dollars were hastily allocated to a Compact of Free Association that would allow the U.S. to maintain their strategic interest. The idea too was that local government would use the money to build a solid infrastructure in the hope that a stable Federated States of Micronesia would in the future continue to favor the interests of the U.S.

The U.S. might have hoped that the local elected officials, most of them a high-ranking elite, would have had the wisdom to use the grant money well. It does not appear that they have. All too frequently islanders themselves complain that those in positions of power have manipulated the national assets for personal gain. The old system is tenacious. Authority is vested in the hands of a few. The ordinary islander cannot imagine rocking this particular boat.

When I suggested to a local lad that commoners should question where Compact money went, he shrugged his shoulder and dismissively said, "They are the leaders, aren't they?"

We needed to accomplish one last thing before leaving Pohnpei. It was necessary to have a blood sample taken from our cat, Mizzen, to conform to New Zealand's strict regulations for importing her. A rabies' test was required six months prior to arriving in New Zealand. The first step towards this had been Mizzen's rabies vaccination in Hong Kong. Now the blood had to be flown to Australia for testing.

There was a problem. In all of the Federated States of Micronesia there was not a single veterinarian! We succeeded in persuading a technician at the local hospital to take blood from our squirming cat and then to prepare it in their centrifuge. We had also to insure in advance that the postmaster would be certain the packet went on the next day's plane to Sydney, the only place in the Pacific where it could be analyzed.

Pohnpei is a sleepy island. The people are languid and laid back. They move slowly and apparently do little work. It is no wonder that neither the Spaniards nor the Germans could compel them to forced labor. Whole family groups idle away the day on porches, swing in hammocks, or loiter by the roadsides. We saw no canoes being carved, or gardens dug, no mats being woven or community projects undertaken. In fact we saw little of the industry commonly evident on the atolls.

Our driver said to us, "The women, they don't cook no more. They just want to go to the store. 'It's too much trouble to climb to the garden', they say. All they make is a big pot of rice."

Statistics support his observation. They show that Uncle Sam's largess is overwhelmingly being spent on imported supermarket foodstuffs!

Nevertheless, people are of a happy disposition. Perhaps the innate security they feel as members of a clan system contributes to this. Everyone has his or her position in the hierarchy along with a measure of personal status. Pohnpei has no orphans or abandoned elderly. Nobody goes hungry. Life is sweet. Peace Corps youths we met with reported that they were swept away by the general gaiety they found. "Pohnpei is Heaven on Earth," they insisted. We too had discovered that our visible dismay and irritation over the mail fiasco at the post office was met only with wide-eyed, bemused smiles. What is there to get excited about, they seemed to say. Time has little meaning on "Upon the Altar," this torpid island given to Sapikini and his heirs by the gods—where, everyday, fruit tumbles from the trees.

18

The Solomon Islands

On the afternoon of July 6, the rainbow-shrouded hills of Pohnpei slipped astern. We had set sail to cross the Equator on what was to be a 15-day, 1,500-mile journey to the most easterly of the Solomon Islands, the Santa Cruz Group. The northeast tradewind pushed us effortlessly through six degrees of latitude. When dirty-looking stratocumulus cloud built up and sheet lightning flashed, we doggedly ignored it to continue on a broad reach.

We crossed the line and in true nautical fashion prepared to initiate the newest Shellback into the ranks of seasoned mariners. Decked out in the best marine grease paint and nautical mop wig, a trident-wielding Neptune climbed aboard, along with Neptune's mate trailing tendrils of crêpe seaweed, who announced the Sea Lord's arrival with blasts on her conch

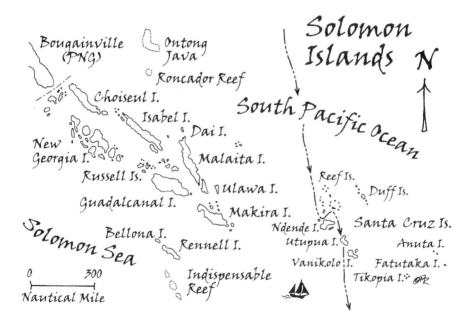

shell horn. Miki, having for the occasion been rudely dragged from her bunk to the quarterdeck, was there anointed, as custom demanded, with saltwater, sardines, and whipped cream over her head. Poor child! Before again departing for his watery kingdom, Neptune presented an overwhelmed, but excited Miki with her traditional Shellback Certificate.

As though Neptune did truly want to bedevil us, the wind suddenly veered. From that time on continuous squalls kicked the sea into confusion. On the tenth day in 40-knot winds we seriously shortened sail. Breaking seas swept SEA QUEST. None of us slept much. The storm raged for four days and nights. Finally on the fourteenth day at sea, as we approached the Solomon Islands, the weather cleared until gradually gentle southeast tradewinds took over.

Our course took us to leeward of Patteson Shoals and to windward of Tinakula's perfect volcanic cone rising several hundred feet, its exhaled vapor visible to us in the starlit sky. The Reef Islands, silhouetted against the rising moon, created a calm lee through which we now sailed. The off-watch crew fell into their first sound sleep in days as we approached Ndende, the largest island of the Santa Cruz group. I felt mean calling Michael from his slumber to stow the sails and make ready to power into Graciosa Bay.

We rounded up to Shaw Point, a cove inside the larger harbor once used by loggers and the only viable anchorage for cruisers. The foreshore of Graciosa Bay is largely inhospitable, bounded by deep water and sheer coral reef walls. Several yachts lay behind Shaw Point. We looked forward to their company. Yet before we could join them we had to launch our dinghy and head across the choppy mile-wide bay to complete the entry formalities at the village of Lata. Before we even had the skiff in the water, a garrulous Kiwi motored over with a terrible tale. There were so many yachts gathered in the bay, he said, because there had been an awful accident.

"What sort of accident?" asked Michael.

The man hesitated a moment. "A yachtsman was taken by a crocodile!"

We were aghast.

"Oh, no! How did such a dreadful thing happen?"

ATHENE III, a Swiss yacht crewed by 60-year old Fritz and his wife Therese, was cruising north from Vanuatu to the Solomon Islands. Thirty-five miles south of Ndende they thought they would stop overnight at Utupua Island. Because the boat was not yet legally entered the couple did not want to draw unnecessary attention. Instead of anchoring near the village they motored deeper into the bay, where large mangroves line the shore.

The water was somewhat murky, but as was his habit Fritz decided to go for a swim before actually dropping anchor to make sure the area was suitably coral free.

"I don't think you should swim here," Therese had cautioned. "I read that there are crocodiles in the Solomons."

"I don't think so," was his cheerful response.

He swam until he could see the sandy bottom near the mangroves and waved back at his wife reassuringly.

Then Therese heard him shout, "Crocodile! Help me, help!"

There was violent splashing and Therese saw a large crocodile thrashing her husband's body.

Several hours later a native found Therese still staring at that dark pool of water. After dropping the anchor she sat as though time had stopped.

"Where is your husband?" the man asked.

"He is sleeping—no! A crocodile took him."

She told those who supported her in the following days that the whole experience had seemed an unbelievable nightmare from which she would wake at any moment.

The village men went that same night with burning torches to scare the crocodiles from their nesting place to retrieve the yachtsman's mangled body. The next day Fritz was buried in the village of Nembao. The local Anglican catechist read from the Good Book. A plain plank coffin was lowered into the grave. Native women keened and Therese wept for her husband buried in a village far from his home and his sons.

The local people helped Therese to sail her yacht on to Ndende where all the other cruisers in the area had also gathered to support her. We felt deeply upset for Therese and extremely sad. It was all of our worst nightmares come to pass.

Because of the tragic business, officials were making the crossing from Lata with unusual frequency. One of them stopped by, offering to check us in right there and then, saving us the trouble of the difficult trip across the bay. Now that the clearance procedure was behind us we turned our attention to scrubbing away the grime and encrusted layers of sun-baked salt accumulated by 15 days at sea. We found a spring-fed jungle pool where we lay soaking like hippopotamuses until our skin puckered.

Ndende has over the past four centuries both attracted and repelled many Europeans. The Spaniard Alvaro de Mendana attempted to establish a colony in Graciosa Bay in 1595, but he and 47 companions perished here. The unhappy survivors called Ndende "a corner of hell in the claws of the devil." Even today, vine-draped jungle cloaks the steamy hills that rise to a height of nearly 1,200 feet. In the hidden mountain villages dark-skinned Melanesians live much as they have done from time immemorial. It is not safe even today to go wandering off on your own in those mountains. Rumor has it that strangers are killed and cannibalism may still exist!

Along the coconut-fringed coast the "wild country, and black, naked, woolly-haired natives" reported by Carteret in 1767 have been replaced by milder, friendlier, Christianized Melanesians. One day we went to a village at the head of Graciosa Bay. As we tumbled out of the dinghy into the surf, women and children reached eagerly for our hands and then thronged around us chattering in a most friendly fashion. A school "Fun Day" was in full swing when we arrived, with big, strong girls hitching their muumuus high to run relay races, while in the next field spectators wildly cheered a boys' volleyball team.

The Solomon Islands are malaria country. Cerebral malaria, common here, kills in only 24 hours. Only the season before a French yachtsman had died in Ndende. Our old nets had perished so Michael, a dab hand at the sewing machine, set about to make a new cockpit screen. When it was finished we could sit outside in the late afternoon and dusk, the time the predatory anopheles mosquito is most active. Since leaving Pohnpei, we had been taking a prophylactic dose of Chloroquine, the medicine commonly used to buffer a severe malarial attack. Drugs like Fansidar, Lariam and Maloprim could only be taken for short times and had many serious side effects. Our supply of these stronger drugs was kept in reserve "just in case."

A mile away from our anchorage a muddy river drained into the sea. Rivers in the Solomon Islands are like broad highways cut into the jungle, a jungle otherwise too dense and dangerous for us to penetrate. More cautious than ever of crocodiles, we checked with the locals to be sure there were none in that river before setting off with our dinghy to explore.

Well up the river we cut the engine to drift in silence. The jungle's gloomy depths were brightened by the undergrowth of red ginger, ferns and palms. Birds flew overhead and flying foxes circled clumsily on translucent wings. Graceful herons with long sharp beaks fished from perches in trees. When two gaudy parrots flying right over our heads screeched, Miki's laughter rang out in sheer delight.

Because Lata is the only port of entry in the southern Solomon Islands, we had a problem. Technically, to explore the Reef Islands we would be required to return again to Lata to clear out. This would add many miles to our trip, and cost us the progress that we would have made to windward. Happily, however, the Immigration officer remembered us with kindness. "It is our policy to say 'No', but we'll make an exception in your case," he told Michael when he stamped the passports. "You know many people in the Reef Islands from your previous visit and you now want to return. That's reasonable. OK."

Archeologists tell us that the Solomon Archipelago was first inhabited by Melanesian hunter-gatherers who migrated from Papua-New Guinea around 30,000 years ago. During the Pleistocene epoch Pacific islanders began to gain enough confidence in their ocean craft to sail between mostly close-by islands. These early Papuan-speaking people were eventually displaced by new arrivals, an Austronesian-speaking neolithic people, who practiced agriculture and established village communities.

Next to pass through, about 3,000 years ago, were seafaring proto-Polynesians. As more savage tribes held the larger islands, they settled the remoter ones. Excavations of proto-Polynesian villages have uncovered distinctive Lapita decorated pottery and obsidian artifacts revealing that these early settlers traded across long distances. Some objects from the Reef Islands originated more than a thousand miles north in either New Britain or the Admiralty Islands. Others came from Vanua Lava Island in Vanuatu several hundred miles to the south.

The present inhabitants of the Solomon Islands bear little resemblance to the ancient Lapita people who, we are told, continued to migrate to the east throughout all of what is now known as Polynesia. In the Santa Cruz Group, though, some of the more isolated islands are today inhabited by Polynesians who arrived about 1,500 years ago in a return migration from the east. On Fenualoa, our present destination, and adjacent Lom Lom, Polynesians have interbred with the old race of Melanesians to create the modern day Reef Islander.

The Reef Island group is a raised seabed of helter-skelter reefs lacking a clearly defined perimeter. You need good light to enter the lagoon safely. Even if our GPS reception had not been deteriorating, it would have been unwise for us to trust that its positions and the reefs drawn on our chart actually matched. And as luck would have it, just as we approached the group, our GPS quit altogether.

With Michael on the spreaders as lookout we ran beside a northwest bearing spur until the coral thinned out enough to cross the shoal, then motored back to windward another eight miles through scattered coral heads and reef to get under the lee of Fenualoa Island. As we neared the magnificent sweep of powdery white beach near the village of Tuwo, a fleet of yelling, happy children in small canoes raced out to meet us.

We headed ashore directly. Seven years earlier, we had come at a time when it was extremely rare for a yacht to visit. As we landed, Old Chief Dudley greeted us by name. We walked through the breezy village and people we had met on our first visit came to warmly shake our hands. A runner was sent to alert Father Cummings, the Anglican priest, with whom we had had long talks in the past.

Chief Dudley led the way through the village. Proudly he pointed to the new steel-frame church. Five years before, he explained, a cyclone had leveled the village and destroyed many important trees. The villagers themselves had rebuilt everything. Yet despite all the new construction, it seemed little different.

During our first visit we had joined in the inaugural

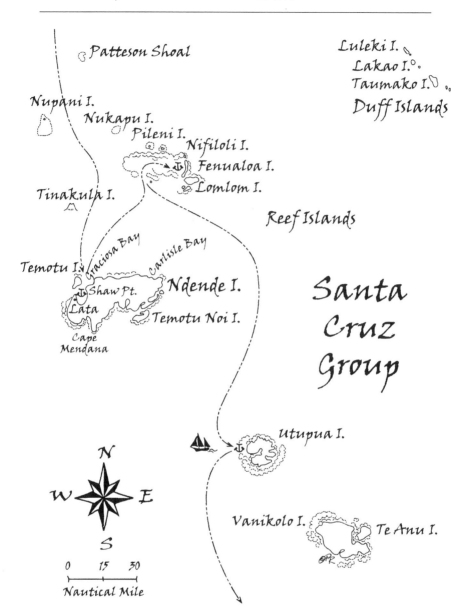

Patteson Shoal

Luleki I.
Lakao I.
Taumako I.
Duff Islands

Nupani I.

Nukapu I.
Pileni I.
Nifiloli I.
Fenualoa I.
Lomlom I.

Tinakula I.

Reef Islands

Graciosa Bay
Carlisle Bay

Temotu I.
Shaw Pt.
Lata
Ndende I.
Temotu Noi I.

Cape
Mendana

Santa Cruz Group

Utupua I.

Vanikolo I.
Te Anu I.

N
W   E
S

0   15   30
Nautical Mile

ceremonies for the new men's house. The thatched structure provided a place where village boys could be taught *kastom*. Father Cummings had blessed the building with holy water, and Michael had made a long speech, in English of course. When he finished Chief Dudley stood in Michael's place and retold the speech word for word in Pidgin English, and then again in the native dialect. What a memory!

Here, the children attend school for just three hours a day. Then on Wednesdays the young boys gather in the *kastom* house for instruction. Girls also attend school here, unlike the girls on many other Solomon Islands. Some even win places at secondary schools and teachers' colleges.

The classrooms are rudimentary. Six students sit side by side at hand-hewn plank desks on plank benches. Dirty, dog-eared books are stacked on the dirt floor. The walls are bare. There is no electricity. The absolute minimum of audio-visual aids a Western child takes for granted are beyond these children's wildest imaginings. They have never seen a computer or a TV screen. Nevertheless, the children do thrive. An 11-year old girl with wild uncombed orange hair pressed near while I sat conversing with a teacher whose mouth was stained crimson with betelnut.

"What is your favorite subject?"

Her quick reply, "Math and English!"

The children all speak at least two or three languages. They speak their native dialect of which there are at least 200 in the Solomon Islands. They also learn Pidgin English to communicate with other islanders. The schoolbooks are written in English, the "get-ahead" language. It is the commercial language of the capital Honiara, as well as the language of academics and professionals. Only by mastering this third language do the gates of opportunity open.

Our visit coincided with breadfruit season. This fruit was known by Europeans to be so wholesome that, when the BOUNTY mutiny occurred, Captain Bligh's ship was transporting a cargo of breadfruit seedlings to Jamaica with the purpose of feeding the Africans brought there as slaves. Here on the Reef Islands it was being roasted whole over open fires in every family compound, to be eaten later with boiled fish. The islanders also preserve breadfruit by smoking it over a smudge fire. It becomes as tough as hard tack and about as dangerous to teeth fillings! But stored on woven racks in the dry cook shed, it is edible for months. Though intended for a rainy day, the fresh chunks were freely offered and as tempting as potato chips.

We saw no fat people in the village. There were more old people with gray hair and supple bone-thin bodies than we had seen since leaving Japan. Unlike Micronesia, the typical diet of Reef Islanders is not basted in lashings of coconut cream. As a result the people seemed much healthier, although the children especially suffer from another scourge. Their torsos and limbs are frequently disfigured by de-pigmented spiral patterns. In worst cases the affliction affects the whole body causing the face to swell and the eyes to weep.

Because the Reef Islands are small and swept by strong winds they are free of the killer malaria found elsewhere in the Solomons. Nevertheless, every environment seems to have a downside. Despite the islanders' relative health we realized how quickly these people age when we brought out our seven-year-old photos to share. The beautiful young girls had turned into work-hardened women. Those who had been in their prime were already old. Glancing from Michael to Chief Dudley and then to Father Cummings, who were all about the same age, I realized that seven years of Michael's life was like fifteen to twenty years of theirs. Its hard to imagine why this may be so when their simple lives seem to be free of one of our main killers—stress!

Fenualoa, an island under five miles long, supports four villages and about a thousand people. Its neighbor, Lom Lom, is bigger and higher, with a population of around 3,000. Reef Islanders refer to Lom Lom as the mainland. Trails lead all over flat Fenualoa to scattered gardens, taro patches and woodland glades. When I asked our guide about the flora he could name a practical use for every plant within range. It seemed as though bush, vine, flower, sap, seed, fruit, root, twig, branch or wood could all be applied to some specific use as medicine, cordage, pigment, food, timber, textile, container, glue or firewood.

The next morning, earlier than we would have liked, canoes began bumping alongside. Stumbling on deck we found the smiling faces of several villagers intent on trading shells for sugar and rice or little luxuries for the children. Occasionally local men and women offered us exotic pieces like necklaces of red oyster, dolphin teeth, *kastom* money, or even hand adzes. More frequently however, they brought woodcarvings.

We always carry some extra food like tins of corned beef, bagged rice, sweets, and also ballpoint pens, balloons, kitchen knives, baby clothes, supermarket cologne and scented soap as well as a stock of large T-shirts. Generally these items are more appreciated than cash. Children often paddled out alone hoping to trade shells. Although I had already accumulated more than I could give away in a lifetime, if I needed eggs or limes, I could promise the ever-circling children a-treat-for-a-trade. With loud squeals of anticipation they would race off, paddling hard in the direction of the island to fetch what I needed. The quality was questionable. Many times I have opened an egg for my cake batter to find a chick inside.

The fruit and shells that accumulated from trading lay about on deck, but could not be ignored for long. Secreted within triton, cowrie, leaf basket and stem of bananas were

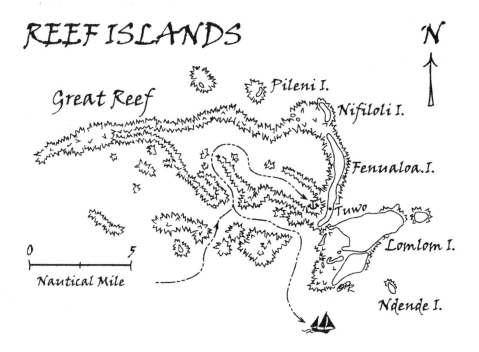

REEF ISLANDS   N

Great Reef   Pileni I.

Nifiloli I.

Fenualoa. I.

Tuwo

Lomlom I.

0   5

Nautical Mile

Ndende I.

185

cockroaches, just waiting for darkness to emerge to find breeding places aboard. Everything they gave me had to be dunked in seawater to force the loathsome insects to swim for shore.

The Swedish yacht SPICE sailing northward with Ulla and Johnny aboard dropped anchor. We socialized over strong drafts of home-brewed Aquavit. They showed us the sailing directions they had for entering the complicated reef pass, sailing directions that they claimed had been photo-copied and passed from yacht to yacht over the years. We laughed heartily when we saw our own name at the top of the page. We had sent the directive to friends after our first trip and unbeknownst to us, it had turned into a chain letter.

Strong southeast winds were still blowing when we bid farewell to both our old and new friends. The shortcut that sliced back through the reef looked too risky to try in blustery weather. Instead we took the long way around, exiting the way we had come. Michael had felt unwell for several days now and the sudden exposure to the boat's pitch and roll as we came out from under Lom Lom's lee made him ill. I was not feeling too hot either although Miki seemed OK. We could only attribute our problems to the fresh batch of Chloroquine we had stocked up on in Lata. We had once before had a similar reaction to malaria pills, causing Michael to feel depressed and both of us to become nauseous.

Because our friendly Immigration officer had also given us permission to stop at Vanikolo, 90 miles to the south, we set a course for that island, hoping to stop there to rest and recover.

By dawn we were still 45 miles dead downwind from Vanikolo tacking against a headwind. The GPS reception continued to be unreliable. Michael pulled out his sextant and took a morning sight through the clouds to get our longitude and then again at noon he took another to determine our latitude. We would not make Vanikolo in daylight. Utupua, site of the recent crocodile attack lay only 20 miles to windward. Though we had not obtained specific permission, under the circumstances we felt we had better take refuge there instead.

As we beat-up the coast in the lee of Utupua's reef, I tossed over the side my homemade lure freshly bound with strips of fluorescent pink and white cloth. We took an immediate strike.

186

A kingfish almost as tall as myself struggled on the end of the line.

After entering through the barrier reef we attempted to hook our anchor on a shoal well out in the bay, but it proved to be as slick as ice. Utupua is an island of primitive beauty with a harbor that cuts deeply into its rugged volcanic hills. Trouble is, the water is too deep for anchoring apart from the muddy confines of the innermost bay, home to at least one man-eating crocodile.

Again we tried to hook the anchor but it again slipped off the shelf forcing us to haul the combined weight of chain and anchor straight up to try again. Acrid smoke wafted into the cockpit.

"Something electrical is burning!" I called out to Michael.

He jumped below to tear out fuses and smoldering wiring from behind our troubled GPS.

As I circled the boat a canoe approached. From it a young man shouted excitedly, "You must anchor near the village. It is a better place than this."

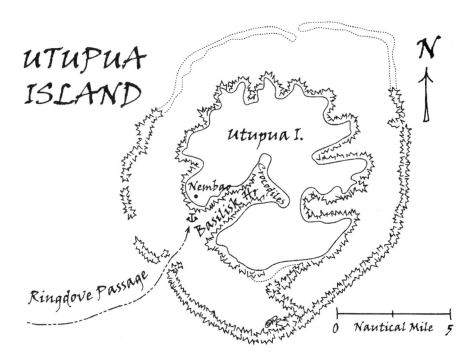

187

With a fish to flay and now an electrical fault to find, dusk was fast approaching. We were ill and very tired and hardly cared about where we would spend the night. Nevertheless, we invited the youth aboard, tied his canoe astern for towing and headed towards the village of Nembao.

Two large canoes packed with men came to meet us. Between the bay and the village is a shallow reef. Just beyond are patches of sand and coral on a narrow shelf where they directed us to anchor. Three tries were necessary before the anchor hooked.

Michael cut two fillets from the tail of the kingfish before delivering the remains into the delighted hands of the grinning youth who had first come paddling out to greet us. We tried not to encourage talkative Willie, Therese's rescuer, now puffed up with self-importance. To the smiling and curious men I said, "I'm sorry we can't invite you all aboard now. We appreciate your help but we are exhausted."

Utapua Island misses out on the yacht traffic. Boats coming from the south must bypass the island to enter at Ndende. Boats heading south must bypass it because they have already cleared out from Ndende to Vanuatu. The local residents are more than happy to bend the rules and let visitors come, but if the officials get wind of it, there can be trouble.

When the villagers returned the next morning, they produced baskets of fruit and an assortment of shells. Negotiating can be an irksome task if you are not in the mood. But my sack of 3-pound bags of rice made excellent currency here.

Later, with Miki to help and several Solomon Islanders peering curiously over his shoulder, Michael began to investigate what had set the GPS wires to cooking. He soon discovered that a short-circuit had developed from the winch motor via the steel hull and the GPS's earth strap, back to the battery. The multi-pin power plug at the back of the GPS had acted like a fuse and melted. Michael constructed another insulator from various materials at hand, including a film canister and a piece of nylon cutting board. By lunchtime the winch was running again.

Although he believed the GPS was now burnt out and useless, Michael rebuilt the multi-pin plug and replaced the melted wires. He hooked it all up to an old cable that ran to a disused aerial mounted on the stern. To his astonishment the GPS immediately picked up a fix.

Late that afternoon we headed across the bay to a beach where we could make a bonfire of our accumulated plastic trash. Then, the noise of falling water drew us through the gloom under large jungle trees. Miki and I looked around nervously. Were they any crocodiles around? A waterfall fell into pools of different sizes and depths that offered us a heavenly choice for bathing. We washed our hair and scrubbed each other's backs. But paradise had a down side here. Chigger-like insects with a ferocious bite devoured us.

When we returned to the beach, after Michael had hauled several five-gallon cans of fresh water from the pools, we found a 50-yard shelf of coral laid bare! It had never occurred to us that the tide would drop so quickly or so far. It took heroic effort to drag our plywood skiff and those heavy jerry cans into deep water.

Before leaving Utupua we wished to pay our respects to Fritz. The Honorable Charles Nathenbe, the local council member, along with a number of attractive mixed-race children led us through the village containing both traditional Melanesian roundhouses and the extremely low Polynesian huts unique to Tikopia. Even a child had to go down on his knees to get through the door openings of these amazing buildings.

In a sandy village graveyard near the thatched church, cuttings had been stuck in the ground to mark a fresh mound, but the palm leaves, glossy green only two weeks before, had already turned a brittle brown, the fading color a reminder of a life so abruptly ended.

Fritz could hardly have imagined a more remote place in which to die. Utupua had no airstrip, no ferry, no regular mail service, no telephones and only a sporadically attended radio. To visit their father's grave the sons would have to fly half way around the world to Australia. They would be airborne another five hours to Honiara and then have to catch a thrice-weekly shuttle-plane to Ndende. Then they would have to hire an open boat to cross (without lifejackets or back-up engines or even safety flares) the 35 miles of open water to Utupua. In the village they would sleep on a coral-rubble floor with pandanus mats for covering. They would wash from an outdoor pipe, use the sea for a latrine and subsist on a diet of local vegetables and fish. Perhaps this extraordinary experience would be the father's final gift to his sons.

Since the grave was unmarked, Michael cast about for some way to remedy the situation. Spying a long chuck of hardwood, still naturally round on one side, but flat on the other, he negotiated to buy it. The balk was floated out to SEA QUEST where Michael set to work with his chisels. Hours later the head post was finished. Under a carved sailboat at the top he had inscribed:

Fritz Messerli
Bern, Switzerland
7 July 1938
"Taken by a crocodile"
14 July 1998

On August 6, having recovered, we departed for what we hoped would be an easy run to Vanua Lava in Vanuatu. A waxing moon rose in the late afternoon sky. The rhumb-line course was 157 miles. The wind had been contrary for everyone that season. Yachts heading north from Vanuatu or south from the Solomons had all been beating to windward.

A strong current carried us to the southwest. The low-lying Torres Group lay under our lee. To force our way eastward, we resorted once again to the Iron Jenny. Against rising winds we temporarily sailed under the lee of magnificent Ureparapara Island, a breached volcanic crater where we had anchored on an earlier trip. Winds slammed us when we left its lee, intensified between Ureparapara's steep crater rim and Vanua Lava Island.

It was nearing midnight as SEA QUEST steadily neared the coast of Vanua Lava. Our destination, Waterfall Bay, was clear of offshore dangers. With a full moon and a good working depth sounder, not to speak of our revitalized GPS, we could find our way safely at night.

As Michael checked our bearings, a school of excited dolphin arrived to escort us. How welcome they made us feel!

Miki, roused from her bunk for the landfall, sleepily rubbed her eyes. I handed her the binoculars.

"Look over there," I pointed. In the gloom, she could just make out a spectacular waterfall cascading into the sea. After Miki passed over the binoculars, Michael exclaimed, "Good God! There are three yachts in there already!" He lowered the glasses. "We'll just have to tuck in behind them."

19

Nakamal

Morning found us at anchor in a turquoise cove surrounded by sprawling jungle. Before us Vanua Lava's narrow foreshore gave way to cliffs and valleys misted by rainbows and curtained in vine. There are no roads on this rugged island where the cloud-catching peaks top 3,000 feet.

The entire Vanuatu Archipelago rides the westernmost edge of the 25,000-foot deep New Hebrides Trench where the Indo-Australasian tectonic plate slips beneath the Pacific plate. The land groans and shakes while half a dozen volcanoes continuously erupt. Scattered throughout this volatile archipelago are countless steaming vents and hot springs. The island group stretches 400 miles north to south. Though commonly described as forming the shape of a 'Y', to my eyes the charted islands resemble a crab claw stretching north towards a few scattered tidbits. The tidbits are the remote Banks and Torres Islands.

Vanuatu, formerly known as the New Hebrides, is a land of tremendous physical and cultural diversity. Its islands and people are as multifaceted as nature itself and as untamed. When it became an independent nation in 1980, Vanuatu briefly riveted the world's attention with the savage massacres of the former French colonists, acts of political violence that seemed to echo its wild geography.

Here in quiet Waterfall Bay, with the sun just topping the vine-hung cliffs a man paddled out to greet us, offering fresh-caught river prawns to trade and a guest book wrapped in a plastic bag for us to sign. Kerely was quiet and unassuming. We invited him aboard. He told us that the sprawling newly rebuilt hut, bright with new thatch, near the water's edge was his. The former owner had probably grown rich enough trading with passing yachts to move down to Port Vila, the capital.

I was hunting for a rare shell that was known to inhabit this area—a shell that would be the prize of my *oliva* collection on which I had been working for years—and I wondered if Kerely could help me.

"Will you help us to look for red-lipped olives?" I asked him.

Kerely seemed surprised at my request, but nodded assent.

Later we made an exploratory foray around the bay together. His young boys collected crabs for bait, but they did not seem to coax any gastropods from the sand. Michael eventually caught sight of a single narrow telltale trail 25 feet below him. From it he scooped a perfect specimen of *Oliva rubrolabiata*. It made our day.

The double waterfall, for which the bay is named, drops from its bluff to a deep pool only a stone's throw from the lapping sea.

"Are we going to do the laundry while we are here?" suggested Michael.

"Why not?" I said. "Didn't we sail thousands of miles to find the most perfect waterfall in the world falling at our feet so we could lug our laundry ashore to wash it?"

Kerely's modest little family and Waterfall Bay were so delightful that we forgot about the calendar, filling our days with diving, beachcombing, climbing the trails and cooking up sumptuous food. We three had just come in from snorkeling and were on the poop deck lathering up our hair when a commotion attracted our attention. An American yacht with two Australian brothers on board as crew was anchored near us.

"What's going on?" I yelled over the water. "Did you catch a shark?"

"Yeah," was the reply. They had hung the carcass of a bluefin tuna on a line over the stern just to see what would happen. "Now what do we do? It's caught around the anchor chain."

"Just don't let it get too close to your inflatable dinghy!" Hastily we rinsed the soapsuds from our hair. The three of us jumped into our wooden dinghy to see what we could do to help.

Michael hooked the shark on the gaff to give some slack while the young man attempted to unwind the line from the anchor chain, but when Miki saw the five-foot shark up close she screamed and beat a terrified retreat to the bow of our eight-foot dinghy. Maybe she thought it would jump into the boat. Michael looped a nylon rope around the thrashing tail and cut away the fishing line. As a rule, we do not kill sharks, but this one was already badly injured.

We towed the limp shark into the shore while Kerely, also drawn by the noise, hurried from his house, closely followed by his wife and little children.

"Kerely," I asked for Miki's benefit, "do these sharks eat people?"

"No," Kerely scornfully replied. "They eat fish!"

"But you eat them, yes?"

He was happy to accept the shark for his own dinner.

At dawn a few days later, we rounded past the lighthouse at Million Dollar Point into Luganville, the natural harbor between Espiritu Santo and Aore Island. During World War II the harbor served as an important naval base, but it affords poor anchorage for yachts because it is too deep.

Espiritu Santo is Vanuatu's largest island. In fact when a Spaniard, Pedro Fernandes de Quiros, first discovered it in 1605 he thought he had found the fabled lost Southern Continent! Had he explored further he would have been disappointed to learn that Espiritu Santo was only a 1,800 square mile island—but he never got that chance. It took him only three weeks to thoroughly enrage the natives who became so suspicious of his intentions that they drove him off. Today areas of dense jungle in the interior containing pigmy tribes are reputedly still unexplored and the highest peak on the island has yet to be climbed.

A sweltering heat had replaced dawn's chill when we approached the main wharf. Along the length of the concrete bulkhead a dangerous swell was running. We were unwilling to risk coming alongside, but a uniformed official stepped out and signaled us to go alongside a pilot boat tucked under the far end of the bulkhead. With both the wind and swell on the beam we had to maintain steerageway as we approached.

We were not halfway in when the official shouted, "Stop!" His warning came too late to prevent us ramming the fallen

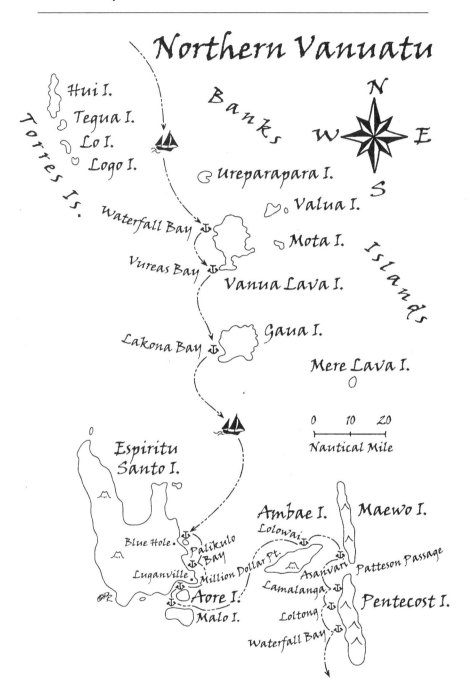

Northern Vanuatu

Hui I.

Tegua I.

Lo I.

Logo I.

Torres Is.

Banks

Islands

Ureparapara I.

Valua I.

Mota I.

Waterfall Bay

Vureas Bay

Vanua Lava I.

Lakona Bay

Gaua I.

Mere Lava I.

N

W

E

S

0   10   20
Nautical Mile

Espiritu
Santo I.

Ambae I.

Maewo I.

Lolowai

Blue Hole

Palikulo
Bay

Luganville

Million Dollar Pt.

Asanvari

Patteson Passage

Lamalanga

Aore I.

Pentecost I.

Malo I.

Loltong

Waterfall Bay

wreckage of the old concrete wharf, invisible underwater. Again we were thankful for our heavy steel keel.

Stepping ashore in Luganville later that day, we realized that we had reentered the "coconut run," the South Pacific playground for cruising yachts we had left nearly five years before. Cruisers were swapping stories over cappuccino and arguing over recommended spots in their cruising guides. Cruising guidebooks are a welcome addition to any seagoing library. However, many assume that the places listed are the only ones worth visiting. Being a trifle contrary, we are inclined to skip some of the better-known anchorages to head instead to coves where unknown adventurous encounters may await us.

There is a brooding, cloud-covered island visible from Luganville that beguiled 100,000 American servicemen stationed there during the war. The native women, sequestered there while their menfolk helped the Allies during the war, were said to be the most beautiful women in Vanuatu. One of those lonely servicemen, young James Michener, wove this fantasy into a novel, *Tales of the South Pacific*, immortalizing Ambae as Bali Hai.

Ambae rises to the 4,500-foot dormant central peak, Vaibindoloua. According to legend the island is volcanically quiet now because the Great God Tangaro removed the worst of Vaibindoloua's fire to Ambrym Island to the south, substituting instead two crater lakes.

Only the northeastern tip of the island offers sheltered anchorage. Lolowai Bay is an old volcanic vent surrounded by cliffs and a narrow beach. The seaward side is marked by a handful of rocky islets and a shallow coral shelf over which boats must pass. We followed the leading marks and, holding our breath, passed over the shallows.

On Sunday morning we rose early and joined other groups walking to church to hear the choir of the Tomisiro Brotherhood. The Brotherhood trains young men to evangelize their Melanesian brothers in the Western Pacific. Youth drawn from as far afield as the Solomon Islands spend three years at the seminary and take vows of poverty, chastity and obedience. But unlike the Catholic Franciscans in the area, these Anglican brothers do not make a lifetime vow. The barefoot Reverend explained. "The church does not have the resources to support the Brothers in their old age. After a few years of service abroad, the men return to their villages, a little wiser and a little worldlier."

The young seminarians, resplendent in white shirt and sarong tied with a broad red sash, sang the service in rich harmonies. It's not all plain sailing at the seminary. Some young aspirants fail to make it through the rigorous training. We witnessed the defrocking of one contrite-looking young fellow who had been repeatedly tempted by the close proximity of a large coed high school. If after several warnings a man continues to err, he is thanked for his efforts, prayed over, and then ceremonially divested of his red sash.

Our next stop was Maewo Island, already crowded with yachts and the square-rigged brigantine SOREN LARSEN with a full complement of 33, mostly paying passengers, to see the special *kastom* dance performance the locals would put on for them.

Ten miles across Patteson Passage south from Maewo lies Pentecost. This island is famous for its skydivers, who hurl themselves from high rickety towers with a jungle vine tied to their feet: the original bungy jumpers. We did not see them. The initiation rites are irregularly scheduled and have become very costly.

We set off to sail along the coast of Pentecost with no plan beyond the need to find more flour to make bread. With binoculars we searched for the tin roof of the co-op we had been told to look for. Anchoring outside a reef that extended well offshore we headed for a small village.

We realized only later how close we had come to causing ourselves no end of trouble and expense. Many places around these traditional villages are taboo. When strangers inadvertently break such taboos, pigs must be purchased and killed for a feast to absolve the error. Fortunately for us, we landed at the beach near women and children lounging in the shade of a spreading breadfruit tree.

The children helped us drag the skiff up the beach.

"What is happening?" we asked one of the women, pointing to a hive of activity around the large traditional meeting-house.

"It is a ceremony for the death of a man."

"Oh! Was he the old man who died at Lolowai?"

"Yes."

"So this must be Lamalanga."

After the service at Lolowai, we had noticed a crowd of keening women on the beach and watched as a coffin was loaded onto a small boat. It seemed an extraordinary coincidence that we now found ourselves here.

We were all invited inside the thatched *nakamal*. Miki and I were cautioned. "See that log over there? You must not sit on it or step over it," the woman said sternly. "Both the log and the beaten circle are *tapu* to women." The log separated the dark interior and a beaten earth circle under the eaves where a few men sat drinking *kava*.

Our eyes took a minute to adjust to the dark interior. Some women were sitting on palm mats scraping and peeling vegetables. Others relaxed on benches of split-bamboo that ran the length of the 100-foot room. A huge earth oven was heaped with stones glowing red. Michael was invited into the *kava*-drinking circle. I started talking with a woman sorting and slicing spinach leaves. She surprised me with her fluent English.

"I am Ruth, the granddaughter of the old man," she said. "It is my job to help with all the food preparation for the mourning period." She paused and chopped a few more spinach leaves, then went on. "For ten days the children of the dead man will provide a feast in his memory—we must prepare much food."

Ruth continued speaking, filling us in with the details. The old man's coffin, she explained, had been discarded on arrival, and then his body had been wrapped in traditional red mats. These valuable mats, about six feet long, are woven from the fibers of the pandanus plant in a laborious process. When ready, they are sent off to one of the artisan clans in the mountain interior: the only clans permitted to do the finish work. There, stencils cut in distinctive patterns denoting the social rank of the wearer are applied to the mats.

More than a hundred relatives had arrived for the funeral, and each had reverently placed red mats over the old man's body. When they had formed a high colorful pile, both body and tribute were gently lowered into the grave.

Michael fell into conversation with Ruth's husband, Ham, who was an important chief and the district representative. He is also the brother of Vanuatu's first Prime Minister, Father Walter Lini, the highly respected political leader who led the new nation out of chaos in 1980. Ham invited us all to walk to his modern concrete house, impressive with tiled floors and a flush toilet.

"We are pleased that you have come," Ham stated. "Yachts never come here."

"We were looking for the Three Hands Co-op so we could buy flour. Otherwise we might not have thought to stop here."

"Stay tonight. You can come to the feast at the *nakamal*."

We felt honored to be included in what was, after all, a family affair.

We headed back to shore at dusk after spraying ourselves with mosquito repellent. Michael was ushered into the *kava*-drinking circle. Miki and I were led into the gloom of the meetinghouse. Shadowy forms, hovering over the huge earth oven, heaved hot stones one by one, onto the bank of ash. I knelt to help the women slide away thick layers of banana leaves to expose steamed cassava, yam and sweet potato. Tucked between them were wrapped packets of fish, pork and lap-lap, a sort of gelatinous pudding made from yams, plantain and kumara.

The food was placed on a bed of freshly gathered leaves. In the soft glow of kerosene lanterns fair portions were allocated to each family. Those waiting quietly socialized. When all the sorting was done, women brought their baskets to be filled.

"You should eat now," Ruth said, handing me a basket.

"Shall I send some food out to Michael?"

"No. The men drink the *kava*."

Miki and I laid out our food on leaves like green paper plates. The earth oven had suffused all the flavors with a pleasant smoky taste. Hungrily we devoured the food.

A woman my age shooed away the children who pressed too

close and introduced herself as Judy. She was formerly a nurse in Port Villa, she said. In her official capacity, she had traveled around the world. Recently separated from her spouse, she had returned with her ten-year-old son to the village of her birth.

"What is it like to be back after so many years?" I asked Judy.

"Things are simple here in one way. In other ways it is more difficult. I got used to doing things my own way in Vila. Here I have many more obligations and I must get along with everyone."

"What sort of obligations do you have?"

"Well, take this affair." She lowered her voice. "I am a sort of cousin. There are two clans, *Tapi-bibred* and *Bule-bibred*. I am *Tapi*. The old man was also *Tapi*, so my family had to give a pig and a lot of food and *kava*."

"Isn't it hard to have extra food and pigs on hand for these unexpected occasions?"

"Yes, we always have to be planting extra and raising pigs."

After a pause I said, "I noticed you have a lot of *tapu* areas around here. *Tapu* areas are mostly forbidden to women. How do you feel about that?"

"It is our custom and comes from the time when men thought women were inferior. We still practice a lot of *kastom* traditions. When men want to become 'big men', they must kill pigs.

"Why do the men strive to become 'big men'?"

"It's for the status, but they have to earn the right by getting wealth."

"You mean by accumulating pigs and mats and food?"

"Yes."

"So, why don't people just raise lots of pigs then?"

"Its not that easy. Our pigs are not very tame. We have to tie them by the foot and feed them. Everyday we must change the rope onto a different foot. The tusks take many years to grow. I'm not sure how long. Maybe five years, or much more to make a circle."

"So all this giving is quite a burden?"

"Well, in a way it is, but it all comes back around. If I hear of a wedding of a distant relative living in the hills, it is my obligation to go there and make a present. But if someone of my family dies there are distant relatives who will help me. We are very supportive of each other."

Outside, in the *kava*-drinking circle, Michael rose clumsily to his feet. He shook his head when I approached.

"I am all right. It's just my legs won't work!"

Two men trailed by fifty amused children supported him down the beach where he was deposited in the dinghy.

Kava is not an alcohol, but a narcotic that numbs the mouth and legs. Today its commercial potential as a tranquilizer has become recognized and the local prices have shot up. Unlike the watery drink that tourists are offered, two coconut shells of full-strength Vanuatu *kava* was all it took to give our big strong Michael double vision and rubbery legs.

For most of our long journey we had either been sailing off-shore under windvane self-steering or the weather had been too rough for Miki to feel fully confident. However along Pentecost's deep shores in a brisk breeze, enlivened with sudden williwaws tumbling from the steep peaks, she had for the first time a perfect opportunity to actually *sail* the boat.

Dropping anchor for the night in Loltong Bay, we found ourselves in a French-speaking port of Vanuatu. Before 1906 the entire archipelago existed as a political no-man's-land. It straddled the British influence in the Solomon Islands to the north and French influence in New Caledonia to the south. The islanders were exploited by traders and preyed upon by black-birders who recruited labor for the Fijian and Australian plantations, often by guile or brute force. Though neither France nor Britain had a strategic interest in acquiring the New Hebrides as a colony, when European settlers began to drift in to establish plantations, neither country wanted the other to have political control. As a result an Anglo-French Condominium was eventually established in which both governments had a say. Jokingly the partnership was referred to as the "Pandemonium." The two governors got along like oil and water. Every public institution in the New Hebrides, from police to hospitals, was duplicated.

Ashore we stocked up on vegetables and watched a lively game of soccer, played without the benefit of shoes. The next morning we went further down the coast to another Waterfall Bay where Chief Isaac and his young grandson met us on the beach. Like a Pied Piper he led us along grassy trails beneath a high canopy of palm through an ancient copra plantation. Behind us SEA QUEST lay framed in a blazing arc of deep sapphire water over brilliant white sand.

Miki, pouting, trailed along behind. We had complained about her choice of clothing. Neither Michael nor I had noticed until we were on the beach that she wore a gauzy, practically transparent dress.

"I wore tights and a mini-skirt in Asanvari. You said nothing."

"But Miki, that was a place where yachts customarily visit. We were part of a large group of foreigners. The natives there charge money for their show and as a result must put up with immodest dress. Here we are on an old man's private farm. We can't please ourselves, but have to show respect."

Unhappy now, with her towel wrapped around her, she shuffled sulkily behind.

The old man led the way up a narrow ravine where two delicate ribbons of water plummeted into pools framed by sandstone boulders. Still fully dressed, Michael and I lost no time diving into the pools, soon shrieking with delight in the refreshing water. Then, from seemingly nowhere, a powerfully-built lad appeared. He stood ankle deep in the water transfixed, staring through poor Miki's flimsy attire. She grew very embarrassed and tried to disappear by cowering neck deep in the chilly water, but of course, when she emerged, the skimpy bikini beneath her gauzy dress was fully visible!

Back at the beach we thanked old Chief Isaac. "Boat, they come everyday," he commented wonderingly. Though he asked for nothing, we gave him some small gifts for his grandchildren. How much longer, I wondered, would his natural generosity hold up in the face of increasing numbers of visitors?

20

Mother of Darkness

Across the channel from Pentecost the clouds over Ambrym lifted to expose the island's entire mountainous flank. A plume of steam rose like a signal from the island's volcano high up on the Ash Plain. "It's only 20 miles to Ambrym from here. Shall we just go?" Michael suggested.

With the wind behind us we scampered across Selwyn Strait to Ranon Bay. Coconut groves swept down to the bay dominated by Mount Vetlam's 3,850-foot peak. We hauled the dinghy up the beach, our feet sinking into coarse black sand that clung tenaciously to our feet, so the three of us looked as though we were wearing dark socks.

A rutted track meandered past a tiny shop or two, locked up now in the late afternoon heat. Half hidden among trees stood thatched houses with black and red woven bamboo walls. The lush foliage stood in such startling contrast to the dark soil that we seemed to have stepped into a differently colored world. We wandered into the grounds of a large school.

A thickset woman, with a child clinging to her hand, approached.

"I am Pamela, a teacher here. Can I show you around?"

With Pamela as guide, we thumbed through notebooks and examined the textbooks, all written in English. Few buildings were constructed of anything more substantial than thatch or furnished with more than a blackboard and a sand floor. Only the library was housed in a cyclone-proof building with a lockable door. Pamela pointed out a large structure without walls, furnished with benches and tables.

"That is the dining room. The school takes in children from the surrounding islands to board here. They grow their own food in the school gardens."

How self-sufficient, I thought.

Pamela's eyes glinted with a hint of mystery, "I will show

you something else if you will take a walk with me." Offering no clue she led us along a coastal track.

"I've heard that Ambrym is known for its black magic," I said as we walked. "Is this really so?"

"Oh yes," she answered. "Only last year a 17-year-old girl at the school was cursed by black magic."

"For what reason?"

Pamela paused, then explained. "Her family in the mountains was involved in a land dispute. The girl at the school got sick and went to hospital, but no one could help her and she died. That is the way. The doctor can't make people well because the spirit is dead—the person dies."

I shuddered inwardly. The same had been the case in the Caribbean where I spent much of my youth. Obeah and voodoo had been commonly practiced there with similar devastating results. The people of Vanuatu call Ambrym the "Mother of Darkness." Even today it remains the Melanesian center for sorcery, witchcraft and other black arts.

Where was Pamela taking us? The late afternoon light gilded the leaves and tree trunks. Then, deep in the shade appeared a cluster of towering totemic heads. *Tam tams!* Slit drums with their bellies split and scooped out to resonate sound, stood almost twice the height of a man. On Ambrym they are still used for pagan ceremonies. The sculpted flat noses and long faces of the stylized heads reminded me of the figures on Easter Island.

On the road again after we had thanked Pamela, a lovely young woman balancing several cabbages in her hands stopped to chat with us. I could not tear my eyes from the cabbages. These were not the faded, tasteless airlifted staples of tropical supermarkets but shiny-green, brimming-with-vitamins, home grown vegetables that only a seriously deprived long-distance cruiser could yearn for!

"Would you like one?" she generously offered.

"Oh, I would love one! But I must give you something. I'm sorry; I have only a few lollipops and balloons." The woman accepted my offerings in good grace.

There was a small Japanese yacht in the bay, the first we had seen out cruising. We stopped by the small 28-foot cutter, YUIGA

Young girl prepared
for festivity powdered
in turmeric, Ifalik

Breadfruit tree canoe under construction. Other pieces will be carefully
shaped and fitted, then laced in with coconut sennit and sealed with
breadfruit sap

Ifalik girls make flower leis
for us on day of festivities

Miki and Lamotrek island girls "posing"

Young women grilling tuna fish liver

Bishop Amando Samos receiving his congregation after mass conversion
to Catholicism

An Ifalik canoe under sail, underway

Young Ifalik girl celebrating her puberty, wearing the traditional "lap-lap", a sarong the islanders weave on back strap looms

Michael happy after a "tuba" coconut beer session

Mortlock Island girls

Tere and Miki overlooking Pohnpei's large harbor

Tere and Michael. Kolonia Harbor in the background

Crossing the equator.
Miki and "Neptune" with
Shellback certificate

Nan Madol, Tere and Miki exploring the main temple

Tere and Michael in Micronesia

Reef Island woman returns from her garden, head laden with casava and spinach

Utupua traditional thatched house

Reef Island women
visiting by canoe

Tikopia girl of Polynesian descent, living among Melanesians of Utupua

Utupua villagers around yachtsman's grave

Michael and Tere at
Waterfall Bay, Vanua
Lava, Vanuatu

Tomisiro Brotherhood at LomoLomo on Ambae

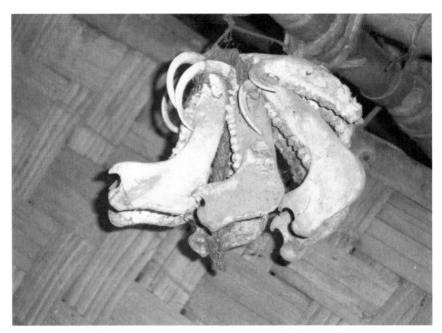

Pig jaws hung in Nakamal to commemorate a "Big Man" ceremony, Pentecost

Interior of Nakamal with women and children sitting on high bamboo benches.

Miki with tam tam slit drums on Ambrym

Michael and Miki relaxing in hot spring in "Butterfly Bay," Ambrym

Baie de Prony, New Caledonia. Red stained sand in foreground

Noumea cottage with mango tree in front garden

SEA QUEST anchored in
Baie du Prony with moon
high in sky

Michael washing clothes in the Carenage stream

Michael about to take down the genoa as the wind strengthens on passage to New Zealand

Michael and Tere on last day of voyage entering port at the Bay of Islands, New Zealand

DOKUSAN, to meet Kaoru and Michiko of Kagoshima. With their four-year-old daughter they had made a great circuit to Alaska, down the North American coast to Mexico, then across the South Pacific to New Zealand. Now they were homeward bound and Miki wanted to compare notes. Over our last precious bottle of sake, we shared sea stories until late in the night.

We left Ranon Bay, still crowded with yachts cowering from an expected northeasterly, to explore what we could of Ambrym's wild coast before the weather changed.

Two active volcanoes, Benbow and Marum, rise from the high Ash Plain. By day they blow cinders; by night they glow like portals to the underworld. The northern and western ends of the island are laid out in coconut plantations but the singed center reveals Ambrym's violent true nature.

This coastline offers a rich study of recent geological time written in layers of ash and lava. The cycle of growth, burning, burial and new growth continues. In 1950 and 1979 this pattern was interrupted by major eruptions that changed the contours of the land, filling in an entire bay. Now there are huge gray ash drifts that are only barely covered in vegetation. Scorched trees and blackened timber protrude like old bones from the eroded shoreline.

We paddled our dinghy into a narrow caldera redolent with sulfur fumes. Sheer walls of weathered black and vermilion rock towered high around us and plunged deep beneath the water. The island held us in its thrall; we were spellbound by its dark magic. We entered a large bay and found ourselves encircled by richly colored cliffs pocked with caves and overhung by bright foliage. The cliffs gave way to a stretch of black sand as brilliantly reflective as a mirror. We dropped the hook close to shore.

A 20-foot-high wall of ash had formed a broad barrier across the beach. Behind it a dry waterfall seemed to offer us a perfect route inland. Finding toe and finger-holds in the twisted black rock, we scrambled up the polished flanks of the cliff. We found ourselves in a towering ravine, a place of enchantment. Lady Ambrym, temptress and Mother of Darkness seemed to be luring us deeper. Studying the alternate layers of heavy boulders and fine rubble, we realized that it was not benign nature that had formed this place, but violent torrents of water. And perhaps not only water, but also abrasive pumice and tuff that had roared down this channel. It was a place of imminent danger.

"Michael, we must watch for flash floods!"

Despite the clear skies I could not shake my sense of uneasiness. Beating a retreat back to the beach we discovered hot water percolating from a cliff face of sculpted stone. We dug ourselves pools in the black sand and lay back languidly soaking up the clean heat. When we were sated we leapt into the cool sea.

"Ah, this is what life is all about," Michael sighed, utterly content.

"Our own private *onsen* bath." remarked Miki.

Butterflies were everywhere. Most assumed somber tones to match the surroundings, but those on the beach were a brilliant lemon hue. We dubbed this unnamed place "Butterfly Beach."

Setting sail again we hugged the coastline to better appreciate the strange landscape. At Baouma Point, a hot water lake had shrunk to the size of a small but delightful pond. Among large rocks we scrubbed our sail-bag full of soiled laundry before rewarding ourselves with yet another long soak. The rising wind grew stronger and now eddied about, chilling us. SEA QUEST tugged hard on her anchor. The promised northeasterly had arrived and it seemed prudent to backtrack a mile or two, where a more protected anchorage could shelter us for the night.

The next morning the winds blustered and smoke filled the sky. Overnight an eruption had spilled a thin stream of lava into the upland valleys igniting the forests. Wisps of wood ash settled on SEA QUEST's decks. The overcast sky, the wind and the flying ashes caused us to feel suddenly lonely and threatened. Fifty-foot ash mounts from an earlier eruption had built ramparts against the sea, out of which dark lava protruded like the twisting tongues of serpents. Yesterday's placid coves were now exposed to breaking surf. As we passed a rugged cove, people ran shouting from huts perched high on the beach waving for us to stop, and we would have done so, had the weather been less forbidding.

208

We pushed on around Dip Point at the western end against strong tidal currents and found shelter at Craig Cove, the site of a Catholic mission and airstrip. But it was scarcely more comfortable than at sea. The heavy swell rolled SEA QUEST from gunwale to gunwale.

Ashore stood a village of large bamboo huts shaded by trees. Behind the bay, 1,230-foot Minnei Peak promised to be a good platform from which to view the interior. We resolved to climb it the next day.

People who want a close up view of Ambrym volcanoes usually pay a substantial sum to be bounced in the back of a truck for two hours from Ranon Bay to a point where they may hike for four more hours to the edge of the Ash Plain. We never seriously considered abusing ourselves like that. People on the beach informed us that Minnei Peak was only "a forty-five minute walk, if you walk fast, and one hour if you go slow." Along the way we rested or fell into conversation with native people tending their mountain gardens. Marie-Willi, a French-speaking 18-year-old, detached herself from a group to be our guide. She was a good-looking, tall girl with frizzy hair bunched into two neatly folded plaits near her temples. Her working clothes consisted of a pair of loose baggy drawers and a long shirt with torn armholes that exposed her black bra. She seemed ashamed of her clothes because all the time we were together she clutched to her bosom a shirt borrowed from her brother that flopped in front like an apron.

"Do you come here everyday?"

"*Oui*. We come every day to the gardens. Every day but Sunday."

Still panting from the long and steady climb, I felt my lungs straining. "Ah, *vous êtes très* energetic!"

The thick bush gave way at last to a grassy summit surmounted by a radio tower and solar panels standing in neat rows. Far below us SEA QUEST had shrunk to the size of a toy. We looked inland across the rumpled valleys to the distant Ash Plain, but smoke from the burning forests obscured the uplands. The erupting volcano was hidden in cloud.

Back on the boat that evening, we listened to the forecast. Strong winds were expected to rise to 30 knots with gusts to 45.

Despite being miserable on a boat still rolling in the heavy swell we took an extra day to recover from our climb before heading out along the southwest coast to Port Vato's wide and shallow bay. We had hoped for a peaceful night under the shelter of the eastern arm, but instead rocked torturously. Despite this the bay did make a splendid vantage point from which to witness the glow of the volcano after darkness fell.

At 5:00 AM the next morning the crew of a coastal trading ship hailed us with a cheery shout, rousing us from our bunks. Groggy still from our restless night we did not even attempt breakfast but lost no time in hauling up the anchor and bidding farewell to the strange charms of Ambrym, "The Mother of Darkness."

21

The Central Vanuatu Islands

Most yachtsmen anchored in Laman Bay were still sitting over breakfast when we rounded up smartly and dropped sail. Offshore more than a mile from the crescent bay on Epi lies a palm-covered islet. From there the villagers paddled their canoes each morning against the wind to work their gardens on the main island. In the afternoon, when they returned from work, they held aloft a palm frond and let the wind push them home.

Laman Bay is a splendid anchorage when tradewind breezes blow from north to southeast, but we knew from bitter experience to beware of southwesterlies. We had been caught here one dark stormy night, as the wind howled and the surf rose up in the shallow bay. Unable to escape because of dangerous overfalls just outside, we were forced to ride the rollers until dawn.

Today in dazzling sunshine, surrounded by a score of anchored cruising yachts, the bay looked deceptively serene. Laman Bay is home to a large school, a scattering of huts and *two* bread shops. Peace Corps volunteers help the resident students not only with their conventional studies, but also teach them about hygiene, animal husbandry, land and building maintenance. We headed ashore where Michael engaged in cheerful banter with local women as they exchanged papayas for sweets and we returned to the boat with hot loaves for lunch.

We set off down Epi's pretty coast to explore anchorages not mentioned in the cruising guide. Just a couple of hours to the south we discovered coral-free Revolieu Bay. Cattle fences barred our way along the beach but the chatter of voices led us to children perched high up in a tree tossing down oranges, amid giggles and laughter. When we appeared suddenly they screamed excitedly and rallied around us. Alerted by the clamor, their father emerged from a nearby hut. I offered him a kilo of rice I had brought along just in case, and he gave us all the oranges we could carry, along with tomatoes and several magnificent lettuces from his well-tended vegetable plot.

But in Vanuatu, lettuce can kill! Vanuatu is host to a small snail whose slime carries a deadly toxin. Miki mixed up a weak solution of potassium permanganate kept for the occasion, and carefully washed each lettuce leaf before we dared to eat it.

As dawn broke the next day, Michael and I donned wetsuits to continue our hunt for *oliva*. A large crab, weighted with lead, attracted some exceptionally dark *tremulina oldi* from beneath the black sand. Elated by our finds, we headed back to join Miki for breakfast.

When the breakfast dishes were cleared, we hiked up the dry riverbed carved through a heavily wooded hilly interior with wild spires of volcanic debris. We found the gully to be sprinkled with large pink land snails, undoubtedly introduced by a French gastronome and killed by the prolonged drought. Here and there garden plots had been hacked from the bush. Then the bed narrowed to a rocky defile, along which we picked our way over polished flintstone boulders while listening to the birdsong and studying the flora. Two miles inland, our way was blocked by fallen stone and we had to turn back.

That night torrential rain fell in solid sheets, as only tropical rain can do. After months of drought it was a washout.

"Tere, look!"

I climbed on deck to see what Michael was excited about. SEA QUEST was floating in a pond of brown muddy water. Ravaged crops torn from the garden plots along the riverbed, where we had walked only the day before, drifted in the tide.

Continuing along the coast, we noticed a wide break in the coral fringe. We picked our way in carefully to investigate. People stared at us from the cover of the foreshore bush. When we came ashore they seemed confused and stepped back into the shadows. Then a very pretty woman appeared; an ex-police officer from Port Vila as it turned out. She introduced herself as Jennifer.

"There has never been a yacht coming here before," she said by way of explanation for the odd behavior.

We were amazed. The white sand beach overhung with shade trees faced a lovely island just offshore.

212

"What is the name of this settlement?" Michael asked.

"Tomali Bay."

We were led to a compound with new thatch huts and communal working and eating places decorated with potted plants. These villagers had returned to Epi to farm what had originally been their family's *kastom* land, sold to settlers a hundred years ago. White planters abandoned their copra plantations in the 1940s when the price of copra took a dive and war began in the Pacific. But it was only in the late 1970s, just before independence, that the government of the day sought out *ni-Vanuatu* claimants and registered their title to the old *kastom* land.

Jennifer remarked, "It's interesting that you stopped by because we are looking for an investor who will build a resort on our island."

The possibility that the government would build an airport nearby made the idea attractive. Yet Vanuatu was a risky place to invest. As they themselves had told us, "Everything in Vila is politics." It was because of politics that their land had been restored to them, but it was also due to politics that Jennifer, whose people were now on the out, had lost her good job. Expatriates have even less protection from politicians' capricious dictates than do *ni-Vanuatu* people. The six-month business license a foreigner requires may, without notice, not be renewed. A lapsed license results in the *automatic* cancellation of the working visa. Without this vital document, business owners are obliged to leave the country immediately.

We were entering the Shepherd Group, an area intriguingly labeled on our chart as *volcanically active with possible major seabed changes*. From afar the steep volcanic islands and islets southeast of Epi are beguiling. Close by, they are challenging. Tongoa, the largest island of the group, is formed from several volcanic cones. Its coast is built from twisted layers of lava covered by jungle. Cliffs plunge to the sea. Rocks tumble in the surf. There are no sheltered bays. The smaller islets are too deep for anchoring.

Old stories tell of a time when violent eruptions and earthquakes ravaged the land, causing it to break apart and sink beneath the sea. A legendary chief led the survivors to find refuge on Tongoa. It is now known that in the fifteenth century the

213

Shepherd Group was part of a large island known as Kuwae. The legends passed down in tales and songs have proved to be exceedingly accurate. Stories that until recently Europeans thought to be mere myth were confirmed as fact when archeologists opened the grave of the leader and found the exact number of buried wives and pig tusks enumerated.

At Lamboukouti Bay on Tongoa, the high island funneled wind into the anchorage, causing SEA QUEST to roll heavily. We rode the surf to shore and then sauntered up the wide beach where local lads were playing an evening game of soccer, and girls played volleyball. A slender young man held out his hand in friendly greeting.

"I am visiting from France," he announced in a charming mixture of French and Bislama. "I was born here, but have not been back for almost 20 years. My mother is from the island."

Indeed she was. A stout, smiling woman dressed in a lace-and-ribbon bedecked muumuu waved and called out to us proudly as she strode up the hill after him, *"C'est mon fils."* She was a dark-skinned Melanesian. He sported a handsome Gaelic nose, skin the color of *café-au-lait* and a mop of blond frizzy hair. He continued, "My father worked here as a volunteer teacher. After I was born, he took us back to France."

He offered to show us around so I inquired, "Is there any bread for sale?"

He pointed to a small dark shed made entirely of corrugated iron with a single locked door. Sacks of copra, obviously the currency of the island, were piled under the eaves. "It is closed." Tongoa's main village is in the interior, he told us. "And we have a Japanese aid worker up there you might like to meet," he said glancing at Miki.

But we were too nervous to stay long, with SEA QUEST in the uncomfortable anchorage. Another villager told us of a bay that was "safe for cargo boats in cyclones" on the south side of Epi, eight miles away. We decided to look for it.

The sail took us through the active volcanic area. Disturbingly, we failed to find one of the charted islets. Had it simply vanished? The thought of the earth giving a great hiccup as we sailed past, swallowing us up like the islet was disturbing. Although we sailed miles we were unable to locate the safe bay.

So we beat back to shelter again under Tongoa, this time below Motomwalau Point. All night inter-island cargo vessels came and went hauling their passengers and cargo through the beach surf.

The dull overcast and squalls cleared, giving us a fresh blue sky and light breezes. Relieved, we carried on with our plan to visit other islands of the Shepherd Group. Just south of Tongoa is tiny Ewase Island. A towering remnant perhaps of the drowned land of Kuwae, it rears almost a thousand feet from the sea.

Michael gunned the outboard as we approached the beach, then shut it down to surf in to shore. Too late he realized that the slope was exceptionally steep and paved with round stones the size of our heads! The dinghy, in the grip of the wave, made its final plunge grating savagely on the rocks. We leapt quickly out and dragged the skiff just ahead of the next breaker.

Once safely ashore, we gazed around in wonder. Narrow streams of cooled magma cut through the eroded cliffs that soared above our heads. Recent rock falls had left craters in the soft sand. This was not a place to linger. Our desire to dive had been swept aside by the sheer violence of the place: the blustery wind, thundering surf and dark sediments swirling in the sea had quickly cooled our enthusiasm. SEA QUEST, heaving heavily at anchor so far off shore, seemed exceptionally alone and vulnerable. After a brief hike along the beach we collected driftwood logs. The surf crashing on the boulders meant that our exit from the beach would be a tricky maneuver. We made a ramp over the boulders with the driftwood to slide the dinghy close to the surf. Miki and I, at the ready, waited, timing the breaking waves until Michael yelled, "Now!"

We heaved the boat forward and stood with the churning water up around our waists for a moment before Michael yelled for us to leap into the boat. Then, with a heavy shove he sent the skiff scooting into the deeper water. Anxiously I held my breath, but with only one pull the outboard sprang to life and we nosed successfully over the next foaming breaker.

The buffeting wind seemed to ease a bit after we returned to the boat. We lay on deck, consumed with lethargy after the anxious moments ashore. "What do you think about staying here overnight?" Michael asked.

I hesitated. "What options do we have? Go five miles across to Bouninga Island where it may be too deep to anchor and, even if we can, we might not have better protection than here?"

"Yeah," agreed Michael. "Or we can sail 15 miles in a direction we don't want to go."

"The weather doesn't look too bad. Maybe the wind will die off in the evening like it did last night. We can make a decision after we've heard the weather report."

The weather promised to be fair. Reassured, we decided to stay put. But by the time the dinner dishes were out of the way the wind was beating in the rigging and SEA QUEST was pitching violently. The surf roared threateningly a quarter mile off our stern. Should our anchor give way, only a quick reaction would keep us off that lethal beach. The night distorts the senses and things usually seem worse than they are. We tried not to overreact, but nonetheless we disliked the situation. Michael stayed in the cockpit and slept only fitfully. At 3:00 AM, I climbed from my bunk and pulled on my clothes. Michael was staring morosely into the dark as I came on deck.

"Shall we just get the hell out of here?" I suggested.

As though to punctuate my concern, another gust heeled the boat over sharply and sent the windspeed indicator needle flying. Without waiting for an answer, I dashed below to check that the cupboards were secure, then returned to watch the wind gauge.

Even Miki was roused by the fury, arriving on deck fully dressed. "What we do?"

"We are thinking of getting out of here," I replied.

"I make cocoa or coffee?"

"That would be nice!"

By the time the cocoa was made and Michael's course calculations finished, the squall had passed and the sky had cleared enough for the stars to poke out again.

At 5:15 AM we hauled up the anchor and moved away from the threatening shore. To our astonishment, the gusting wind settled immediately into a light breeze. The mountain had fooled us. It alone was responsible for our nightlong misery. Relieved now of our anxiety and on an easy beam reach, we laid a course towards Efate. Clear skies and the brilliant bright sea gave no hint of the drama of the night.

The volcanic peaks of Makoura and Mataso islands rose from the sea ahead. Mataso rises 1,620 feet from sea level but plunges another 2,300 feet to the ocean floor. More volcanic peaks high enough to snag clouds lie near Efate's northern shore. Little Pele Island stands between Ngouna and Efate; it was under her lee that we sought shelter. To avoid numerous coral patches as we entered Undine Bay we hugged Ngouna's southern shore, keeping a sharp lookout. Beaches of white sand backed by lush coconut trees reflected deep green into the bright, inviting shallows. We felt a sense of relief when our anchor dug into the sandy bottom and SEA QUEST lazily tugged at her chain.

Michael set to work to fix our kerosene stove that had been acting up. Then we went to explore the village on Ngouna Island. School had just been let out so fifty overexcited children welcomed us. Fortunately an authoritative teenager arrived followed by a schoolteacher to shoo most of them home.

It was on this island 140 years ago that John Renton, a Scot, was ambushed and eaten by natives. They had become angered by the relentless forays of blackbirders and did not realize that he was there only to protect their interests. As a government inspector, Renton accompanied ships on their way to recruit native labor for Australian sugar plantations. His background was remarkable. As a young lad he had been shipwrecked in the Solomon Islands and kept by a cannibal chief as a pet. He soon realized that to stay alive he had better adopt the ways of his captors. In due course he was initiated as a headhunter and tattooed all over. He married the chief's daughter, fathered a child who died, and finally, seven years later, escaped on a British trading vessel. He wrote a book about his captivity, *The White Headhunter.*

So pleased were we to be in a secure anchorage again that we made no move for several days to depart. Instead we used our time to touch-up the numerous "canoe bites" and other bruises that marred SEA QUEST's painted topsides. Michael cleaned the engine room. Miki and I worked on the letters we planned to mail in Port Vila. Afternoons were kept free to snorkel on the surrounding reefs. But we could not linger indefinitely.

Unlike the volcanic islands to the north, the island that contains the capital, Port Vila, is made entirely of limestone. Efate is characterized by a distinctive stepped profile created by a series of cataclysmic upheavals. Moso Island, just offshore, has cliffs honeycombed with caves and scores of white sand beaches. The land generally drops into deep water but shoals of reef may surprise the unwary. Several hours after leaving Undine Bay we dropped anchor to dive in a bay unnamed on our chart.

We were still exploring the bay's rich diversity when dolphins approached us curiously but proved too shy to make more than a few tentative forays near us. Believing that a larger bay further down the coast might be safer for the night, we continued another five miles to a place we nicknamed "Bombie Bay."

The sun was so low when we arrived that we could discern no color changes in the water, which made the task of anchoring exceedingly difficult. Several times we dropped the anchor only to have it drag over the scoured limestone seabed and then we would swing over yet another previously unseen bombie, an isolated coral head rising from deep water. After four tries the anchor caught in a fissure and there we stayed.

The next morning we took advantage of a rare opportunity to enjoy a real downwind sail. Wing and wing we rode the northerly breeze to Toukoutouk Bay. In the old days sailing ships waited here for favorable winds before attempting to weather Devil's Point to enter Port Vila. Surrounded by cattle farms, we spent a peaceful night.

Port Vila, with a line of yachts moored Mediterranean style along the waterfront, nestles behind the pretty resort island of Uririki. Yachts swung at moorings in the inner bay. Near a big yellow quarantine buoy, the newly arrived lay at anchor awaiting the Customs and Immigration officers.

Port Vila is a mixture of French charm overlaid by British efficiency. It is a civilized outpost of about 14,000 people. Two thousand European and Vietnamese expatriates live here alongside the indigenous Vanuatu people. Duty free shops and boutiques, craft stores and banks jostle one another along a main road thronged by sunburned, scantily clad tourists. Though we had been satisfyingly self-contained in the outer islands, now sitting in a shaded courtyard with a steaming cappuccino in hand and anticipating a Camembert-filled croissant, we were not immune to the sheer luxury of life in a town.

At the Post Office, with its façade dominated by a colorful mural, we called at the *Poste Restante* window. "We have only one letter for you," said the young man with a dismissive shrug.

"Only one?" We insisted that he go back to the stacks and search some more. So long did we wait that we became convinced he had taken off on a lunch break. When he finally did return however, he bore several manila envelopes and a rueful smile that said, "It's not my fault!"

In a downtown supermarket stocked with French cheeses and fine wines, we bought locally grown beef for a long anticipated steak dinner. Miki, as independent as ever whenever we were in port, set off to do the town alone. Michael and I selected a different coffee shop each day where we could sit and watch a fascinating stream of people pass by. Although sunburned cruise ship passengers dominated the sidewalk scene, *ni-Vanuatu* women in beribboned muumuus added welcome splashes of color while the deeply tanned and smartly dressed expatriates, who sat near us, spoke French. We also met other yachtsmen in town burdened by heavy bags of groceries, happy to stop for a yarn.

In the early evening on the Waterfront Restaurant's lawn we exchanged news with sailors who had until now only been known to us as a voice on the radio. "Where have you cruised? Where will you be going during the cyclone season?" we asked them.

The season was drawing to a close. The harbor was now full of yachts poised to sail to New Caledonia and then west to Australia or south to New Zealand. We hoped to stop at Tanna, one of the most southerly of the Vanuatu Islands. It has always been a difficult place to visit legally and in recent years the officials have become even stricter. Yachts have been fined thousands for breaking the rules. You cannot normally complete the clearance papers required for leaving Vanuatu at Tanna. Instead yachts must return to Port Vila 125 miles to windward.

A notice pinned to the yacht club bulletin board read: *"Boats wanting to clear out from Tanna, write your name here."*

If enough yachts joined up, all could share the cost of flying a Customs/Immigration officer to the island to clear us en masse on October 20, a date that suited us perfectly. We added SEA QUEST's name.

That gave us three weeks with time to spare for visits to both Erromango and Tanna. We still had to complete the cat's papers so that she would be allowed into New Zealand. The

Kiwi veterinarian seemed surprised at our arrival, and complimentary about all we had done towards performing the necessary tasks. The results of Mizzen's rabies tests had been sent to New Zealand's Ministry of Agriculture and then forwarded to us in Port Vila. In less than five minutes he had signed the official paper.

Just days before arriving in Vila, a fatigued flexible section of the generator exhaust pipe had fractured and our engine room filled with greasy black smoke. Michael had temporarily mended the hole with our handy standby, Bostik's Blu-tack, a material designed for attaching posters to walls that had proved invaluable on the boat. It seemed to be unaffected by heat, fuel oil, or moisture. We had a length of flex-pipe among the spares under the bunk. Michael took the whole assembly to town to be welded. After re-installing it, he ran the engine to bring the freezer down to its normal icy temperature. The following day Michael scrubbed clean the sooty bulkheads in the engine room. But when all was sparkling, he cranked up the generator only to find that more black smoke billowed out. He was fit to be tied! The welding shop was now too busy to rush. The frozen food became squishy, and the skipper grew irritable. But when the re-repaired part was at last ready, it did the trick.

While roaming around, Miki had struck up a friendship with the manager of a local charter-boat company who generously invited all of us to her home for Sunday lunch with her family. Veruja was a professional who had turned away from traditional ways. Both assertive and articulate, she felt confident enough even in the presence of her banker husband to voice her opinion. Their two-storied house was comfortable. A shiny four-wheel drive truck sat at the curb. A relative, who acted as housemaid, looked after their three children. Veruja and her husband are representative of Vanuatu's new bourgeoisie.

Although *ni-Vanuatu* drawn by imagined opportunity flock in the hundreds from the outlying islands to Port Vila, most of them lack the necessary education to reach the hoped-for prosperity. Between traditional culture and the new commercial reality, there exists a hard-to-bridge gap. The shantytowns grow alarmingly. Only a fortunate few complete more than a couple of years of elementary school and girls are at a significant disadvantage. In a country committed to a trilingual school system, secondary education is exceptionally expensive. Parents must contribute heavily, a task well beyond the reach of most.

During a drive around the island, we had met an expatriate New Zealand couple who invited us for afternoon tea. She taught at an elementary school. "It's heaven teaching here. I never want to teach in New Zealand again!" she exclaimed.

"Why? What makes teaching here so great?" I asked.

"The kids are motivated," she responded. "There is so much competition for scarce places in the upper schools that they really want to learn. I don't have to deal with the behavioral problems I had at home."

The population growth remains high in Vanuatu and is expected to double to nearly 400,000 in the next 25 years. With bride price still exchanged at marriages, women are expected to pay back the family's investment by producing an average of seven children! Only the most sophisticated resist producing such large families.

As the time to leave Port Vila approached, we bought market vegetables and good local meat. Then we moved to the fuel dock to load diesel, the first refill since leaving Pohnpei in July. After Miki and I had scrubbed every inch of deck with a brush and detergent, it gleamed like it had not done for months. Taking advantage of the generous fresh water supply, we took turns shampooing our hair. It was late in the afternoon before we finally cast off the lines and motored far enough out from Port Vila so that we could lay a clear course towards Erromango, 70 miles to the south.

22

Children of Light

Morning brought us to Dillon Bay where we dropped anchor. We stayed aboard to make repairs to the dinghy, more seriously damaged by our wild ride through the surf onto the boulders at Ewase that we had at first realized. Michael powered up the tools and sanded the dinghy bottom down to bare wood, then applied fiberglass reinforcing. Coming on deck to help, I found the entire foredeck dusted with dark blue paint chips. The virtuous effects of yesterday's scrubbing had just been eliminated.

The William's River lets out into a cove over a boulder-strewn beach. The river's name is all that is left from one of the many Protestant missionaries killed and eaten here in the early nineteenth century. Erromango was so unkind to its missionaries that it quickly earned the name Martyr's Island. The missionaries would have saved themselves a lot of unnecessary agony had they heeded Captain Cook's prophetic words recorded in his log in 1774: "No one would ever venture to introduce Christianity into Erromango because neither fame nor profit would offer the requisite inducements."

However hostile the locals, the Europeans of the day, at great risk to their lives, were fatally drawn by the search for the precious and aromatic sandalwood. After Fiji's forests were depleted it was the Irish trader Peter Dillon who first managed to exploit Erromango's rich forest stands. The "rascals" who followed brought smallpox, influenza, and whooping cough that killed much of the local population. When in a few years time the sandalwood was gone, the traders took to blackbirding raids to keep their vessels in cargo.

With the new paint barely dry the next day, we motored up William's River until shoals of rock barred our way. Women and children washed clothes in the fast moving stream. The island had few roads and only a handful of vehicles. We hiked a steep track. From a heavily wooded valley far below roared busy chainsaws. Today government grants are funding local labor to replant sandalwood for the future.

Later we walked through a village, shaded by a canopy of spreading banyan trees, past dilapidated houses of woven split bamboo or corrugated iron. Near the river mouth stood a whitewashed church, testimony to the eventual success of the missionaries. A trading store was painted in red and blue vertical stripes. Next to it, a tiny concrete block edifice had a sign nailed to the eaves that read, "National Bank of Vanuatu." But its window was boarded, the tin door locked.

Two bone thin dogs scratched at fleas and then lolled listlessly in the dirt. Girls sat gazing towards the river. Miki amused herself and several children by stringing frangipani flowers on

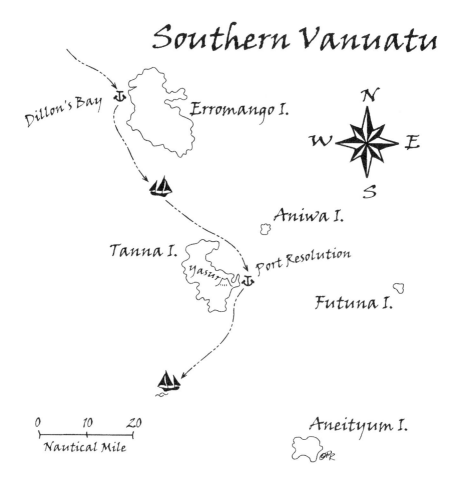

coconut fiber. An old woman stoked a fire beneath a raised oven in preparation for baking bread. Silence settled like a shroud, the jungle sounds crept closer, flies buzzed.

I joined the shy girls on their bench. They told me they were of marriageable age and were just waiting. "When a young man from another village is ready he will visit and pick one of us for a wife. His parents will arrange the bride price," they explained. Though the couple will scarcely know one another, marriages here generally thrive as everyone has been raised under the same traditional laws.

Not all are so lucky though. I later spoke to a very pretty girl. She already had a baby but was not yet married. In the villages illegitimate children are generally treated as equals to legitimate siblings and share in the inheritance of land. However, this girl, having become a mother so young, now had adult responsibilities thrust upon her. She was expected to work, not idle away her time with the other 18-year-olds. Today she helped her mother load dozens of loaves into a hot oven, while her young brother kept an eye on the baby.

Tanna lay 50 miles southeast of Erromango. At 5:00 AM we got underway. With no offshore reefs to worry about we hugged the coast and watched the scenery until the blazing sun poked over the rim of the island, blinding us. On the horizon Tanna floated like a pale shadow while Erromango sank slowly in our wake. For 11 hours we motorsailed. With binoculars we picked out the dark ash crater of Mount Yasur, Tanna's active volcano standing in stark contrast to the green of the surrounding hills. Steam vapors rose from its summit. Around us red ash dusted the limpid water flowing under SEA QUEST's prow and the depths were filled with tiny scintillating flecks.

Captain James Cook named Port Resolution, on the eastern tip of Tanna, after his ship when he discovered the island in 1774. The title seems a little grand for a bay so shallow that yachts may penetrate only about halfway. Yet it is a wonderful haven. The villagers have made visitors their business, creating the Nipikinamu Yacht Club, a pretty collection of round grass guest huts and a dining area overlooking an emerald bay.

The western headland of Port Resolution is composed of dramatic layers of eroded red and black volcanic ash. Where the

225

tides lap its walls, scalding water pours from steaming fissures. The villagers use the spouting hot water to launder their clothes and cook their food.

After trading for several crayfish, too large to fit into any of SEA QUEST's pots, I asked the young trader to show me where I might cook them. "Come," he said, climbing into our dinghy, which he directed across the bay to a tumble of wave-washed rocks. "But be careful. Don't slip," he warned. "This water is very hot!"

Steaming water gushed from the crevice where he placed the freshly woven palm leaf basket he had made for the crayfish. They rapidly reddened. A few minutes later he lifted the basket and announced, "They are done!"

One pitch-black night when any stirring of the water set alight countless phosphorescent plankton to shine like miniature galaxies, we left SEA QUEST to head ashore. Atop the bluff where the yacht club stood there was not a single electric light but spread below in the bay the dozen or so gently swaying masthead lights created a splendid tapestry. We had come ashore to join others for an overland ride to the "Cargo Cult" village of Jon Frum. We made ourselves as comfortable as possible on the steel floor of a Toyota truck. Though we were strangers to most of our fellow passengers, it would not be for long as we bounced in intimate proximity, while the vehicle twisted and wound through the hills. "It's a short ride, maybe fifteen or twenty minutes," we had been told.

Fireflies glowed. Tall tree ferns framing the night sky over our heads were eerily lit by the back-glow of headlights. Large fig trees towering 100 feet above us flashed past.

Emerging from lush forests to the ashy skirts of Yasur, the fire-mountain, we drove along the crumbling edge of a wide and shallow lake that shone in the night like dull silver. The truck slued and tipped. White-knuckled we gripped the sides. The wheels spun loose. The driver stopped dead; then cautiously moved forward. The wheels caught and slowly we clawed our way from the soft ash. Soon we were again jolting along rutted tracks. All conversation ceased: we concentrated on bracing ourselves against the chaffing bumps. Glancing at my watch I saw that a full hour had passed.

The truck slowed to a stop. Dust covered and stiff, we climbed down. Wide-eyed children, wrapped against the chill in layers of printed cloth, shyly held out their hands for us to shake. "Hello, hello," we greeted them, grasping each tiny brown hand in turn.

In the distance voices raised in song could be heard. Today was Friday, the start of the Jon Frum Sabbath. The villagers celebrate their holy day by gathering from dusk to dawn to worship with song and dance. In the open-sided meetinghouse men with guitars huddled, tuning their strings. Sitting in a close circle near them were village women, their calico shawls pulled tight. We were led to high uncomfortable bamboo benches. Outside, in a large dirt rectangle, stood a group of village women and girls wearing intricately dyed grass skirts and T-shirts.

With their visitors settled, the Jon Frum congregation resumed its singing and dancing. After an hour perched upon the bamboo seat, I got up to stretch. Michael joined me. Watching and listening I swayed gently to the music. All the participants seemed mesmerized. Sedately the women took three swaying steps forward, three retreating steps backward. That was all. A group of pre-adolescent boys flailed energetically but in a mechanical sort of way, endlessly repeating the same movements until their eyes lost their focus. Beyond the dancers reared the massive, almost menacing form of the glowering volcano, Mount Yasur.

A man suddenly appeared by our side. His face was narrow, crowned with thick black hair, his chin embellished by a thin beard. His eyes, dark fathomless pools in the night, were the most arresting. Impaled in his unruly frizz was a single sharp stick. He somewhat resembled a narwhal. As I stepped back a pace to avoid the pointed stick that threatened my face he bent forward close to me.

He said, "I am Royal. You are welcome to dance. Women dance at the back. Men dance at the front."

Realizing he was making an oblique reference to my body's gentle swaying to the rhythm of the music, I replied, "Is it OK to just stand here?"

He stepped closer, the stick again jabbing forward. "Oh, yes. That's OK."

With another quick step to safety I asked, "Can you tell us what this is all about?"

"Now they are singing in English," he said. "Can you understand?"

I could just make out the words, *Thy kingdom come, Thy will be done . . .*

"They are singing the Lord's Prayer?"

"Yes."

"But why do they use Christian themes if Jon Frum was anti-Christian?" Michael interjected.

"Jon Frum was not anti-Christian. The Christian missionaries were anti-Jon Frum!"

"The people are praising Jon Frum," he went on. "He brought the teaching. All the songs are about Jon Frum."

"What *was* Jon Frum then?"

"He was a Spirit-Man, not like you and me. He came to give a message that the people should not turn their backs on *kastom*—their dance, their songs, *kava* drinking and all the other things that the missionaries wanted them to give up. Jon Frum told the people that Christianity was all right, but it must not replace their own traditions."

Adherents of the Jon Frum religion, like other Cargo Cult religions of the Pacific, believe that all their needs will be met by the unseen forces of the supernatural. Jon Frum's early prophecies said that the struggle for European money was no longer necessary: In the early 1940s the cult gained notoriety when its members squandered all their money or just threw it away. At that time the big silver birds were dropping the supplies of war, like gifts from heaven. Perhaps Jon Frum was right. Why go out and labor manually, when visitors will now *pay* to view the normal weekly worship?

The music ceased abruptly. The singers and musicians filed from the shed, men by one exit, women by another, joining the now motionless grass-skirted dancers. In unison the group turned to face the slopes of the dark volcano rising before them like a monstrous sacrificial stone. In voices so low that I could not at first distinguish them, musical cadences rose and fell monotonously, then rose again. The fiery crater, quiet before, now began to glow brightly until it cast its wild and livid effulgence into the murky vapor above. The earth beneath our feet trembled violently. Then the mountain slowly darkened again. The group shuffled back single file to resume their guitar playing, singing and dancing.

"Does Jon Frum have something to do with the mountain?" I asked Royal.

He bent and whispered so close I could smell his heavy breath. "Yes. He came from the mountain and although we cannot see them, there are others like him there, other Spirit-Men."

Later on the long trip back to Port Resolution in the back of the bouncing truck, I kept thinking about what Royal had said. The concept that spirits exist in the high-energy center of the crater fascinated me. Moses, Jesus Christ, and Mohammed all experienced revelations on a mountain where God's voice emanated from a burning bush or the like. Is it not highly appropriate for each religion to have its own prophets? Why should we arrogantly dismiss the spiritual beliefs of a primitive people? When analyzed, are our own any less ridiculous? Most of our beliefs evolved in a time when we too were rather simple. It is easy to forget that blind adherence to the idea of a devil personified as Lucifer and Christian notions of angels and heaven after death, are, from the point of view of science and logic, just as irrational as believing a Spirit-Man lives in the mountain!

"What a waste of time," one of the yachtsmen who shared our long ride home grumbled. The Jon Frum village had not put on the polished floorshow he and many others expected. The ceremony was, after all, only the weekly reaffirmation of their faith.

A dugong lived in Port Resolution and late one afternoon we set out to find him. In the area where he was known to swim we cut the outboard engine and drifted. Just moments later his strangely padded head surfaced close-by for a long look at us. We slipped into the water. Michael and I were a little uncertain at first about swimming with such a large creature, and Miki, although she had very much wanted to come, kept moaning aloud.

"Shhhh . . ." said Michael, holding a figure to his lips, "not so much noise."

Water magnifies. The dugong, only a dozen feet away, seemed alarmingly large. Dugongs are mostly harmless. His head resembled a stuffed-stocking granny doll, bumpy and square, as though inexpertly made from lumps of kapok. A pendulous nose and small myopic eyes in the side of his head gave him quite a comical look. The eight-foot long body was perhaps three times heavier than that of an average man. He looked like an elephant, I thought. My guess was truer than I had imagined. Dugongs and elephants are distantly related.

So that the dugong would not fear us, I swam a little way from the sheltering dinghy, tentatively, reaching out a hand. He studied me, considering the wisdom of trusting, then moved a little closer. I ran my hand over his head, and then gently along the length of his pale gray body, sparsely covered with bristly hairs as sharp as baby barnacles. Gaining confidence, he circled and drew closer to Michael, who also ran his hands along the body but as the dugong turned away Michael clung playfully to the tip of his tail to let the animal pull him along.

The dugong returned and teased us. He turned belly side up and tried to embrace me with his stubby fore-flippers. I wriggled from his grip but he clutched my fins. How strange it was to swim with such a beast.

Then Michael made a mistake. He dove underwater towards the dugong. Did the dugong, with his poor eyesight, think Michael was an attacking competitor? It reacted swiftly, ramming his head into Michael's chest. In a welter of spray, Michael was catapulted to the surface, gasping. Only with a strong sideways thrust did he manage to push clear of the dugong's head to swiftly return to the shelter of the dinghy.

Dugongs are mammals and loyal mates. The females nurse their young, holding them in their flippers. They graze like cows on sea grass in sheltered bays. In Vanuatu and the Solomon Islands they make a welcome change from fish and are a favorite meal. Natives hunt them for their meat, their hides and the tusks of the males. Fortunately old taboos and clan's totemic relationships partially protect them. Here in Port Resolution, there once lived a second dugong, but rumor has it that the rival village ate her.

The surviving dugong was reputedly a male, but as yet had no tusks. At an evening drinks party ashore Michael jokingly questioned, "How do you sex a dugong?"

"Get it excited," said a voice in the darkness.

"And how do you excite a dugong?" another voice asked.

"I thought Michael was doing a pretty good job of it!" was my retort.

Where the Nipikinamu clubhouse now stands there was once a church, in which lived a spinster lady, *Misibran*, meaning "missionary female." A yellowing sepia photograph of her frowning face hangs from the clubhouse wall. The inscription on a crumbling gravestone nearby bears testimony to her fate. As on nearby Erromango, most of Tanna's missionaries suffered from the locals' extreme animosity, causing most to end up in soup pots. Misibran tried to avoid that fate by never venturing beyond her church doorstep. She ate and slept in the church and had rigged up a long rope from inside to ring the bell for services. Although black magic was strong in Tanna, the stalwart lady would give no quarter to pagan fancies. The villagers mentioned one day that whenever she ate a banana she must consume it all.

"Why should I?" she wanted to know.

"Should a banana be only partially eaten," they explained, "and the remains fall into the hands of a sorcerer, deadly spells might be made over it."

"Pshaa! What unholy nonsense," she scoffed. "Here. I will eat a half a banana. You give the other half to the witch doctor and you'll see!"

A few days later the Lady of Faith was laid to rest.

A party of us hired another truck to transport us to the Mount Yasur's crater. It was another rough ride, but this time done in daylight. Once beyond the tree line on a windswept slope of ash ominously sprinkled with black boulders, we eagerly clambered over the tailgate to make the final climb on foot. Our chests heaved in the thin air. At our feet the mountain's great maw opened, exposing sheer smoking black and gray-streaked walls and a pair of molten-lava filled caldera. The ground under our feet shuddered. From within the terrible abyss came swishing and crackling like tides and waves and the sighs of nightmares. A thunderous boom caused us to leap back in fright. People screamed and fled. Sulfurous smoke billowing from the crater engulfed us, searing our lungs. Choking and gasping we bent close to the ground and stumbled downhill.

But some fascination drew us back to the crater edge and held us there waiting for darkness to fall. The volcano seethed and occasionally tossed cascades of fiery rocks through the charged atmosphere. In the past rocks like these have killed people. The mountain grew very quiet. The sun's blazing disc descended behind the crater's rim while our eyes remained riveted on roiling vents that were like openings to the underworld. For long moments the crater, as though holding its breath, would silently darken but for the reflected glow of the bubbling, blurping pools of lava.

The ominous silence intensified. Then, with a shattering blast, a furious inferno of fiery rock and sparks poured forth in the blazing finale that we had unconsiously anticipated.

Turning to retrace our steps across the boulder-strewn ground, we were astonished to see that everyone else in our party had long since returned to the truck.

23

New Caledonia: La Grande Terre

Eighteen yachts cleared from Port Resolution on Tanna, glad to pay the little extra it had cost to fly the Customs and Immigration officers over. Not a whisper of breeze ruffled the bay, and the officers did not object to us delaying our departure an extra day. But, on the next day when the weather also remained windless, we left under power. Miki and I were below deck, sliding a hot tray of biscuits from the oven when Michael called for us to hurry on deck to see the sunset.

Nearby clouds had been transformed into fantasy creatures. Coral pink suffused the sky while the sea face reflected soft blues. As darkness deepened, no wave rippled the glassy surface. The sky above was a magnificent jewel-studded canopy, its constellations mirrored in the dark waters. Such was the radiance that, although moonless, the night was not truly dark.

At 1:30 AM an easterly breeze allowed us to silence the

New Caledonia
The South Lagoon

0   10   20
Nautical Mile

engine and drift along quietly. Another late-leaver from Tanna drifted two miles to starboard. It was a novelty to have the companionship of other yachts close by. By dawn the night breeze gave way to the sun's searing rays. The sails slatted, the boat wallowed; things clattered in shelves. On the southwest horizon a black squall gathered, then bore down on us to blow 25 knots from the south-southeast. We had planned to sail from Tanna south around Ile Maré. Fortunately, we had already made enough southerly progress under power to now clear the island and lay a comfortable course to La Grande Terre. We noted, however, that many of the fleet had taken a rhumb-line course from Tanna to Havannah Passage. They now struggled against headwinds and seas in the slot between Lifou Island and New Caledonia.

The tide through Havannah Passage on the southeast tip of New Caledonia can be riotous. The heavy current had already turned against us as we approached the pass. Worse, the cloud cover rendered the water opaque making the many hazards invisible. Carefully keeping the three range markers on the high bluff lined up, we motorsailed into the channel, and then, as the afternoon lengthened, beat along La Grande Terre's south coast. Although tempted to stop at Baie de Prony, we knew that New Caledonian Customs officials frown on sailors staying there before officially entering Nouméa—particularly if they leave their boat and venture ashore. However the passage to Nouméa inside the lagoon is very long. When daylight failed we dropped anchor at Ile Ouen flying our yellow Q flag to show we had not yet cleared.

La Grande Terre, as New Caledonia's main island is called, rises boldly from the surrounding lagoon. Row upon row of mineral-rich hills extend over a rugged area of some 10,000 square miles. But barren mining scars and landslides spoil the once pristine beauty of the hills. Although this southern region is relatively dry most of the year, heavy seasonal rains wash out ravines and bleed away the soft red soil staining many beaches a dirty ochre color.

The cause of this wounded land is the open cast mining. New Caledonia's nickel reserves are the third largest in the world. At the height of its production in the late 1980s the country exported 2.8 million metric tons of nickel ore, as well as tungsten, cobalt, copper, manganese, iron, and chromium. It is primarily from the exploitation of nickel that the French immigrants, about 37% of the population, have become rich.

Although New Caledonia may have been inhabited for as much as 30,000 years, indigenous people remained undisturbed by outsiders for millennia. Then traders in search of sandalwood and *bêche-de-mer* brought with them the first taste of European contact and portents of disaster. When European missionaries had no luck converting the indigenous people they thought that trained native Polynesian missionaries might stand a better chance. The first two trainees were deposited at Maré and Lifou Islands in 1841 and 1842 where they manfully struggled to make even a single convert. Although the local chief protected the pair, it was for political reasons. He hoped to benefit directly one day from trading goods and guns with Europeans. However, others wanted to get rid of the missionaries without delay. *The Works of Ta'unga*, compiled by R.G. and Marjorie Crocombe and written by one of these young missionaries, give some gruesome insights into the life of Melanesian natives of the time. The letters were all written to the bishop of Ta'unga when the missionary expected each day to be his last.

Scanning the notes I had hurriedly jotted down in the Pohnpei library I read, "Warfare: they never stop fighting day in and day out, month in and month out . . . their reason is vindictiveness and to satisfy their hunger for human flesh. . . . Relatively few people are taken in open warfare . . . a greater number are obtained by stealth like kidnapping. They do rituals to all their gods for head and hands, insides, eyes and ears. . . . Women stay behind the fighting groups, but when a man is killed, even one of their own, they whoop with glee and rush out with a big basket on a pole to pick up the body. They scramble for it, cutting up the pieces and placing them in their baskets, shouting (happily) because their wants (for human flesh) have been satisfied. Both sides do this . . . when an enemy is captured they grab him and while still alive, cut him to pieces. The thighs particularly are cut up small. The men each take an arm and consecrate it before placing it on the grave of their parents. If a chief has been killed every person—even every child—must partake of it, lest they all die."

After four years Ta'unga and the other missionaries were forced to withdraw. The French government, envious of the British foothold in Australia and New Zealand, was keeping an eye on developments. In 1853 Emperor Napoleon III made his move. He ordered the annexation of New Caledonia, the sixth largest island in the South Pacific—as a penal colony. To populate his new colony he shipped out 20,000 French convicts. Later another 4,000 political prisoners, many of them artists, writers and Communards were shipped out to forced labor on Ile des Pins.

But the death knell for the indigenous people was finally sounded when Jules Garnier discovered nickel in 1864. Twelve years later mining began. The French government attempted to relocate natives from tribal lands to reservations, which naturally caused the tribes to unite and revolt. Inevitably the *Kanaks* were defeated, their ancestral lands forfeited. The Grande Terre natives were forced to settle in 150 new villages at the far north of New Caledonia. By the turn of the century, severely traumatized by disease and warfare, their population had declined from 70,000 to around 30,000. They have been displaced to only 10% of the land. The rock of *Le Caillou*, the local name for New Caledonia, had been cut from beneath their feet!

I was up early the next morning to make bread before getting underway for Port Moselle. But first I had to pick weevils out of the flour. The ship's stores were now a year old. The weevils had invaded everything edible: the nuts and seeds, the dried prunes, the wheat germ, and the pasta. They had even munched into the carefully rationed chocolate-covered almonds. But they would not touch white flour, only resting disconsolately within the folds of the paper packaging. They had discovered that the bleached denatured stuff would not "build healthy bodies 12-ways," as I had been led to believe as a child. However, they thrived in the stone-ground whole-wheat flour, fattened, multiplied and emigrated to populate the world of SEA QUEST. At night when I snuggled under my light to read, they even crawled up under my clothes.

Before my twice-weekly baking I sieved, shook, and picked

from the flour as many weevils as I could. My secret and ulti-mate solution was to add linseed to the mix, thereby making it impossible for the unsuspecting to identify exactly which pro-tein he was ingesting.

The strengthening east wind gave us a thrilling sail. We tacked into Nouméa's harbor past the notorious penal island, Ile Nou, where the first unlucky convicts had been incarcerated. At Port Moselle Yacht Club, we took possession of one of the overnight berths provided for newly arrived boats, where Customs and Immigration officers could come and clear us in at their leisure. We lost no time in taking full advantage of the hot showers and looked forward to a few days of sophisticated dockside life. Michael re-assembled and oiled up our rusting tandem bicycle and we set out to explore.

Nouméa sprawls along miles of coastline and encompasses several bays. The commercial sector is near the port, as is the market and the Latin Quarter with its old French townhouses. Beyond are Orphelinat Bay and Baie des Citrons where many local yachts moor. Tourist hotels like the Park Royal and Club Mediterranée have been constructed along the beach at Anse Vata, the site of the Allied South Pacific Command during World War II. Greater Nouméa is a patchwork of suburbs spreading across several steep hills up over which we now puffed on our rickety, complaining steed.

A couple we had met in Tanna stepped from a coffee shop and waved us in. They had abandoned their friend's boat to spend the remainder of their vacation in a hotel. It was the typ-ical story. A week aboard is fun, two weeks tolerable, but three weeks is usually the absolute limit with even the best of friends. We were grateful to have achieved a working balance with Miki. Because of our mismatched ages, she was more like a daughter to us. And Miki was emotionally self-contained. Tak-ing another person on board, though it can lighten the burden of work, is a big risk because nothing spoils a trip faster than an emotionally charged atmosphere.

At Anse Vata many women were sunbathing topless. Young or old, public exposure makes little difference to the French. Michael's neck swiveled dangerously and the tandem careened while he took in the sights. Young people promenaded on side-walks, indulged at fast food shacks, powered noisily on rented jet skis or skimmed lightly across the bay on wind surfers. Darker skinned *Kanaks* rested beneath shady trees or swam modestly, away from the main beach.

For a full week Michael and I enjoyed the delights of the town while Miki had all but disappeared, socializing with a younger set. We made forays to the markets and stores, to return laden with baguettes, French cheese and other small luxuries, conscious that the buying-power of the US dollar was small. We nibbled pizza and sipped espresso while watching well-dressed shoppers pass in the street. Sophisticated French women lived up to their reputation with elegant clothing. Nouméan girls would not be seen dead in flat shoes or rubber thongs; heeled sandals were de rigueur.

A Kiwi family with a flashy new catamaran and a handsome 20-year old son tried to steal Miki away. She left with them for a two-week cruise to Ile des Pins. With the boat to ourselves we thought we would kick back and relax by sailing down the coast a ways.

On Ile Ouen we waded up a streambed. I later learned that exceptionally fine jade is found here. Every step in the water stirred up a cloud of red silt. From atop the riverbank we could look around. The surrounding valley floor was carpeted in sedges, grasses, bracken, lilies, orchids, wattle and shrubs displaying tiny leaves. A closer look showed us the striking similarity to Australian flora. Some trees had thick peeling bark used by native people to make medicinal oil.

We sailed on to the Baie de Prony. The ravaged hills made the surrounding landscape depressing until we penetrated its sheltered recesses. In geological terms New Caledonia is slowly sinking, the narrow valleys flooding. We motored up a fjord-like waterway to an anchorage called the Carenage, a fine cyclone refuge. With a hot pool in one inlet, and a rocky river in the next, it was the perfect place to do boat maintenance, followed by leisurely scrubs in hot or cold flowing water.

One day, Michael asked me, "What do you want for your birthday?"

Impetuously I suggested, "A lemon meringue pie!"

"And just how do I make a lemon meringue pie?"

The pie was perfect. We had no lemons of course, but he used lemon juice we had squeezed into a bottle just before leaving Tanna. For peel, he grated our breakfast oranges.

Cooking aboard is one of the most satisfying aspects of cruising. Food is more than just nourishment, it becomes one of life's pleasant pursuits. With all the time in the world, some humble ingredients and a little patience, we can turn out wonderful inventions. Like the crayfish soup served up to guests in Nouméa. After consuming the tails at Tanna, we sautéed the pickings with a little butter and garlic, and froze the result. A week or two later, defrosted, dressed up with a splash of sherry and a dollop of cream, the dish absolutely stunned our visitors.

We returned to Nouméa to wait for Miki who returned with ciguatera poisoning. It turned out that the crew had accepted a large fish from an effusive Frenchman who assured them it was all right to eat. The fish was served up as dinner and the four on the yacht plus their two guests were all poisoned. They were exhausted and wrung out when they arrived back in Nouméa, with skin scabbed from scratching and puffy faces. The skipper, in addition to the other afflictions, also suffered for over a week from hiccups that left his chest muscles excruciatingly sore. The irony for Miki and her friends was that the Frenchman had also offered the fish to locals who had said to him, "Throw it away!"

Ciguatera poisoning is common in many tropical places, including the Caribbean. Because Michael and I had frequently seen people suffer from it, occasionally for months, we had as children almost lost our taste for fish, especially barracuda. The larger the fish, the greater the danger. Toxins are said to accumulate in fish that feed on damaged coral reefs. Larger fish eat smaller fish. The bigger fish accumulate more toxins. Barracuda, as a predator at the top of the food chain, is the worst. Victims sometimes even loose their hair and teeth. Most suffer an overwhelming lethargy, and can take a long time to recover. There is no known cure.

By the middle of November, most of the seasonal yachts had departed. We planned to monitor the progress of others sailing south to get our own feel for this year's weather patterns. Strong southeast winds, caused by lows rolling off Australia, were steadily blowing. In a safe anchorage it is easy to forget that the ocean, and particularly the Tasman Sea, is wild and untamed beyond the barrier reef.

A terrible wake-up call that shocked cruisers who had perhaps become a little complacent happened in 1994. An intense tropical low swept through the northbound cruising fleet just a few days after it left New Zealand's shores. Seven yachts and three lives were lost.

In June 1994 the regatta fleet left port on a prediction of steady 20-knot winds for the following 24 to 48 hours. It was unexpectedly engulfed by a rapidly deepening depression later dubbed "The Bomb." Winds gusted to 90 knots. Had the awful weather conditions been limited to a few hours, all the boats would have made it, but the storm continued unabated for four interminable days—a lifetime for crews and skippers who had to endure each agonizing minute. The furious winds produced mountainous seas. Boats rolled, masts broke, ports were smashed, rudders fouled and people were injured. An entire crew was swallowed without a trace. Six other yachts were dismasted and eventually abandoned.

Some light displacement racer-cruisers were pushed up to speeds of 16 knots and could not slow down. The twin-rudders of the three catamarans lost were smashed or fouled when the boats slid sideways down the waves.

Such conditions require a skilled helmsman at the wheel. Self-steering gear is simply not good enough to ride down waves. Steadying a careening boat on the billowing back of a wave demands proficiency. The necessary strength and expertise is often in short supply among the usually shorthanded and inexperienced crews. Few yachts attempted to trail heavy rodes or sea anchors. Many crews were terrified and just wanted to abandon their yacht, whatever the cost. They subsequently risked not only their lives, but also the lives of their rescuers to do so. In fact most of the yachts that were abandoned actually survived the storm, being later beached or picked up at sea. The boats were abandoned not because they were sinking, but because of crew fatigue.

Tropical depressions such as "The Bomb" occur only a couple of times each year. It was just bad luck that so many yachts happened to be out there at the time. More yachts seem to be getting into trouble simply because many more yachts, in fact hundreds of them, now sail annually to New Zealand.

Tuning in the radio for the yacht check-in to see how those at sea were faring, we heard that flares had been seen in New Zealand's Great Exhibition Bay. WOODY GOOSE had been swept ashore and the skipper's wife drowned. Sadly the accident raised many questions. The SSB and the VHF radios, the autopilot and the masthead lights had all failed due to water damage when the boat was on a reef in Fiji. Questioned was the skipper's absolute reliance on GPS and the use of only a small-scale track chart with few details. There are several lights on this part of the coast from which a fix could have been obtained and the bluffs and steep cliffs to the south are easily discernible by radar. There were questions too, about why the skipper chose to anchor on a lee shore instead of sailing well away!

Now, amid the crackle of the airwaves, while we listened to check-in, a feminine voice caught our attention.

"Things are pretty dire out here, Des. We don't know how much longer we can manage. If you don't hear from us at the morning sked, send out a search!"

The yacht, a Moody-40, had lost its mast several days earlier in calm weather due to gear failure. Russell Radio put the couple on ENERGETIC directly in touch with Taupo Search and Rescue. The same bad weather that had overtaken WOODY GOOSE now also had them in its grip.

"We are surfing and fear that we will be rolled," Aileen continued in a steady voice.

What she did not need to clarify to those listening was that without a mast and steadying rig, they had little margin for error. They would then be entirely reliant on the auxiliary engine for control. If it quit working, the storm would overwhelm them.

While Bill and Aileen survived, others did not. Only 50 miles north of ENERGETIC's position, 53-foot JANNAMARIE II, en route home from Australia, was struggling in the storm. Aboard were the owners, Richard and Jan Lay, along with their younger brother David and Mark Mart, an Australian boatbuilder, as crew. The yacht was overtaken by a wave that rolled and dismasted it. Mark, at the helm, was washed over the side. Water poured into the main cabin from a broken hatch. Then as the yacht righted itself a surge of seawater sucked David out through the hatch to his death. The U.S.S. SHILOH later rescued the stricken owners.

A week passed. ENERGETIC sailed into Lord Howe Island under jury rig, took on a load of fuel and then, still under short rig, returned eastward to New Zealand. Spinning off from the slow moving highs, were a series of depressions, most of them shallow. Some of these depressions linked up to the Equatorial Convergence Zone troughs where the weather, though unpleasant, is seldom dangerous. One depression however, on which all eyes were now focused, rapidly deepened to 986 Mb. and became nearly stationary. Centered southwest of Norfolk Island it posed a danger to a number of boats. Yachts scrambled to flee. The delivery crew of one yacht prudently turned back to sail directly north again. In Nouméa we continued to wait. For the hundredth time we wondered nervously if our own luck would hold.

24

The Untamed Tasman Sea

Storms continued to roll off the Australian continent. Perhaps a hundred boats were poised for departure from Tonga, Fiji, Vanuatu and New Caledonia. Anxiously we listened to the maritime net as the dramas continued. The weather forecasters had not predicted that the depression lashing the Tasman Sea would become so bad that even large ships would be forced to seek shelter.

Two American yachts, only 100 miles northeast of New Zealand, were now in the midst of 70-knot winds and 30-foot breaking seas: not a nice place for small sailing yachts. SALACIA, a Tayana-37 was the first to be knocked down. Michael Fritz was sailing out of San Diego, California, with his companion Julie-Ann of San Carlos, an inexperienced hand who had just joined the boat in Tonga. As the storms continued, Julie-Ann suffered from bouts of seasickness and mild hypothermia. SALACIA did not carry an EPIRB or a liferaft. This is not altogether uncommon for US registered vessels, though New Zealand registered yachts are required to have all of these inspected items on board. SALACIA, like WOODY GOOSE, had also grounded on a tropical reef earlier in the season, damaging her steering. On the passage her engine had broken down. The heavy displacement Taiwanese-built Explorer-45, FREYA, out of Bellingham, Washington was just ahead of them and had offered to tow SALACIA through the calm before the storm approached.

About the time of SALACIA's knockdown, FREYA, with three members of the Burnham family as crew, was nearing the coastal shelf where the seas grow dangerously steep in rising winds. Concerned, Des Renner at Russell Radio offered to keep in touch through the night; however the Burnhams declined the offer. Early the next morning though, when FREYA failed to check in, Des alerted Taupo Maritime Rescue. They picked up a faint EPIRB signal. A plane was sent out to search. FREYA had

capsized five times in the night, losing her mast, her liferaft, and the sea anchor she had been trailing. The boat's interior was knee-deep in water and filling faster than the three of them could pump. If Marianne and her 13-year-old son Heath had not taken turns to continuously broadcast on VHF, it is likely the family would have been lost, because the EIRPB signal had died away soon after being activated.

Once they were located, a volunteer crew aboard a New Zealand Northland Electricity helicopter set out on an extremely risky operation. Fifty-four-year-old Trevor Tuckey was lowered down into the raging waters and dragged towards the yacht. Before he could climb aboard, he unfortunately slammed his head into the yacht's side. Dazed, he had to be winched back to the helicopter and needed to rest before he was able to try again. Eventually he managed to bring each family member to safety.

As soon as the Burnhams were safe, the helicopter was diverted to search for SALACIA. Twelve hours had passed since their Mayday, sent over a marine radio channel, had been intercepted. After the first call, there had been silence. Everyone feared the worst. By the time the helicopter located SALACIA, the rescuers were short of fuel and had to return to shore. Meanwhile the container ship, DIRECT KOOKABURRA, the only vessel in the area large enough to maneuver in the awful conditions, was directed towards her. Though Michael Fritz and Julie-Ann saw the big ship approaching, they did not seem to realize that it was on its way to rescue them in response to their Mayday call and went back down below into the shelter of the cabin. In interviews later, Fritz told reporters that *he* had not sent a Mayday. It was never made clear if he had any knowledge of Julie-Ann having made one.

Although SALACIA's engine was not working and the rudder was giving trouble, her rig stood and the uninsured boat was not sinking. Fritz, who had lived aboard for years, said he had not believed the situation to be severe enough to abandon his boat.

The captain of the container ship tried to create a lee for the yacht, only to have a massive sea lift and roll her onto SALACIA, tearing out the mast and rigging. The couple scrambled on deck to catch the liferings thrown down to them. As they were about to jump into a scramble-net, the container ship again collided with the yacht's hull, this time splintering it. The impact knocked Fritz into the sea where somehow he managed to grab onto another floating lifering and was hauled bouncing up the ship's side. But Julie-Ann slipped out of hers and was lost.

We were stunned. The whole harbor of yachts poised to depart was shocked by the news. Four boats lost and now four dead! Seventeen devastating days of November had claimed more lives than the 1994 Bomb. The Southern Ocean had proved again that it is no plaything and now we faced our final passage—the culmination of our 14-month voyage from Japan.

We took extra precautions. We rigged car tires on lines to slow our speed should it become necessary. We screwed down locker lids under the bunks and floor. We bent on our heavy weather storm sails. Though the water temperatures that spawn tropical cyclones were steadily rising, we remained determined to stay patient and wait the weather out. We felt certain that the unpredictable, dangerous spring lows would give way to the big stable highs that we normally expected at this time of year. Only in such conditions would this passage be a safe one.

Daily a couple of the skippers, waiting so anxiously in Port Moselle, made the 20-minute walk to the Meteolorogical Office at the top of one of Nouméa's highest hills. The weathermen, amid their flickering console screens, would point out significant features on the weather maps. Later, at the informal skippers' meeting, the photocopied information would be discussed ad infinitum. There was little agreement on the conditions that were most favorable for departure. The visits to the Met Office served mainly to confirm that the lows continued to slip relentlessly off the Australian coast. Finally, at the end of November a pair of enormous highs floated off the Indian Ocean to drift across Australia, one obediently tagging behind the other. The time had come to depart.

The German skipper shook his head. "You are going now?"

"Yes, we will leave as soon as we get the dinghy on deck and lashed down."

"But the highs are still far away and more lows may still develop!"

We had heard all the arguments. Some wanted a high to be right over them before making a move. Others liked to hitch on to the back of a passing low, even though at first the sea would be rough. Kiwi friends Lyn and Sue aboard JOIE had done just that. They had left 24 hours earlier and sailed 150 nautical miles.

"You may be right, but experience tells us SEA QUEST needs a bit of wind to get her going. Those big highs will becalm us."

The German wished us well, but rowed away shaking his head. We later heard that he had waited until Christmas and then *motored* all the way to New Zealand across flat, windless seas.

Amedee lighthouse dropped astern. It was December 1. The southwest wind was light and so was the cloud cover. Michael and I were upbeat and cheerful. Miki was lovelorn and sulking. She had fallen for the heady charms of the boy on the dashing trimaran. The boy had invited her to sail with him to Australia. We urged her to remain aboard SEA QUEST, to complete the voyage she had set out to do. Later, if she still wanted to, she could join the young man.

That evening, the wind veered to the northwest and our German friend radioed. He seemed all too anxious to tell us that a new trough had formed west-northwest of New Caledonia. By 2:00 AM the wind backed 180° to southeast and rapidly strengthened. The barometer fell while the mounting seas pummeled us and sheets of cold rain swept SEA QUEST. Fifty-knot winds shrieked in the rigging. We unhanked our big genoa and dragged the wet dripping sail below. We continued under double-reefed main and small jib. From time to time a solid wall of green water tumbled across the decks to flood the wheelhouse and drip miserably on us. In preparation for nightfall Michael rigged the storm trysail, a tiny handkerchief of cloth. Stiff and hard to handle, this sail had never before been broken out. But with it up and SEA QUEST hove-to we settled into a more comfortable pace. Hunkered down in the cockpit, we were grateful for the respite from endless sail changes.

The sky was still leaden but the southeast wind had eased by day three. Down came the storm trysail and up went the main and genoa. The storm winds and current had pushed us well to the west of Norfolk Island's longitude. Our present course was an excellent one, had we wanted to sail to Sydney! As the day progressed and the sky brightened, we dried our clothes and tidied the boat.

In the wee hours of day four we decided to tack, but the only course we could hold would return us to New Caledonia. After seven hours we gained just ten miles. Defeated, we jibed back to the southwest again. Pressure ridges in the clouds seemed to indicate a change.

As I came up on deck to serve dinner I noticed the fishing line stretched taut. "Whoopee," I yelled as I dashed aft. "We've caught a fish!"

And what a fish! The 200-pound test line was stretched to its limit and neither Michael nor I could move it.

"Why don't we give it another try after we have eaten dinner," I suggested.

By that time the fish was nearing exhaustion. Together we worked it close, but when the fish saw the boat's hull a surge of adrenaline sent it thrashing wildly, pulling the heavy line back out through our hands. Whipping a bight around a nearby cleat, we prayed that the gear would hold.

Bit by bit we worked the fish closer.

"It's a tuna! A yellow-fin," I yelled, as Michael sunk the gaff into its jaw.

"Grab a line!" Together we gradually pushed a loop first down the gaff, then the body, to snug tightly around the tail.

"Miki. Come help us!" Michael called.

Miki had remained stubbornly withdrawn since leaving New Caledonia. Even catching a fish worth a fortune in Japan failed to move her. She was giving us a cold shoulder. But at Michael's direct order, she roused herself.

Michael continued, "Get the second line around the tail and both of you haul!"

It took our combined strength to get the struggling fish out of the water, through the lifelines and onto the deck. The tuna probably weighed 100 pounds or more, the largest fish we had ever caught.

Our freezer was empty because New Zealand quarantine regulations prohibit the import of meat and dairy products. But fish was fine. Great steaks of crimson flesh were sectioned off, enough for 500 sushi dinners! When the job was finished, our 32-cubic foot freezer was packed full.

The 50-foot ketch JACARANDA was ready to leave Suva. Des on Russell Radio told the crew, "Best you wait until this blows through."

The trough that had already buffeted us with 50 knots had now turned into a low threatening all in its path as it rampaged to the east. But in our part of the Tasman Sea, the weather had completely cleared and the night watches were glorious spectacles.

That afternoon we broke through Miki's wall of silence.

"It is my life," she had said. "I should not have obligation. I free!"

Gently I reminded her that she was the one who after all had insisted on joining SEA QUEST despite her lack of experience. It was she who persuaded her mentor to use his considerable influence to place her on SEA QUEST. All of us were bound by the promises we made and now it was fair for us to have some expectation of the adventure's successful outcome. The primary purpose had always been that as a character-building exercise the voyage would help harness Miki's considerable talents and focus that strong will of hers so that she could successfully carve out a life for herself, in or out of Japan, where she would flourish.

It was difficult for her to live up to her end of the bargain. She had rebelled first against her parents, later her mentors, and in Nouméa she had tried to rebel against us.

"The total freedom you crave is an illusion," I said. "Every relationship implies an obligation of some sort. To deny this leads to taking without giving. If you do that you must be very strong and very independent, because that behavior generally leads to a thankless existence."

"But I want happy. If I obligation I *not* be happy!"

Though we might have preferred a less emotionally fraught crew, we felt it was Miki's privileged upbringing speaking. Her headstrong choice to act so radically as to run away from Japan aboard SEA QUEST had taken her to many stormy shores, both figuratively and actually, that she had never known existed.

Along the way she discovered that her choice encompassed not only a physically tough journey, but a psychologically tough one too.

Michael and I did not try to push things further but sank back in the cockpit cushions. Soon the gentle undulations of the calm ocean produced their usual tranquilizing effect. There was no wind. To make up the distance we had been blown to the west, we motored east for all of our fifth and sixth days out.

"More of the same," was the message from Russell Radio that night. "There are no isobars in your area."

JOIE was 300 miles to the south of us. They were beginning to pick up the stronger winds of the higher latitudes. Though our destination was the Bay of Islands on the sheltered eastern side of New Zealand, JOIE was bound for Wellington. There, even ordinary winds are amplified in the frequently gale-lashed reaches of Cook's Strait where the weather is funneled between the North and South Islands.

Today was ideal for whale watching. Within minutes of taking up the search we sighted a pod of about 20 pilot whales. Miki, who had made a remarkable turnabout since our talk, scampered on deck.

Pilot whales are actually large dolphins. The largest grow to about 20 feet and migrate long distances. In some places like Tonga and the Solomon Islands they are still killed for food. Circling at a distance, we noticed the twisting and erratic course of a shark's fin. He waited for some easy pickings.

At dusk when a blue-faced booby wheeled around SEA QUEST, we knew we must be nearing Norfolk Island. We shut down the engine to drift. Norfolk Island lay just 35 miles to the east. In the darkness, the quiet sea gleamed like polished black ice. Wrapped in a big blanket to keep off the dew, Michael and I remained on deck all night to enjoy the full spectacle of the stars that wheeled and danced around us. SEA QUEST's gently swaying masts cut a romantic silhouette. One of us kept watch while the other slept. Only when the day had begun did we finally power up the engine. Norfolk Island lay so close by, we decided to go sightseeing.

Norfolk has eroded to a fraction of its former size and its two islands now sit on a shallow shelf above the ocean floor.

When Captain Cook first noticed uninhabited Norfolk and Philip Islands and the surrounding rocky islets, he formally claimed them for Britain. In his notes he suggested that the fine stands of straight pine and flax would be suitable to make masts and sails for the Royal Navy.

The first settlement was established in 1788, only two months after the arrival of the First Fleet to Australia. The island's population, subsidized by the navy, peaked at 1,100 souls but in the early nineteenth century it was found that neither pines nor flax were as suitable as intended. The colony was abandoned in 1814 and to discourage undesirables, all the public buildings were destroyed. Then in 1825 Norfolk became a prison colony and was operated as such for 30 years. The convicts built substantial roads, bridges and stone buildings. However, the brutal excesses perpetuated by the prison staff raised such a public outcry that the prison was eventually shut down and the island again abandoned. In 1856 Queen Victoria invited the entire population of Pitcairn Island, nearly 200 mixed Polynesian/British descendants of Christian Fletcher and the Bounty mutineers, to settle the Norfolk Islands. The buildings and works of the penal colony would prove to be a fine legacy for them. Queen Victoria declared Norfolk "a separate and distinct settlement," to operate under its own local laws. Each family was allotted 20 hectares. Over the next century some families returned to Pitcairn Island. Today Bounty descendants populate both islands.

White terns swooped about SEA QUEST, while petrels sat like ducks on the water. Bluebottle jellyfish and Portuguese men-of-war floated past. We steered a course that would take us into Sydney Bay between the twin peaks of 960-foot Norfolk Island and 840-foot Philip Island. Although yachts sometimes anchor in the lee in calm weather, poor conditions are notorious. The weather shifts so rapidly that on occasion crews ashore have been unable to return fast enough to save their boat from wrecking.

Wind swept the smooth sea into a flurry of ripples. The sky now held some stratocumulus. Was the back edge of the huge high finally passing over us? Or was this a local effect caused by the contours of the land? To our surprise, a six-foot swell was running in Sydney Bay. To anchor in such a place seemed foolhardy.

Michael pointed out that the long ocean swell was being forced abruptly up over the shallows of the Norfolk seamount. At the same time all the energy contained in that swell was being squeezed between the two big islands. The horizontal and vertical compression had magnified the effect, setting up a violent and confused sea.

Behind a solid line of breaking surf was Kingston, the island's only town. Beyond the combers and spume were stone colonial buildings. Circling as close as we dared we studied them with our binoculars. Many were two-storied. Others seemed to be settlers' cottages. With the aid of a map given to us in Nouméa, we picked out the old beach store, the settlement guardhouse, the legislature and the Royal Engineers' cottage. We could also see the police station and flag house, the boat sheds, and even the prisoners' barracks. Higher up the hill the governor's mansion was a picture of grace and elegance. Near the beach were the old salt works. Apart from a couple of modern homes on the overlooking hills, Kingston looked much as it must have done in 1855, when the penal colony was disbanded.

Rounding up to set some sail, we tacked away into the short bucking seas that swept around Nepean Islet, just offshore from Kingston. We speculated that with a 200-mile fishing zone as an asset, and a strong tourist industry that would pay big dollars for great game fishing, the islanders might take a leaf out of the Japanese's book and build an artificial harbor. What a boon it would be! If it can be done in Japan it could be done here.

Even where delightful small coves break the shoreline, landing at nearby Philip Island is also reputed to be dangerous. The island was once heavily forested, but the early settlers felled all the trees. Subsequent erosion has washed the thin soil from the steep terrain. Today the birds use it for their sanctuary. Hundreds of petrels, shearwaters and terns, as well as white-capped noddies, masked boobies and others nest there. I watched a red-tailed tropicbird beeline towards us from the shore. It circled once and then returned to the land.

Miki prepared lunch. Her happier disposition had reasserted itself and we lounged in the cockpit together. Half-jokingly Miki said with a smile, "I give you much trouble this trip. I am sorry. I am much unhappy about many things. I confuse. But I learn much!"

Our thoughts drifted back over the events of the past fourteen months.

Since our departure from Wakaura, after the whistles and horns of our escort faded, our relationship had steadily become more affectionate. For Michael and I the journey had been richly rewarding. Miki, we sensed, had now reached a new level of maturity.

Noiselessly we slipped through the water. The clear high gave way to low cloud. Though barely moving we were determined to sail. We had no itinerary after all, except to get home by Christmas. JOIE was far to the south. For several days running they had been beating into southwesterly winds. They were now caught up in a new pressure system whirling up from Tasmania. Double reefed in 40 knots and more, Sue and Lyn, though tired, knew that they could expect little change. They were seasoned Wellington sailors, well used to the kind of foul weather that would wither most of us.

On our ninth day we sighted our first albatross. We were sailing the Whale Route that streams thousands of miles northward from the polar regions of the Antarctic to the Coral Sea. We watched a young wandering albatross skim wave tops, drop into troughs and then wheel skyward, almost never pumping his wide wings. When they are not breeding these incredible birds remain at sea. We were soon rewarded with the sighting of yet another circumpolar species, the magnificent black-browed mollymawk, a smaller albatross.

Two more days passed, then the breeze began to veer and our course improved. Now, just over the horizon lay sacred Cape Reinga, believed by the Maori people of New Zealand to be the leaping off place for the spirits of the dead.

The southwesterly swell gradually shifted west. We tacked, we drifted; we set the spinnaker. We even motored a little until Michael sang out, "Land ahoy!" *Kia ora. Aotearoa*—Greetings, Land of the Long White Cloud.

North Cape lay abeam, a pale smudge on a gray sky. The long awaited wind suddenly sprang up, rapidly gaining strength until it was blowing 30 knots. As darkness fell we stood well offshore to avoid the rough seas churned up along the edge of North Island's undersea shelf. We knew only too well that it is not in the deep sea that the greatest dangers lie, but in the approach to the unknown and unforgiving shore, especially at night.

At dawn an opal sky etched Cape Wiwiki and its companion, Tikitiki rock. It was December 13. Cape Brett brightened as though brushed with gold by the rising sun. Tikitiki and Cape Brett are the two rugged landmarks that define the boundaries of New Zealand's Bay of Islands. They spelled home.

I wanted to wake Michael and Miki. Instead I held back to savor the moment. The deeply shadowed hills, only moments before in darkness, were now tinted gold at their peaks. A welcoming party of birds encircled the boat. Several big yellow-headed gannets along with tiny blue-penguins, called *kokora* locally, drifted on waters ruffled now by only a faint breeze. The penguins scuttled away rapidly from SEA QUEST's path while the handsome gannets sat imperturbably watching.

Our 10,000-mile journey was complete. For a moment I imagined bus schedules, supermarkets, crowds and phone bills and felt a visceral contraction. And yet there was also heady anticipation for the touch of New Zealand's moist and fragrant earth, and to walk again among familiar faces.

Although our son and daughter now lived in the States, Michael's British born parents still lived in New Zealand. We had been out of reach of the old people for a long time, but we looked forward to being within shouting distance.

Michael, although a heavy sleeper, seemed to sense the poignancy of our homecoming. Silently he emerged from below, his curly hair tousled from sleep and a twinkling look in his soft blue eyes. For long moments he just stared out, drinking in the golden landscape, not saying a word. Then he put his arm around me.

Softly he whispered, "We've made it—and in one piece too!"

254

"Can you believe that we are really home after all these years?" I murmured. "I never imagined it would be eight years!"

"Oh, but what a time we've had." He squeezed me a little closer, paused a moment as though considering, and then in hushed tones spoke fateful words.

"I just hope that we don't somehow get stuck here so that we can never sail away again!"

Michael-the-Adventurer was already restlessly planning the next cruise—although we had not yet set foot on dry land! Any ideas that I might have been nursing of a cottage and a rose garden would have to be put on hold.

The voyage of SEA QUEST began with Japan's 1997 northeast monsoon and ended in New Zealand just before Christmas 1998. *Aotearoa*'s green hills never looked greener; her safe estuaries had never felt more like home. Delightful scenery, a secure anchorage, the embrace of friends and family threatened our plans to eventually sail on. Yet we realized that before we became helplessly enmeshed we must set a date for departure—however far in the future that might be.

Three years to enjoy local life would be about right, we thought. Long enough to make new friends, catch up with old ones, and take temporary jobs. Long enough to have time to share, after eight long years away, with Michael's parents. Now in their eighties, they still retained enough enthusiasm for our lifestyle to encourage us to continue. Michael found jobs managing a shipyard and later as a marine cabinetmaker. In between jobs he and I both devoted time to refitting SEA QUEST, now nearly twenty years old.

Miki left SEA QUEST soon after our arrival in the Bay of Islands, her baggage filling two skiffs. She set herself up in a tourist hotel where for a couple of weeks she reveled in unaccustomed luxury and hot showers. Christmas was our last time spent together in the country home of Michael's parents where we enjoyed an English-style celebration of turkey and ham and all the trimmings. "It is like a picture book or the movies!" Miki exclaimed when she saw all the food set out.

At first she wandered New Zealand wide-eyed, a babe in the woods, exploited by some of the people she met. Born-again Christians, wildly enthusiastic fanatics, tried to make her one of them. Although she conceded they were nice people and she had lots of fun, she soon tired of prayers throughout the day or evening.

She was next befriended by a sophisticated young woman, wowing Miki with female confidences and promises to launch her into the modeling business, even offering to share her home in Auckland while Miki found her feet. Miki assured us by phone. "Very nice lady. She say because thousands Japanese tourists come, New Zealand need models for brochure and magazine. She say with her connections Miki easily get lots high paying work!" After Miki spent money for modeling courses and photographic portfolios, her friend closed in for the kill. As Miki fretted about diminishing funds and lack of work, she offered "in the meantime" to find her work in a *massage* parlor!

Warning bells woke Miki to reality. Immediately she moved into a rented room. Her new landlords were a warm-hearted Dutch-English family. Not only did she charm the parents but their youngest son Mike was soon head-over-heels in love with her.

Miki and Mike were married in 2002 and remain in New Zealand, although traveling occasionally to Japan where her parents have unbent a little. Miki says she is very pleased with her new life and her gentle, accommodating husband. She loves her work climbing up the management ladder in quality jewelry stores. After-hours she paints and makes jewelry of her own design. In New Zealand her creativity and personality have found room to blossom.

Miki recently wrote to us. "Look at Miki now! I am so happy and have made my own life here. It all came from your support from 7 October 1997. That was the start for everything."

She went on to say that sailing aboard SEA QUEST was the most important event in her life. "Now, whenever Miki come face to face with big problem, Miki just think of my time on SEA QUEST, what my Captain and Ocean Mama would have done. Then Miki just go on—like you do."

The date for our 2002 departure neared and we began to drop out of local activities. Our friends were incredulous. "How can you? You have so much going for you here!" Without doubt the idea of staying home, enjoying our comfortable lifestyle and engaging friends was inviting. But life seemed too short for that. How could we explain that to stay in port would spell the end of ambition? We still felt an urge to continue to explore the world. We had dreams to cruise French Polynesia. The almost untouched atolls in Micronesia also beckoned us back again. Beyond all that awaited the mysteries of Southeast Asia. If we gave the future a chance to unfold we hoped it would lead us along watery highways and many more enriching encounters beyond imagining.

258

GLOSSARY

Amah	Chinese nursemaid
Aotearoa	Land of the Long White Cloud (Maori, New Zealand)
Bai	Traditional men's meeting (Belau)
Bancas	Outrigger canoes (Philippines)
Bislama	Pidgin English (Vanuatu)
Byoin	Hospital
Calamar	Squid (Spanish)
Dekinai	Forbidden
Dhur	Sarong (Micronesia)
Fafalithi	Earth oven (Vanuatu)
Fugu	Puffer fish (poisonous)
Gaigin	Foreigner, usually European/American
Gujisan	Shinto Priest
Gunto	Chain of islands
Hashi	Bridge
Hashi	Chopsticks
Hinoki	Cypress
Hiragana	Phonetic symbols for writing Japanese language
Hong Kong	Fragrant harbor
Ikitai?	Want to go?
Kaikyo	Channel
Kami	God
Kami Kaze	Divine wind
Kampai	Bottoms Up
Kanak	South Sea Islander
Kastom	Traditional ceremony
Katakana	Japanese phonetic alphabet
Katau Peidi	Place of the sunset
Kava	Narcotic drink from root of pepper tree (Fiji)
Klidm	Ancient carved stone heads (Belau)
Ko	Harbor

Kokora	Blue Penguin (Maori)
Kuroshio	Warm ocean current flowing north-eastward past Japan
Lap-lap	Gelatinous yam pudding (Vanuatu)
Matsuri	Festival
Mikan	Tangerine
Mikoshi	Portable shrine (for festivals)
Misaki	Cape
Motu	Small islet on atoll reef edge
Nada	Sound, enclosed water
Nahnmwarki	High Chief (Pohnpei)
Nakamal	Meeting house (Vanuatu)
Nihon-jin	Japanese person
Nihon-shu	Distilled rice, sweet-potato or sugar alcohol
O	Great (honorific)
Obon	Buddhist festival
Okusan	Lady of the house
Oni	Devil (rude term for foreigner)
Onsen	Hot spring
Palu	Micronesian navigator (literally 'man')
Pidgin	Simplified English/island language
Pohnpei	Upon an Altar
Retto	Chain of islands
Ryokan	Inn (traditional)
Sakau	Narcotic drink from root of pepper tree (Pohnpei)
Sake	Japanese rice wine
Samurai	Warrior
Sayonara	Goodbye
Sento	Public bath house
Seto	Strait
Seto Naikai	Inland Sea of Japan
Shima	Island
Shochu	Distilled liquor from rice, yam or sugarcane
Shogun	Military ruler of Japan

Shoto	Islands
Soba	Buckwheat noodles
Sugi	Japanese Cedar
Suido	Channel
Tam-tam	Slit drum made from a log (Melanesia)
Tatami	Thick floor mats
Torii	Gate to a Shinto shrine
Tsunami	Tidal wave
Tuba	Alcoholic drink made from coconut tree sap
Wan	Gulf
Yaki	Ceramic ware
Yukata	Light bathrobe

WEATHER FACTORS

Northern Temperate Zone

Southwest monsoon
   March/April until October/November
Typhoon season
   June until November
North East monsoon
   November until April
Equinoctial gales (*haru ichiban*)
   April

Northern Tropical Zone

Typhoon season
   May until November/December
Sailing season
   December until May

Southern Tropical Zone

Cyclone season
   December until May
Sailing season
   May until December

Southern Temperate Zone

Sailing season
   December until May
Winter gales
   June until November

Sea Quest's Voyage

October—December
> From Japan to Hong Kong, with the north-east monsoon behind us

January—June
> Philippines and Micronesia

July
> From north to south in the Convergence Zone

August—November
> Solomon Islands to New Caledonia

December
> Tasman Sea to New Zealand

INDEX

Other books of interest

RETURN TO THE SEA
Webb Chiles
In his newest book, Webb Chiles describes his voyage from Boston through Portugal,
Brazil and Cape Town to Sydney, thereby completing his fourth circumnavigation.
"Chiles is philosopher, adventurer, confessor, seaman par excellence and, of course, survivor.
Above all, he is a consummate storyteller who, like a true pugilist, pulls no punches, but lands his
blows with the sensitivity of a poet."—*Yachting Monthly*

THE LONG WAY
Bernard Moitessier
"Moitessier was the original mystical mariner and inventor of the charismatic French
boat-bum persona: there's no denying Moitessier's impact on bluewater sailing. This account
of his most legendary exploit, in which he blew off winning the 1969 Golden Globe
round-the-world race so he could 'save his soul' in high southern latitudes, is a bible
to ocean sailors with a metaphysical bent. His decision to quit the race and keep on sailing, in
more ways than one, marks the point at which ocean racing and ocean cruising went
their separate ways."—*Cruising World*

THE LAST GREAT ADVENTURE OF SIR PETER BLAKE
edited by Alan Sefton
"A new book is on the shelves that commemorates Blake's life and relates the story of his final,
remarkable voyage. It is memorable not only for page after page of vivid photography but for
Blake's own take on the wonders unfolding before him. He proves to be an excellent
correspondent and a keen observer of the natural world."—*Cruising World*

THE OCEANS ARE WAITING
Sharon Ragle
"Sharon Ragle is a woman in perpetual motion, and her rollicking tale about her personal ad—
'attractive lady sailor seeks SWM for cruising future and beyond'—and marriage and four-and-a-
half-year circumnavigation aboard the Tartan 37, TIGGER, with said SWM (a great guy named
Dave) is written in her brilliantly impulsive style of life."—*Cruising World*

SEASONED BY SALT
A Voyage in Search of the Caribbean
Jerry Mashaw & Anne MacClintock
Mashaw and MacClintock are not your average sailors. Their story brims with humor
and high adventure and reflects a deep respect for and understanding of the history,
people, and economy of the many Caribbean islands that they visit.
"...captures the feel of sailing among the Caribbean islands and
realizing what matters in life."—Daniel Hays

Sheridan House
America's Favorite Sailing Books
www.sheridanhouse.com

Other books of interest

READY FOR SEA!
Tor Pinney
"...an easy read, packed with good advice. Even experienced cruisers will pick up a thing or two from this one."—*Latitudes & Attitudes*
"...presents clearly and concisely what it takes to provision a boat and sail it confidently..."—*SAIL*

HANDBOOK OF OFFSHORE CRUISING, Second Edition
The Dream and Reality of Modern Ocean Cruising
Jim Howard
"...an immensely practical work. This encyclopedic volume has become a standard reference for bluewater sailors, particularly those planning extended cruising in mid-size sailing vessels."—*Charleston Daily News*

THE *SAIL* BOOK OF COMMONSENSE CRUISING
Patience Wales
The sailing world's best-known writers offer practical advice on many aspects of cruising, from choosing a crew and passage planning to preparing meals and navigating at sea.
"In these pages you will find a plethora of practical tips and hard-won experience that it would take a lifetime to gain."—*Yachting Monthly*
"...all really good common sense stuff...a must for every cruiser."—*Soundings*

THERE BE NO DRAGONS
How to Cross a Big Ocean in a Small Sailboat
Reese Palley
"A delightful blend of information and stories, with emphasis on the human aspect of sailing. Witty, irreverent and inspirational with as much 'why to' as 'how to.'"—*Cruising World*
"...funny, raucous, insightful, anarchistic, entertaining, instructional; seamanship with a difference."—*WoodenBoat*

INSTANT WEATHER FORECASTING
Alan Watts
"Gives the layman the magical art of weather forecasting..."—*Motor Boat*
"...a sure-fire bestseller..."—*The Yachtsman*
"...another gem that's a dog-eared favorite..."—*Coastal Cruising*
"...a popular forecasting guide since its first printing in 1968...particularly useful for the boating aficionado."—*Bulletin of the American Meteorological Society*

Sheridan House
America's Favorite Sailing Books
www.sheridanhouse.com